Lilly

Lilly

*Reminiscences
of
Lillian
Hellman*

Peter Feibleman

William Morrow and Company, Inc.
New York

Grateful acknowledgment is made to the following publications for permission to reprint material from:

"Eulogies to Lillian Hellman." Copyright © Vineyard Gazette, Inc. Used by permission.

"An Interview with Lillian Hellman" by Fred Gardner, recorded in 1969 on audio cassette. Reproduced with permission. Excerpt from taped interview (46 minutes) available on cassette from Jeffrey Norton Publishers, Guilford, Connecticut.

Interview with Lillian Hellman by Nora Ephron. Used by permission.

Interview with Lillian Hellman by John Phillips and Anne Hollander in *Writers at Work: The Paris Review Interviews,* Third Series, edited by George Plimpton. Copyright © 1967 by The Paris Review, Inc. Reprinted by permission of Viking Penguin Inc.

From *Eating Together: Recollections and Recipes* by Lillian Hellman and Peter Feibleman. Copyright © 1984 by Left Leg, Inc. and Frogjump Productions, Inc. Used by permission.

Pentimento: A Book of Portraits by Lillian Hellman. Copyright © 1973 by Lillian Hellman. Used by permission.

"The Autumn Garden" in *The Collected Plays* by Lillian Hellman. Copyright © 1951 by Lillian Hellman. By permission of Little, Brown and Company.

Library of Congress Cataloging-in-Publication Data

Feibleman, Peter S., 1930–
    Lilly : reminiscences of Lillian Hellman / by Peter Feibleman.
      p.   cm.
    ISBN 0-688-06188-5
    1. Hellman, Lillian, 1906– —Biography.   2. Dramatists,
American—20th century—Biography.   3. Feibleman, Peter S., 1930–
—Friends and associates.   I. Title.
PS3515.E343Z68 1988
812'.52–dc 19
[B]   88-4702
                                               CIP

Printed in the United States of America

First Edition

1 2 3 4 5 6 7 8 9 10

BOOK DESIGN BY ELLEN FOOS

Grateful acknowledgment is made
to Rita Wade, whose memory for the
chronology, detail, and impact of
certain events is better than my own.
—PF

CONTENTS

Special Effects

>>>>> I

FROM THE DECK of the house you can see an osprey. It wheels, banks, then tilts on the wind, doubling back in circles over the beach, wings arched in terrific silhouette against the dawn rays, the first of a white September sky. Under it an obese ferryboat, sleek in this landscape, moves without sound in a long thin glide out of the morning.

The early sun angles and breaks: slivers of light jitter on the surface of the water like minnows and the smell of seaweed and other tidal morning rot rises and floats onto the shore, fresh and foul and visceral. The wind shifts to the west, visible now in the witty little blades of dune grass, and the earth seems to stretch and grunt. A gull hovers, flutters, drops a clam onto the rocks of a jetty—bursting the shell, feeding—backed by the faded look of summer's end, the hand-me-down trees of the shore across the bay. Then the day opens and thick slabs of saffron light lie over the sea, as heavy and still as amber.

I came here first in the early sixties to spend the summer with a friend in this same quiet house, her house, my house since she vacated the premises and left it to me a couple of years ago. Her name was Lillian Hellman and in the years since her death I've come to think of it as home. The house overlooks its own beach and a small peninsula called East Chop and part of the harbor of Vineyard Haven, the name of a settlement in the town of Tisbury. The high front windows are lined with rosebushes three to eight feet high, planted by Lillian a quarter century ago and still producing unkempt slatternly blossoms that turn translucent at noon, a pale inviolate pink, the color of sunrise. I remember stopping short at the sight of the big obscene roses the day I first came, landing early one evening by plane in answer to a letter I keep, mailed in May of '63: "Stop stewing, it's unserious of you. We all get stuck. The thing is to get unstuck. Come to my island, Lillian."

It was mid-June when I came and the roses were floating open like sea anemones in the wet heat. I had been complaining in letters and phone calls and in person about my troubles with a new novel and Lilly had listened to my whining with a kind of secret gentleness combined with a merciless attitude of assault she had learned from her closest friend, Dashiell Hammett, who showed no pity to writers. But Hammett had been dead over two years and my visiting her on the Vineyard was a new turn in a relationship that had already existed in some form for a long time, because I had known Lillian since I was ten; since then I had published three books of fiction, had a play on Broadway and then come unglued, which didn't seem fair. "You think too much about fair—none of it's fair. Writing is just writing," she said. "Unpack your things and come down for a drink."

I did as I was told. The house faced east. There was no wind. The ocean looked as though a layer of skin had been pulled taut over it with a surface tension much like the one I was feeling. The sun lay low behind the house and a glaze of orange light touched the tree line and presently the water took on a viscous quality, patches of rainbow drifting across it, oily places caused by gurry, the cut-up guts and junk thrown overboard by fishermen. To the right before the harbor was an angled stone breakwater and a lot of boats at anchor, sailboats and motorboats, boats for cruising and boats for fishing, all of them pointed like seabirds into the wind. Halyards on aluminum masts clunked and tinkled. Every so often a ferryboat slid back and forth in front of the house on its way to the mainland or Nantucket and I sat on a sofa where I could watch it.

I did not know the Vineyard well and the bay in front of the house that led to the ocean looked aloof and unfriendly except for the passing ferries, their lights beginning to blink on in the heat-thick evening. Water and sky had merged into a solid grayish blue—the color of gravestone slate—and for a long time I stayed in my place on the sofa staring out the window. Beyond the roses was a smaller flower garden and in front of that a vegetable garden with a pine tree on the left and a peach tree on the right. Then there were some horseradish plants, some low dune bushes with berries and then the beach. Just then, looking at it, I felt empty and lost. I have almost no sense of compass direction but I asked Lilly for a map in the dim hope that an overview of the island would help orient me in a general way, not so much by telling me where I was as by showing me where I wasn't. She found an old gas-station map in a kitchen drawer and we spread it out on a table and sat down to examine it.

The island of Martha's Vineyard is in the Atlantic a few miles off the southeast coast of Massachusetts, twenty miles long and ten miles wide at its broadest points. From the air it appears as a drunken triangle fretted with inlets and bays, big saltwater ponds and small fresh ones. With the map in front of her, Lillian frowned; she had even less sense of direction than I, though her confusion was on a far grander scale—a kind of cosmic disassociation—and for a long time we stared at the map in silence. We were seated side by side at the kitchen table and something about it looked wrong.

"This must be Noman's or one of the Elizabeth Islands," she said finally, "it doesn't seem anything like the Vineyard." I had been trying to decipher the names of the roads with no success and I put my glasses on. "It's upside down," I said after a considerable while. "How can you tell?" Lillian said. "The words," I said, "are upside down." "I think that's brilliant of you," she said, "I love people who notice things." I said I didn't think I noticed things, I thought we were both crazy. "I don't want to talk about it," Lillian said.

LILLIAN: *July, wasn't it?*
PETER: *It?*
LILLIAN: *The first summer you came here.*
PETER: *May, I think. June.*
LILLIAN: *It was July.*
PETER: *Couldn't have been.*
LILLIAN: *Forgive me, but your memory isn't very good. I have a diary entry.*
PETER: *All I remember, I was nervous as hell about coming.*
LILLIAN: *You're right about that, you were nervous as hell.*

PAUSE. SOUND OF MACHINE CLICKING.

LILLIAN: *I wonder why—you had no reason to be. No reason at all.*

PAUSE. SOUND OF LILLIAN COUGHING.

LILLIAN: *Why were you nervous?*
PETER: *I don't know. Because we'd never lived together in the same house, I guess.*
LILLIAN: *It's not enough to say we'd never lived together in the same house. That doesn't explain it. We'd had nice times together over the years, a lot of them, especially the winter before in New York—you were there over a week.*
PETER: *Two days.*
LILLIAN: *I wouldn't bring that up if I were you. If it was only two days, it was because you only wanted two days. You were very unpleasant to me afterwards. Very unpleasant, you caused me great pain. I think in some ways I never got over the pain of that experience.*

PAUSE.

PETER: *All I did was go to Mexico.*
LILLIAN: *It's not all you did. You'd have left New York without . . . never mind, let's not argue. I don't want to talk this way, it's prideless. Let's talk about something else.*
PETER: *I'm willing.*
LILLIAN: *Oh, sure.*

PAUSE.

LILLIAN: *Now you've upset me.*
PETER: *Sorry.*
LILLIAN: *What's the use speaking that way and then saying you're sorry? It's cruelty in space.*

PAUSE.

LILLIAN: *I wonder sometimes if you know your own angers about women.*

PAUSE.

LILLIAN: *I think I'll have another drink.*

But how do you tell about someone you loved and have lost? I'm better at inventing people than describing friends that are gone, partly I guess because the evocation of a scene or a person is a novelist's business but more because my reaching back for someone I cared about is too angry at the feeling of abandonment: too cynical or sentimental. I make villains and heroes of the past, the way some children make a devil of one parent, an angel of the other. But Lillian wasn't either and in my world she is not in the past: I have notes that were pushed under my door, notes left on tables and countertops, piles of letters she sent me from various places over the years, her voice in sixteen hours of tape we made at last hoping to put together a book of spoken memory in the final years, the years when she couldn't see to write. I have Christmas and birthday presents with memos and commands and demands and complaints and telegrams over the decades. I have pieces of a journal. What I don't have is Lillian.

LILLIAN: *You want to call Elaine May?*
PETER: *Do I want . . . no. Why would I want to call Elaine?*
LILLIAN: *I'll tell you after a while.*
PETER: *Tell me now.*
LILLIAN: *No, I don't think so.*
PETER: *Why not?*
LILLIAN: *I just don't want to . . . I mixed two drinks and I'm not feeling very well.*

> PAUSE. SOUND OF MACHINE CLICKING. SOUND OF LILLIAN COUGH- ING. SOUND OF ICE IN GLASS.

PETER: *That ought to do it, let's see if it works, okay?*
LILLIAN: *Sure.*
PETER: *Say something.*
LILLIAN: *Testing, testing, test . . .*
PETER: *Don't just keep saying testing, it's silly.*
LILLIAN: *What else am I going to say?*

> CLICK.
> PAUSE.

LILLIAN: *What kind of recording machine is it?*
PETER: *A JVC.*
LILLIAN: *JDC?*
PETER: *No, honey, that's the Jewish Defense Committee.*
LILLIAN (laughing): *The what?*

PETER: *Something like that. Or the Jewish Joint Distribution Committee.*

LILLIAN: *What's this thing, then?*

PETER: *I don't know what JVC stands for, it's just a machine.*

LILLIAN: *Is it off?*

PETER: *No, but if you want to say something private, say "turn it off" or press the button.*

LILLIAN: *I won't remember.*

PETER: *I will.*

LILLIAN: *No, you won't.*

PETER: *Yes I will, I'm much more discreet than you ever were or would be, how's that?*

LILLIAN: *Not discreet about me. Just maybe discreet about yourself.*

> *PAUSE.*

LILLIAN: *Okay, go ahead.*

> *PAUSE. SOUND OF LILLIAN COUGHING.*

LILLIAN: *Maybe we can get a book out of it. Be nice if we got a book out of it.*

> *PAUSE.*

LILLIAN: *Turn it off. We're wasting tape, Peter. Tape's expensive.*

PETER: *So what?*

LILLIAN: *How can you talk like that? . . . you talk like a slum child. You weren't a slum child.*

PETER: *I am now.*

LILLIAN: *No you're not. You can't just be a slum child—can't get into groups. You have to be born into them. Can't elect where you're born. You're stuck with your father and mother whether you like it or not.*

PETER: *Thanks, I feel better already.*

> *PAUSE.*

LILLIAN: *Well, I can't think of anything to talk about. What about you?*

PETER: *Bupkus.*

LILLIAN: *What's bupkus?*

PETER: *Goatshit.*

LILLIAN: *What a pair of dopes we are.*

PAUSE.

LILLIAN: *How about if one of us tells a story?*
PETER: *What kind of story?*
LILLIAN: *A true story.*

PAUSE.

LILLIAN: *How about if one of us tells the truth?*

The trouble is, it's hard to tell the truth about a close friend without telling the truth about yourself—at a certain depth the truth is tricky. I for instance like to think of myself as quiet and steely and intractable, but the truth is I'm too babyish for that kind of courage and I talk too much. The courageous are often quiet about their friends as the timid go around saying things like "I can't help saying what's on my mind," a mouthwash remark meant to precede pure spewed malice. Not the way to begin a story, even a true story—and yet you have to begin somewhere.

The day I first saw Lillian's house, that day in the sixties, there were two guest rooms—one with twin beds in it, the other with one. The one that had one bed was small and I took to it right away. It had the feel of a cell, with enough space for the bed (an antique sleigh bed with a broken box spring and mismatched mattress), a bedside table, a couple of lamps, a dresser, a chair, an old tin card table set up for me to work on, a portable typewriter. The two guest rooms shared a bath that was out in the hall.

I had brought with me six bulky suitcases swollen to bursting, not because I needed everything, but because I was full of the sort of swallowed anger that makes choices of any kind impossible. I kept the suitcases under the bed or stacked in a heap at the foot of it: I wanted to think it was possible to get away on a moment's notice, a desire that didn't escape Lillian's attention, though she never mentioned it. She was at least as manipulative as I, in a different way, careful in a different way, as delicate about certain kinds of talk as she was indelicate about others.

The house smelled nice. It had been built by her set designer, Howard Bay, to Lillian's exact specifications, and the shape of it told you something about the shape of the woman, since you were never quite sure whether you were stomping in by the front door or sneaking in by the back. It was set into the side of a hill facing the water, so the road led to the back and stopped at the top—at what people had every right to expect was the proper entrance, save for an announcement pasted on the upstairs door which said, in cheap gold-edged black print, TRANCE DO STA RS, all that was left of some hardware-store letters indicating Lillian's wish to have visitors enter by means of the outside staircase, a precariously steep wooden affair leading down to the main floor. Her friends all obeyed the sign but nobody else did. Nobody else could read it. As a rule, delivery people came to the upstairs door hoping it was the kitchen (it wasn't; the kitchen was downstairs, next to the front door) and found themselves on the bedroom floor by accident. The whole thing gave you an uneasy feeling, as though you had forced your way into a lady's bedroom without knowing it was her bedroom and then weren't sure whether to apologize for the invasion or for the not knowing.

The problem was trickier than it sounds and during the two decades of summers I visited the house people persisted in arriving at the wrong level three or four times a week, till John Hersey and Jules Feiffer and Art Buchwald colluded and convinced Lillian it was because of the sign. Then she went out and bought another sign that said ENTER and placed it at the foot of the driveway. Not even her friends knew what that one meant. But she didn't change ENTER to ENTRANCE, with an arrow pointing to the outside staircase, until the year before she died.

I couldn't get my bearings in the house for a long time. The second or third day a brassy cooking odor swam out of the kitchen where a woman with a tense face was heating olive oil with garlic and fresh basil from the garden, under Lillian's too sharp orders. Just before dark the voices began to sound belligerent and I wandered downstairs to the bar and asked Lilly what she wanted to drink. "Scotch with charged water," she said, "one piece of ice. Is it your feeling we should have wine with dinner?" I said that sounded fine. Lillian said: "Spaghetti with pesto. Then bluefish. White wine if you believe in such rules . . . I don't. Maybe you'd like red." I said I liked red fine.

"You're not trying to help," she said, "knock off the charm and tell me what you want."

"You have something against charm?"

"I have something against charmers," she said, "they're hell when they're cornered. The charm gets relentless." I said I'd just as soon have a beer and she went to the icebox to get it and I sat back and took another look around.

The sun had set and a tinged muggy breeze was blowing the roses high against the screens. The breeze had a gassy acid smell from the seaweed blown in by last week's northeaster. The west side of the room was filled with bookshelves topped by the wine-colored ninth edition of the Encyclopaedia Britannica and the dining table was at the east side, facing the sea.

The south wall, or a large part of it, was taken up by a slender green Victorian piece of furniture that looked rickety and was; it was the sofa from the original production of *The Little Foxes,* the one Tallulah Bankhead had draped herself on in the third-act scene when Regina denies her husband medicine while he tries to make the staircase and collapses. You had to sit on it carefully now and several people collapsed in it over the next few years despite its being sent out for repair three times. The major reconstruction it needed would have cost a mint and Lillian was tough about such things, often unable to spend money at all, a habit not unrelated to economy in work: a play is a dialogue of limited length because an audience will only sit still for so long and many skilled playwrights have been scared of going broke.

When she came back with the beer she sat in one of the two white chairs and I took the other. The chairs were so old the stuffing in the cushions edged out on all sides like the slowly leaking innards of some extinct species that has come into fashion too late to do it any good; but they faced each other and they shared the Queen Anne table, a good arrangement for Lilly and a friend, considering the cigarettes and ashtrays and cups and pots and lighters and books and papers needed all day and into the night. "What's playing?" she said.

I said not much.

"Yes there is," she said. "You've been thinking since you got here. What's on your mind?"

What was on my mind was too convoluted for speech and I was still feeling edgy. The crickets had started and so had the gulls. We went on sitting in silence at the Queen Anne table for some time.

LILLIAN: *Remember the first month you came here when you took to locking yourself in your room during the day? You remember that?*

PETER: *Sure.*
LILLIAN: *I was very, very hurt by that.*

PAUSE.

LILLIAN: *God knows it was your right to be alone. Everybody's right to be alone. I need to be alone myself a lot of the time—I always did. But locking your door, that was done against me, I think. I'll always think that now, so don't let's argue.*

PAUSE.

LILLIAN: *Certainly you can't imagine I'd have opened your door.*

PAUSE.

LILLIAN: *Do you imagine I'd have opened your door?*
PETER: *Yes.*
LILLIAN: *Forgive me, but you ought to know better. In my whole life I don't think I ever tried to open a locked door.*
PETER: *Then how did you know it was locked?*

PAUSE.

LILLIAN: *You have an answer for everything, don't you? It's not a very serious way of thinking, if you'll forgive my saying so. What did you imagine I was going to do, disturb you in some way?*
PETER: *No.*
LILLIAN: *You must have thought so.*

PAUSE.

LILLIAN: *You must have thought so, or you wouldn't have locked the door.*

There were good days of work that first month and bad days for me when I didn't know what I was about—one of those times you can't remember your reason for living—and Lillian was gentle with me, though people might not have thought so from the way she spoke. But I thought so.

Up till then I had never shown unfinished work to anyone since all suggestions about writing made me hostile and the occasional delicacy of an editor—"I wonder if I'd do that section *quite* that way"—didn't strike me as delicacy. Lillian's way of making a suggestion was, I thought, what delicacy was all about.

She would hold up the manuscript in front of her, set her head back into a long ladylike curve, and shout: "What the fuck do you think you're doing?" in a booming voice that appeared to reverberate like the call of a demented mermaid off the rocks of the breakwater. It carried the sound of passion and it washed over you like a warm sea surge in the wake of a tropical hurricane. Anybody who cared that much about you could say what they liked without offending and Lillian's affectionate rantings produced strength and bred stamina. In the world of the word, things are often backwards, and she had perverse celestial credentials: angels rush in where fools fear to tread.

Lillian was bombastic, opinionated, dazzling, enraging, funny, peevish, bawdy and about writing at least, accurate—she had a way of saying what you didn't want to hear so that you did— and there was a lot I didn't want to hear. Whatever it is that bubbles up from the helplessness of babyhood like poisonous fizz and causes people to corrode or corrupt had stopped me from living, let alone writing; my early work had been overpraised, I knew, and public luck hadn't helped private sense of failure. What helped was Lillian, who was beginning to be for me what Dashiell Hammett had always been for her. She was twenty-five years my elder, more than twice the age difference there had been between them, with another difference. She was stiff about work but she was careful too—she had some feeling for the emptiness, the crippling sense of dread writers get when they go blank or go wrong. "I'm not like Dash," she said, "I'm too easy."

We were sitting on her beach—it must have been midsummer by then because I remember the wet heat, the sting of the sand flies and the ominous glassy ripple of the water.

"You ought to write about growing up in New Orleans," Lillian said suddenly, loud. She said it as if she had been thinking about it for a while.

I watched her but I didn't get it.

"It's a funny city to grow up in," she went on, "New Orleans does odd things to people. It did odd things to me too."

"That's not what you meant," I said.

"No," she said. "But it's almost what I meant."

I sat there a while, then I got it. When I first met Lillian, I was ten and she was a successful playwright of thirty-five who had come back to New Orleans for a visit. I was by then what is

officially called a molested child, having been taken to bed at
nine by one of the people who worked for my father, a black
man in his twenties. That year, my tenth year, was not a successful year—I had started out lonely and seductive and wound up
frightened and empty. "Child molesting is an old American cus-
tom," I said, "but your politeness is appreciated. You can call it
growing up if you want to."

"You can go to hell, and I wasn't being polite," Lillian said,
"it's disgusting of you to take that tone. You're full of self-con-
tempt, that's the truth, and anybody who loves you is bound to
come in for some of the contempt—it's a terrible price some of
us pay for an offer of decency in this world—a terrible, terrible
price."

She sipped some wine and lit a cigarette.

"It's bad for everything, that kind of thinking—very bad.
Most children are seductive."

I said I had been more seductive than most.

"Well, don't be so goddamn proud of it," she said. "What
did seduction ever get you besides sexual abuse and unhappiness?"

"You," I said.

Lillian threw her head back and laughed for a couple of minutes. "Maybe you should just go to hell," she said. "There's
something you haven't told me, isn't there?"

I kept still. There was something, but it had to do with my
mother not me—not yet anyway.

"I thought so," she said, "you'll tell me when you're ready.
I've long since given up trying to force people to talk. What's the
matter now? . . . Why are you grunting?"

I was grunting because my neck was stiff.

Lillian blinked and radically changed her tone.

"How about a nice swim-poo," she said, "in the sea-pie?"

I said I wished she would cut the baby talk—it didn't
bode well.

"Pay me."

"What for?"

"I don't cut baby talk for nothing," she said, "Dash once
paid me five dollars an hour not to baby-talk. All the way from
Philadelphia to New York in an old Ford, and it was years before
they built the Turnpike. I made over forty dollars."

I wanted to know if he'd paid up.

"Certainly he paid up," she said, "the man wasn't a crook."

She got up and went in the water and dog-paddled for a few minutes and came back. She was moving slowly and I was mulling over what she had said about New Orleans. "What are you doing now," she asked, "making notes?"

I wasn't, I was doodling on a pad; I didn't need notes to remember my conversations with Lillian, I would have needed shock treatments to forget them. I swore at her and she chuckled and lit a cigarette and I asked what Hammett had done when he thought her work bad.

"Whatever he felt like doing—he pitched a draft of *Autumn Garden* in my face and told me if I wanted to write like Rodgers and Hart to go live with somebody else," wrapping a beach towel around her shoulders, "Hammett was tough past belief. If tough is the right word. I'm not sure it is."

There was a silence and the double toot of a ferryboat. "Dottie Parker said he was more than tough. 'It can't be news to you that Dash is a cruel man.' She was right, I think, but I don't think it much matters in the end . . . the word, I mean. He didn't like bad writing." There was another hollow silence and Lillian said: "Dash didn't like a lot of things. He didn't like lying, and he didn't like Hollywood. He didn't like homosexuality when he noticed it."

I asked if he had noticed it in her.

"I don't know," she said and looked away.

By then each of us knew a little about the other's early troubles and Lillian had often told about a period during which she and Hammett would get rowdy drunk together and sometimes take another woman home, not an unusual thing to do in his time, his world, and I had been curious about it ever since.

"What about the partying?"

"It went on now and then till I put a stop to it. Dash had a taste for whores. It never happened again."

"Why not?"

"Because I got scared."

"Of hating it?"

"The opposite."

I said being scared hadn't made her quit other things.

"Serious things, not comedy things. I always thought sex like that was comedy stuff."

I said I thought it was too.

"You ought to act on what you think," Lillian said and walked back to the house.

So we shared, among other things, a certain aimless tone of bravura, as rebels of different generations often do, especially Southern rebels who romanticize their pasts for some of the right and all of the wrong reasons. We had both grown up in New Orleans—had both been uprooted and moved to New York in our teens—had both been impossible cutups. We had both been experimental in sexual ways and other ways and had both paid a price for the experiments.

I was, by then, very happy around Lilly and was not, by a long shot, the only man who was. Lillian knew something many Southern women know—and many Northern women do not even seem to know about—she knew how to make a man feel as if he had done her an enormous favor by merely walking into a room: she didn't just blush, she glowed, and at her best she glittered. Few qualities are as attractive as a certain combination of the bawdy and the shy.

And in a lesser sense, the jealous; but in that sense Lilly overshot the field. If all jealousy is sexual, which it probably is, as opposed, say, to envy, she was more jealous than anyone I've ever known—jealous of all her friends, regardless of race, creed, color, religion, class, marital status, gender or age, let alone occupation—and if any two of her friends got together and collaborated on something that excluded her, there was trouble.

LILLIAN: *Jules and I had an appalling conversation the other night.** You know, Jules and I are really devoted to each other. He made a passionate speech, he was very tight— Are you sitting upside down?*
PETER: *Sort of.*
LILLIAN: *Why?*
PETER: *I'm drunk.*
LILLIAN: *You are?*
PETER: *A little, so are you.*
LILLIAN: *I'd like to get very, very drunk for a change.*
PETER: *This is pretty good stuff for a cheap California Bordeaux. Is there another bottle?*

---

*Jules Feiffer remembers this episode as "the time Lilly got mad at me because she found out I had a new girlfriend I hadn't told her about."

LILLIAN: *In the closet and it's not cheap.*
PETER: *It is by today's standards.*
LILLIAN: *I don't live by today's standards and neither should you. Anyway, Jules had been drinking. His girl left him and Lally Weymouth thinks that's what it is. I don't think that's what it is. I think he's upset about her leaving, but I don't think that's why he's drinking.*
PETER: *Does Jules need a reason for drinking?*
LILLIAN: *Is there some reason you keep interrupting me?*

    PAUSE.

LILLIAN: *We were at Milton Gordon's house for dinner.*
PETER: *Who?*
LILLIAN: *You know, the rich character who gives money to the charities of the famous every year and then invites them to dinner. You know him.*
PETER: *You introduced me to him.*
LILLIAN: *Sure, blame it on me. Blame everything on me.*
PETER: *I try.*
LILLIAN: *Anyway, he gave some money to my Committee for Public Justice, so he had us to dinner, and I don't know how Jules and I got on the subject of* Carnal Knowledge *but we did, and . . . well, you know how I feel about* Carnal Knowledge *. . . I told you, I cried the night I saw it in a projection room with Mike. —Mike directed it. And Jules wrote it. They collaborated. The two of them.*
PETER: *I saw it.*
LILLIAN: *Up till* Carnal Knowledge, *Mike always showed me the scripts he was going to shoot, but not that one. So Jules said: "I know you don't like it, I know you feel . . ." and in an attempt to stop him from talking about it, I said: "Jules, I certainly never blamed* Carnal Knowledge *on you. I'm afraid I blame it on Mike." . . . Well, that he misunderstood. He thought I meant Mike had written the picture. So he began to explain his part in the writing. And that began to irritate me. You can see why.*

    PAUSE. SOUND OF CORK POPPING. SOUND OF LILLIAN COUGHING.

LILLIAN: *Because I was saying almost the opposite. Without saying it in words, because I wasn't going to attack Mike, but the fact that Jules didn't understand me—and it was now in front of people—was irritating me, if you see what I mean. Are you pouring wine for me or just for yourself?*

PETER: *I switched to brandy. Your wineglass is there.*
LILLIAN: *Where?*
PETER: *By your right hand.*
LILLIAN: *The lights in this room are disgraceful. It gets darker in here every day. Isn't it dark to your eyes?*
PETER: *No, Lilly.*
LILLIAN: *I hope I'm not going totally blind, I don't think I could manage blindness.*
PETER: *Then don't put off the eye doctor.*
LILLIAN: *I won't.*
PETER: *You already did.*
LILLIAN: *Don't chivy me, Peter, it's too . . . I can't . . . I was talking about Jules. —So I said: "Jules, knock it off." I said: "It's a picture that so demeans relations between men and women that I can't talk about it. And I don't want to be told in a movie or a book that the sign of a whore going down on Jack Nicholson is corruption, because I don't believe it's corruption." And Jules said: "You don't understand—it's a picture about men's hatred of women." He said: "All heterosexual men hate women . . ." I said: "You'll forgive me, but that statement makes me very, very angry."*

    PAUSE. SOUND OF HICCUP. SOUND OF FOG HORN. SOUND OF LILLIAN COUGHING.

LILLIAN: *I said: "I went through a lifetime with heterosexual men and whatever trouble I found with them, I found no hatred . . . I found other things to complain about, including infidelity—including often anger or meanness or greed or many other things, like jealousy—but I never found hatred." Is there still some wine in my glass?*
PETER: *Hang on . . . there is now.*
LILLIAN: *I said: "You're talking about homosexuals." . . . Jules said: "No. Homosexuals love women. And heterosexuals hate women."*

    PAUSE.

LILLIAN: *What he means of course is that homosexuals love a certain kind of woman. And a certain kind of woman loves homosexuals. He means a man who thinks he's an unattractive small fellow has a tough time.*

PETER: *I wonder.*

LILLIAN: *Then I made a very great mistake. I said: "The proof of what I'm saying is that Mike told me once that he, John Calley and Buck Henry were so upset about the picture, they all decided to get married." —And Jules said: "Buck Henry had nothing to do with the picture—nothing to do with it—didn't write it," completely misunderstanding what I was saying. Are you following me?*

PETER: *I'm trying to, honey. We're both plastered.*

LILLIAN: *Well, who can blame us for getting plastered? I mean if people are going to go around saying things like all heterosexual men hate women. One would accept the statement in other terms, of course—there's an enormous amount of hatred in almost any kind of love. And some men hate women.*

PETER: *Everybody hates women a little, Lilly—even women. In fact, especially women.*

LILLIAN: *I don't think that's true, Mike doesn't hate them enough.*

PETER: *Enough for what?*

LILLIAN: *For himself, of course. I've known Mike since, say, twenty or twenty-five years. In those years he's had four or five serious love affairs. Living with one woman after another. In a house.*

PAUSE.

LILLIAN: *Every woman but me.*

PAUSE.

LILLIAN: *The idea that you can find that many people you want to live in a house with is absolutely bewildering to me. And each time it's over, it's completely over, as if he'd never known the woman at all.*

PETER: *True of me too. It's true of a lot of people.*

LILLIAN: *Is it?*

PETER: *Sure.*

LILLIAN: *Why sure?*

PETER: *There's nothing deader than dead passion, Lilly, not even dead fish in the marketplace.*

LILLIAN: *I guess not, but I wouldn't put too nice a light on it if I were you—I think it shows a kind of contempt too—and I'm afraid in Mike's case some of it's moved over to me, without ever having slept with me.*

PETER: *Meaning?*

LILLIAN: *I think Mike wishes to be rid of me now too.*

PETER: *You're wrong.*

LILLIAN: *I'm almost sure I'm right. On various signs, including the last conversation I had with him, in which . . . well, it's too boring to go into in detail, but something I'd said to Lally Weymouth got misquoted.*

PETER: *How the hell did we get back to Lally?*

LILLIAN: *I'm about to tell you—quiet down. What is the matter with you?*

PETER: *Got the hiccups.*

LILLIAN: *Peter, you are the only person I've ever known in my whole life, outside of a comic strip, who actually gets the hiccups when he gets drunk.*

PETER: *Can't help it.*

LILLIAN: *Where was I?*

PETER: *Lally.*

LILLIAN: *Yes, Lally. So all I'd said to Lally was, "I don't know when Mike's coming to visit me on the Vineyard—he's lost an actress, and he's recasting the play he's directing—I guess he'll come when he's recast." I said: "I've long ago given up Mike and dates, so I don't know what the date of his arrival will be." And Lally said . . .*

PETER: *I'm getting confused.*

LILLIAN: *It doesn't matter whether you're confused or not. Why don't you try holding your breath? The point is, I like Lally, but she's a mischief-maker. She called Mike up and said: "Lilly tells me she's tired of your backing in and out of dates, and she doesn't want you to come to the Vineyard." She . . .*

PETER: *She who?*

LILLIAN: *Lally.*

PETER: *How do you know she said that?*

LILLIAN: *Annabel told me.*

PETER: *Annabel?*

PAUSE.

LILLIAN: *Peter, please don't stand on your head like that, you'll hurt yourself. It's not going to cure your hiccups. Peter, are you listening to me? . . . So I said: "Mike, I'm not feeling very pleasant this minute. Annabel tells me that you're angry with me for something that Lally told you, and I'm extremely offended that you believe Lally." I said: "It seems to me that you have every reason to know I've been intensely loyal to you, and if I made some kind of foolish joke, you certainly should have known it was a joke, and I'm very offended. Not at Lally, although I'd be glad to take it up with Lally if you'd like me to—but I think the offense lies with you. If you can be so easily shaken about me, then something has been very wrong for a long time, and I think we're in trouble." And Mike said: "I think we're in trouble too."*

SOUND OF CRASH.

LILLIAN: *I told you you were going to hurt yourself.*

PAUSE.

LILLIAN: *Oy. Are you all right? Why don't you get up and sit in a chair?*
PETER: *I like it here.*
LILLIAN: *Well, try to keep your face out of the fireplace. So Mike said: "When you come back, I think we should have a talk." — And I said: "That's up to you . . . I don't feel I've made the trouble, so it's up to you." . . . I haven't heard from him. When I get back to New York, I guess I'll call him. Something is very wrong, I don't know what. But it sounds to me like—I don't know . . . Sounds . . .*
PETER: *Sounds like Mike loves you, Lilly.*
LILLIAN: *Oh, well. Sure.*

PAUSE.

LILLIAN: *Love.*

Listening to her voice on some of the tapes—tapes made a few years before the end of her life, when time was beginning to strip her of defenses and make her sound different: not old exactly, but maybe her kind of old: when all I could do was get silly-drunk and clown with her, because she was already three quarters blind and one quarter dead and couldn't face it, wasn't ready to accept what had to be accepted until it had to be—I miss the other woman. I miss the vigor of Lillian.

I miss the swimming, fishing, laughing and cooking and carousing and working and wild woman of that first blaze of summer, who wouldn't stop. Who had more energy than children.

Who, then, in late middle age, had already run a farm and written a handful of plays at the same time; had been forced to give up the farm in the McCarthy days when she was blacklisted, and gone to work, she said, first as a saleslady, and then in the accounting department at Macy's under a different name; had survived all that, and then survived Hammett.

The facts of her life were simple. She was born in 1905 on Prytania Street in New Orleans. Her father ran a shoe store, her mother's family was rich and felt that her mother had married beneath her. Her mother's family was a hornet's nest of money-grubbing middle-class horrors according to Lilly, who used her maternal grandmother as a model for Regina in *The Little Foxes.* It was because of her mother's family that she was attracted to the rich and hated them all her life. She never came to terms with growing up, and the outraged heart of childhood lasted through old age; she was an angry and uncompromising loner, not what is thought of as pretty, but she was sexy, and there was a shower of sparks under the flint in her voice. After her parents moved to New York she kept to herself, went to school and college, got a job reading manuscripts for Horace Liveright. Then she went to Hollywood and read for a studio and got married to Arthur Kober and divorced him and met Dashiell Hammett.

Hammett was a successful writer who had almost reached the end of his writing career: he impressed her, she interested him, and they lived together while Lillian discovered she couldn't write short stories and tried writing plays. She was not very good at intricate plots, but Hammett was, and he stood behind her. Lillian wrote *The Children's Hour* and became famous. From then on she was not just the best-known female playwright in the world, she was practically the only one. Her second play was a failure, her third and fourth and fifth and sixth international successes. She was a vehement anti-Fascist and in the thirties thought of herself as a Stalinist, though she never joined the Communist party as Hammett and many of their friends admittedly did. She was declared an alcoholic, went into treatment and was declared cured. She went to the U.S.S.R. during World War II, met Prokofiev, met Shaw in England, met the people she wanted to meet and lived a rowdy life of independent discipline. Her bond with Hammett lasted till he died and was full of bumps and grinds and contortions and all the other helpless movements of passion, though the affair itself was short-lived: they were furious lovers and tender friends.

In the fifties, at the height of the McCarthy period, they were both called upon to testify, she before the House Un-American Activities Committee, he before Senator Joe McCarthy's subcommittee. It was fashionably safe in the fifties to rat on your friends and many people did: Lillian did not. When asked "Are you now or have you ever been a member of the Communist party?" she answered no. Then a letter she had written to the committee was read into the court record, saying she would be willing to answer all questions about herself but no questions about anyone else, that she believed that was the only stand to take, the moral stand for an American, and the last paragraph of the letter contained a sentence that was to become a kind of slogan: "I cannot and will not cut my conscience to suit this year's fashions."

She later took the protection of the Fifth Amendment to stay out of jail, but she never did inform on others. The experience of the HUAC took the wind out of her and she was blacklisted for ten years afterward so she couldn't make a living. That was when she sold her farm, "Hardscrabble," in Pleasantville, N.Y., and she didn't have the heart to write another play for a long time. When she did, it was a success, but the luster of her fame as a playwright had dulled over and it never quite came back.

One morning on the Vineyard I found her pacing around the living room as if she had forgotten where the door was. It was early and through the bleariness of mind-fog I saw a chunk of the Sunday *New York Times* doubled up in one of her fists and she started speaking as I walked in.

"This is foolishness. God knows I've taken it before, so have you—we all have, and I will again—but not now. I have to do something about it now, it's the wrong time, the wrong day. The coffee's on the stove."

I went and poured a cup from the Chemex that was kept every morning in a pot of warm water and came back. Lillian was still pacing. I asked her what had happened.

"What makes you think anything's happened?"

I kept quiet.

"One could make out a case it should be ignored," she said. "It has no importance—it's the timing that's wrong. There are people who can stand to be forgotten and people who can't. One day I may have to stand it, but not like this—I'll feel crippled if I leave this alone, it's not my nature and I'm stuck with my nature now. I'll just have to act on it."

She went on for a while and I swallowed some coffee and got another cup and waited for her to simmer down. After two cups I still didn't know what she was talking about. What she was talking about was an article in the drama section of the *Times* that referred to the three major living American playwrights as Williams, Miller and Albee, with no mention of Hellman. The piece was written by a Hollywood director who was pushing one of his movies and trying to sound literary; it wasn't meant as a slight. Most Hollywood people try to sound high-minded and so most of them talk art, partly on the assumption that talking art makes artists, and partly to avoid thinking of themselves as what they are—industrialists—though they don't seem to mind referring to the movie business as "the industry." "You worked in Hollywood," I said, "you know how they talk."

"Certainly I know how they talk. He's trying to sound like a literary swinger. He wants to know the hip and the fashionable. Whose work counts and whose doesn't."

"Exactly. So what?"

"So mine doesn't," Lillian said.

"You care what movie people think?"

"No, and I'm not taking his word."

"Whose word, then?"

"Whoever he paid to write that article," she said, "are you blind? *He* didn't write it. That's halfway decent English."

She went out and made a fresh pot of coffee and came back and paced some more. It was the first time since I'd known Lilly that it had seriously occurred to me she cared about such things, so I missed the point of what she was saying and missed it cold.

That was the morning I made the mistake of thinking of her as a frail and failing writer and feeling sorry for her. I never made the mistake again because that was the morning she made the decision to write a memoir, and long before she had published the last of the four books that were to follow it was clear that no one would overlook her work again in her lifetime. From then on, she became a kind of self-propelled American folk heroine whose face was so famous that the same people who had taken mild pleasure in ignoring her began to think it their duty to attack her, and presently they found a reason.

There is a literary elite in most societies whose members are so learned that they spend their days savoring their opinions—so old they have reduced sex to gender—and so dry that every time they cough, dust comes out. Many are saints by their own admission, having dedicated their lives to saving literature, and Lillian was not one of them: her mind didn't work that way and her glands were never that dry. She'd already bowled her way past such people in her first career and she guffawed her way through them in her second. But what impressed you was not so much the force behind it as something else.

It's not exactly news that talented people tend to go on too long with what they're doing and so wind up as Hemingway did, a parody of himself. For an aging writer the only antidote to the poison of self-imitation, apart from silence, is the most stinging geriatric salt. After the failure of her last play Lillian tried going on with the theater for a while, mainly because she wanted to finish the story of Regina—the one she had begun in *The Little Foxes* and continued in *Another Part of the Forest*. She had meant those plays as two parts to a trilogy and so she spent months on the third, a play that had the same woman, now in her late seventies, living on the French Riviera with a string of young lovers. But Lilly scrapped it after writing a couple of acts on the grounds that it was the wrong choice—Regina would not have ended like that—she would have gone on living in Chicago where she was headed at the close of *Foxes* to become a reigning society hostess.

Regina in Chicago was the right choice but the play was never written because Lillian had quit writing plays. She was evasive about her reasons and in public interviews spoke up about the death of serious theater on Broadway and what was happening to ticket prices Off-Broadway. But when cornered by a friend she said simply: "The theater has passed me by," and let it go at that. The bright day of the well-made play was done—at least for the present—and to go on with it would have been to parody plays of her own already under attack as melodrama, so she went another way. Having trained herself to think in dialogue for one career, she took a sharp turn and trained herself to think in prose for another. It was a little like a sculptor learning to paint, but she had seen it coming, and she managed it by teaching students to write English prose at Harvard, Berkeley and MIT—teaching herself along with them. She refused to teach playwrighting or to talk about it.

The Vineyard house in the sixties was a nesting place for the try at a new career and the combined noises on the bedroom floor during the mornings would have sounded psychotic if there had been anyone to hear them. Happily there was not. My bedroom was sealed off at one end of the hall, Lilly's was at the other. I was working on a novel about Spain and the flow of Andalusian gutter talk from my room was as constant as it was unnecessary, though I seldom spoke above a whisper.

Lillian on the other hand was very loud—spoke English— and spoke in several voices. Ever since I'd known her she had had an imaginary companion, an elderly woman whose name, God help her, was Nursey, and the two of them often got into fights before noon when Nursey told Lillian to mind her manners or put on another dress or have some sense about what she was writing. Nursey was a boring old crank but she meant well and she had been there so long I was used to her: I no longer paid any attention to her patronizing Lillian or to Lillian's high angers at being patronized. The two of them wouldn't have upset me at all if a third person hadn't appeared on the scene.

I became aware of the third lady slowly because I was too self-involved to listen much but once in a while I couldn't help noticing the new voice, which was both different and unpleasant. One night at dinner I asked Lillian who she was and after a long silence Lillian said: "Her name seems to be Mimsey."

"I hope I didn't hear you right," I said.

Lillian laughed. "There's no use going on about it," she said, "that's her name and that's that."

"Mimsey's so damn cute for a name."

"Sure is. Cute as pigshit," Lillian said.

"How long has she been around?"

"Two or three weeks."

"Is she planning to stay?"

"I hope not," Lillian said.

But she was. For most of July and August Mimsey took up squatter's rights in Lillian's mind, tapping her foot lightly and patiently while the other two argued. She never spoke much, but she was always there—a kind of referee. From time to time she would say things like "Well, what would *you* do in my position?" in a clear calm nasal tone that made you want to slap her till her teeth rattled. If she was that irritating to me I knew what she must be doing to Lilly and I sympathized, but after a while I couldn't take any more of her.

It was mainly because of Mimsey that I took to locking my door during the day. I never admitted that she was the reason, for fear of reprisals—I had the feeling, despite her cool, that Mimsey was capable of sharp and rather ugly behavior—but the reprisals came anyway, and they came from Lillian.

And so we fought and argued, with ourselves and with each other, and worked happily through the summer and into the fall.

With the exception of John and Barbara Hersey I didn't want to see much of anyone else that summer because my work had started to go well. But Lillian did want to and she asked people to dinner once or twice a week. I was paying two hundred dollars a month as my share of household expenses but I didn't like being consulted about meals and I kept pretty much to myself. I sometimes surfaced when she had company, not always, since in those days I thought of myself as a very private person (a euphemistic way of acknowledging that I was afraid of exposure at almost any level) and the change in our relationship would never have been noticed if we hadn't been living on an island, or if Lillian hadn't talked. But she did talk. For most of her life Lilly had an awkward habit of telling secrets to all her friends on the phone—usually prefaced by "This is one thousand percent for you"—and before the middle of August it was common cocktail chitchat around the Vineyard that we were more than just friends. It was an unfortunate time to have it said that we were lovers, because it was a delicate time for both of us in different ways and because it was true.

But it had not been true for long and I was still wary of it for all the obvious and some not so obvious reasons. The Vineyard itself was one of them; the summer population was another.

Rather than try to describe the virtues and problems of Martha's Vineyard, Lillian took me for a drive one Sunday and walked me around town; it's a curious aspect of Vineyard time that when I took the same drive by myself last week the general feel of the island was not much changed. New shops, new houses buried down dirt roads, new condominiums have appeared in the intervening quarter of a century, but there are no high-rise buildings, no big hotels, and the impact of the place is the same.

The town of Vineyard Haven looks as comfortably untidy today as it did the morning she walked me through it: a convocation of gray-shingled houses with green trim, old rose-lined fences made of picket or stone, the earth around them strewn with elm and oak and red-leaf Japanese maple. In size Vineyard Haven is more of a village than a town but it is real, it does not look self-consciously quaint and isn't. Its backbone is an infinitesimal segment of the same Main Street that slices all the way through New England—the street that once ran across America—only a few blocks long here, with a grocery store, a bookstore, a cheese-and-pasta store, a barbershop, one small movie house and two drugstores, an odd assortment of specialty shops threaded among them.

The Sunday after the Vineyard Haven tour we drove out to see Edgartown, about eight miles down-island. Here it seems worth explaining that down means east, up means west in this part of the world, due to sailors and ship captains consulting maps and charts upon which degrees of longitude go down as they go east. People all over New England talk about going "down to Maine" when they mean they're going north or northeast, and a disoriented Southerner like me is in constant trouble. The effect all this had on Lillian is hard to define but one evening when we were driving to Jules Feiffer's house for dinner she gave me her best direction thus far: "Two miles before you come to a little lake, turn left." I accused her of poisoning my thinking and she accused me of not listening.

Edgartown, the day she took me to see it, was impressive—the largest and oldest settlement of its kind on the island. There used to be a back lot at Warner Brothers in Los Angeles that had a permanent movie set built just like Edgartown: a small white church, a white town hall, a string of white wooden clapboard houses with white picket fences, white bedrooms, white kitchens, white people, green shutters, green grass, green leaves. If you watch the Hollywood movies of the thirties or forties you will think that most of America looks like Edgartown, largely because the European immigrants who made the movies thought so. It isn't true. Only Edgartown looks like Edgartown. Or at least that was the case until the early fifties, when suburban people all over the States took to remodeling their homes to look like the Warner Brothers movie set, which resulted in the immigrants' vision of America becoming America.

Edgartown itself—the original—is a splendid-looking collection of crisp white houses overlooking one of the brightest and prettiest little ports in the country. If it lacks the scruffy, lived-in look of Vineyard Haven—if it is a little self-conscious in its architectural purity—you can't blame it, considering it has been ripped off so often that most visitors who come here think they've seen it before. There are more cases of déjà vu in Edgartown than anywhere else on the North American continent: that's enough to make any place a little vain and the town rises before dawn and starts posing long before the tourists are out with their cameras. I used to have the feeling if you woke Edgartown up in the middle of the night it would look like Vineyard Haven.

The point of all this is not so much the towns themselves as the sort of people who have summer homes in each of them. With certain exceptions the Edgartown residents tend to be dressy, politically conservative, rich and WASP—as opposed to the towns of Tisbury (Vineyard Haven) and West Tisbury, which have a bohemian tang that serves to attract liberals in summer and fresh or seedy intellectuals of all kinds all year. As an ex-radical and a Jew, Lillian was more welcome in Tisbury and up-island than she was down-island in Edgartown but there were people in both camps who would have enjoyed seeing her make a fool of herself, either because they disliked her politics or because she had made fools of them. Most of them were harmless enough but a few had clout.

In recent years Martha's Vineyard has been in the press more than usual and it's no longer a secret that the crowd of summer residents includes (or has included) Walter Cronkite, Mike Wallace, Katharine Graham, Jacqueline Onassis, Kingman Brewster, Bishop Paul Moore, Carly Simon, James Taylor, Beverly Sills, Mia Farrow, André Previn, Christopher Reeve, Patricia Neal, Mildred Dunnock—and—Dashiell Hammett, Thornton Wilder, John Hersey, Art Buchwald, Anthony Lewis, Robert Brustein, Shel Silverstein, Herb Gardner, Jules Feiffer, John Updike, Philip Roth, Carlos Fuentes, John Marquand, Jr., William and Rose Styron and a slew of lesser-known writers.

The island is awash with shellfish and writers and it's as easy to dig up the one—if you know how—as it is hard to avoid the other if you don't. In the first group there are steamers, littlenecks, cherrystones, quahogs, lobsters, shrimps, crabs, scallops, mussels, squid, conchs and sea snails. In the second group there are successful writers, failed writers, promising writers and talentless writers lured here by the lyrical look of the other writers.

The glitter of the summer residents has earned the island a reputation that isn't always accurate: *Paris Match* called Martha's Vineyard *"l'île chic"* the same year the American press started to refer to it as the "rich liberal's island," a term as deeply resented by the reactionary residents of West Chop as it was by the conservatives of Edgartown. The truth, of course, is a mixture. If the island has certain money-green oases inhabited by rich liberals where no necktie is ever seen, where seldom is heard a discouraging word except about the government, where women affect the simple woolly look of Eleanor Roosevelt and frayed cuffs for men are de rigueur—it also has areas inhabited by people who are as rich, who are given to formal country attire and who affect English accents and fake-aristocratic facial tics worthy of a William F. Buckley, Jr. You can find extreme affectation anywhere if you're looking for it but there's less of it on the Vineyard than in other places of its kind.

Given the gaudy extravagance of this stage set and its cast, the play of island gossip can be as casually lethal today as it was two decades ago. It was dangerous then to a loving relationship and intended as dangerous. Lillian knew how to batten her hatches better than I since she knew the game and the stakes better and the cardinal rule—the unassailable attitude of not caring what was said or not said—came more easily to her than it did to me. Most of the folks who were out to take a swipe at Lilly would cheerfully have used me if they could. There was nothing they could do at the moment; but I wasn't so certain of the future. A summer of sleeping together is one thing, but what about winter, is a thought that has entered the heads of better and more responsible men than I was.

Summer jabber on the Vineyard starts around Memorial Day with who is sleeping with whom and ends around Labor Day with who isn't. Because of what Lillian referred to as her angers, she had already alienated a large gaggle of geese that year and sexual malice among intellectuals is rampant at best. The whole damn scene made me nervous and I didn't know how to get unnervous. Trouble was coming—that I knew. Whatever went on upstairs, I was never entirely comfortable downstairs when people came to dinner.

LILLIAN: *I still don't see what in hell you were so nervous about,*
Peter.
PETER: What finally happened.
LILLIAN: On the Vineyard, you mean?
PETER: The mainland.
LILLIAN: Oh, that.

PAUSE.

LILLIAN: Oh. Oh, that.
PETER: Yes, that—Jesus Christ—that. What else was there to be
nervous about?
LILLIAN (chuckling): Don't exercise yourself, honey, I just asked
a question. No offense intended.
PETER: What are you laughing at?
LILLIAN: Can't I laugh?
PETER: No.

SOUND OF LILLIAN LAUGHING. SOUND OF LILLIAN COUGHING.

LILLIAN: *It's a miracle we came out so well in the end. It's largely*
due to my stubbornness if you don't mind my saying so.
PETER: Oh sure. Take all the credit for yourself.
LILLIAN: I'm not taking credit—I didn't say loyalty, I said stubbornness.
PETER: What's the difference?
LILLIAN: Loyalty is too self-serving a word for a tasteful lady to
use, honey, it would sound boastful. You know I never use such
terms about myself—I'm far too modest.

PAUSE.

LILLIAN: I'm famous for my modesty.

PAUSE.

LILLIAN: I'm famous for my gentility too.
PETER: You are?
LILLIAN: I'd like to see the cocksucker says I'm not.

PAUSE.

LILLIAN: I have a darling nature.
PETER: I wish I had a darling nature.
LILLIAN: Never mind, honey, you have a charming nature. Some-
times it's too charming.

PETER: *Yes, I know.*
LILLIAN: *How do you know?*
PETER: *I know because you've been telling me so for twenty-five years.*

By the last week in August the heat was out of the air. Early autumn is the best season of all on the Vineyard—a time when days are crystal and nights are cool. Flocks of migratory birds skeeter over the earth and drift down into it out of a chill sky like black confetti. In the afternoon after the wind dies the sea takes on a curious light, deep and delicate, dark with a hint of violet, its surface as smooth and impenetrable as molten glass. This is the true time of bonding, when island people begin to drift into couples against the cold of winter, many of them to drift apart again in April with the first thaw.

Lillian hadn't brought up the question of where we would go in winter any more than I had and the subject sat in a corner or between us like a good child, seen but not heard. Sooner or later it had to be discussed, but for the moment work carried us. It was as if we had fallen accidentally into the right answer for friendship despite the age difference and the difference in what Lillian called our natures. Not enough has been written about the virtues of shared time and space, as too much has been said about love: if affection is meant to endure, just plain hanging out together may be the deepest bedrock of all.

Some mornings we'd sit and read out loud from yesterday's work, then go for a walk on the beach. Reading a few pages and talking them over was to become a sort of habit for the next years, so that afterward—when the witch-hunting and red-baiting started all over again—the habit came in handy since I already knew what was made up in Lillian's work and what wasn't, and didn't care.

But that was for later. For now we were content and I had not expected such contentment, having somehow come to trust exclusively the worst in people. The best in people, I figured, could disappear on a dime, but the worst is always there. I was in my thirties, too young and too old for my age.

⊱⊱⊱⊱⊱ II

WHEN YOU SENSE trouble coming you tend to freeze but if it's a certain kind of trouble it can wait you out for years.

August spilled into fall and still the problem of what to do with winter did not come up. Lillian had an apartment in New York, I had been living between New York and Spain, we both liked living alone. The act of drifting through the summer together was by now a weightless force something like gliding, not so much planned upon as used: every day was the same day, so today never passed. Nights were different, nights went by too quickly, but the speed of darkness is faster for lovers of any kind than the speed of light, and the sleep that knits up the raveled sleeve of care is bullshit, since there's no difference between raveled and unraveled in the first place.

LILLIAN: *I didn't sleep a bit last night. Not one bit.*
PETER: *Sure you did. I came in and saw you.*
LILLIAN: *I wasn't sleeping. I was thinking.*
PETER: *You snore when you think?*
LILLIAN: *I don't want to talk about it.*

SOUND OF LILLIAN COUGHING.

LILLIAN: *I had an aunt who told me once she hadn't slept all summer.*
PETER: *No Southern lady worth her salt ever admits to having slept.*
LILLIAN: *Oh, shut up.*

PAUSE.

43

LILLIAN: *There's a tough streak in you—tough as nails. It's not always pleasant.*
PETER: *Flattery.*
LILLIAN (laughing): *You're mighty sure of yourself, professor.*
PETER: *I'm mighty sure of you.*

   PAUSE.

LILLIAN: *Just don't be too sure.*

The first Sunday in October I rented a Jeep and Lilly filled a picnic basket with sandwiches and chicken wings and fruit and a bottle of wine. She owned a handkerchief-sized piece of beach property up-island in Gay Head with a shack on it and we started for it and then changed our minds.

I turned the Jeep around and drove to Katama, then out onto the beach and along it, all the way around Chappaquiddick to the end. At the foot of the Cape Poge lighthouse there is a length of sand about half a mile long, angled in such a way that the earth behind it recedes and the sea before it stretches out and tilts over the end of the world. In the October afternoons when the days shorten, just when you are least expecting it, the sky lifts and the light whips across the water to the horizon and dazzles there, as though it were flirting with something unseen. To the east, between Cape Poge and the mainland, wild swans feed in the lagoons and come exploding out of the water on foot if you get too close, wings spread and necks high in attitude of attack, making a harsh ugly sound, like death in ambush.

We put the picnic basket down on the long spit of sand and spent the day on the beach where we could watch the light and wander in and out of the water. I had brought the metal card table from my bedroom and a beach umbrella, along with two portable typewriters and two collapsible chairs. I was trying to imitate Hammett, who had sometimes gone to the Gay Head cliffs that way: he had lowered everything on a rope one by one, Lillian included, from the car to the beach, so that the two of them could spend the day writing and eating and swimming. It is not a good idea to follow in another man's footsteps if you're the kind of klutz I am and the man was as good with his hands as Hammett was and I got sand in the typewriters and a little in Lilly. But she was a good sport about it, she only made a fuss over the typewriters for an hour or so, and then she shrugged it off and in the end laughed and gave herself over to the vagaries of the day.

It's worth noting here that Lillian had the most spontaneous and helpless laugh in the world. From time to time she gave in to it, and then it went on so long it sounded as if she had gone into spasm and quit breathing. Other facts about her altered from decade to decade and over the years her face changed with age as faces do, but her laugh had the feel of an infant's laugh all her life, so that the gurgle of the cradle and the guffaw of the office and the cackle of the wheelchair were as one—as though she had learned in laughing to stop time. There are things in most of us unworthy of trust and there were things you could not trust about Lillian. But you could always trust her laugh.

Standing by the lighthouse that day she laughed for a long time. Then she stopped with her back turned, facing the water, and stood for several minutes the way a person might stand who has just seen with great depth of clarity something either very small or very far away. Just then without warning she turned.

I have a thing to tell here that I don't know how to tell, because it's an awkward thing, a thing I didn't understand when it happened. There is sometimes, for me, a part of the anatomy that strikes me as the physical embodiment of a person, so that it seems with time to become the essence of that person. It may be because something was left out of me that I have no way of taking in the total awesome suddenness of another human face, no way of recognizing the whole, and so I panic and tend to fasten on the particular. A foot or a finger or the turn of a jaw becomes the distillation of a presence. I never know what part of the body is going to do it, but the part of the body that struck me most in Lillian was her back. She had a habit of coming right up to you and turning her back, in order to think, that was both abrupt and infinitely touching—like a child who has wandered in off the street and for no apparent reason found you comfortable enough to stand next to. But it was not so much the gesture as the back itself, posture and fiber and bone, that moved me, and I have no idea why.

That day when she turned she caught me staring at her back and I looked away at the beach. My gaze fell on a shape on the sand no more than three or four feet off and the shape looked wrong. It was one of the wild swans from the lagoon and it was lying dead on the beach in a grotesque cruel form as if it had been twisted out of the sky by some big malevolent hand. The swan was a travesty of itself: one eye was open and staring and the sweeping arc of its neck had been mangled so that it was sick-making to look at. I was looking at it when Lillian said: "Light me a cigarette, will you?"

Ordinarily I would have refused, since she smoked too much and needed help quitting, but to keep her from noticing the dead bird I got up and took the lighter out of the picnic basket and lit her cigarette. I needn't have bothered for her sake—Lillian had no sentimentality at all about animals and if the swan had been alive would probably have tried to kill it for dinner—but for my own sake, because of something nameless and awful I couldn't stomach, I didn't want her to see it. The bird had made me ashamed. When she turned away I edged over and kicked some loose sand over it, feeling less like a man than a sneaky little boy hiding some private obscenity from view. It was an involuntary action, one of those things you do mainly to keep your heart from beating so fast, and when it was done I felt relieved, as though I had managed to cover up a disgusting and unimaginable secret.

When I looked up, Lillian was gone. She had vanished from the beach as completely as though she had never set foot on it. She was not off swimming or walking—she was just absent— plucked out of view like something wiped out in one stroke by a clumsy painter, or maybe a graceful painter who thought better of his work and started over. I looked all the way around me but she was not in sight.

The sun on the sea was so sharp it was blinding, a long wave causing a mirror that burst as it broke, splinters of light flying up out of it like long slivers of jagged glass. My eyes watered and when they quit and I was able to see again, filtered through the light and shimmering in a heat wave, was Lillian smoking a cig-arette. The whole thing, from the time she asked for a light to her reappearance, had lasted maybe two minutes and if I were capable of believing in any form of mysticism this would have done it but I'm not, so all it did was make me angry. I felt re-duced by what had happened, I felt ten years old. It was as if she had caught me doing something contemptible and played a nasty trick on me to teach me a lesson. But I couldn't ask her about the trick without admitting to burying the bird and I stayed in an irritable mood for the rest of the day. During lunch I grumbled about the food, about people so genteel they cut crusts off bread and make dainty little doily sandwiches that aren't any good at all if you're hungry.

Lillian chuckled but her mind was off on some tack of its own and she wasn't listening. After lunch we lay back with the half-empty wine bottle and two plastic cups and she asked me to tell her a story. The story, she explained, was to begin with the day we had met and to go on with how much I remembered of the times we'd spent together since that day. "Tell it slow," she said, "go on, professor—your turn to tell a story."

It was my turn, she was right, but I wasn't up to it and I kept silent. This was like the breaking of a minor covenant between us, since we had discovered years ago that we had in common a kind of autoeroticism about retold stories and from then on it was only a question of whose turn it was to tell, whose to listen. New Orleans was a favorite topic, growing up a running theme, and there were stories of her aunts, my family, the South in general, the Jewish South in particular, stories of old loves, stories of new friends, part-truth-part-fiction stories that one of us fixed up for the other in accordance with the day's requirements, the teller from time to time decorating the trunk or branches of an old story with new baubles—what the French call ornamentation—small bright additions placed among the twigs and leaves to lend more sparkle where sparkle was needed. Before and in between and after other events there were always stories, some of them long, some short, their beginnings like the deep lacy roots that held together the fabric of turf we had chosen for friendship that summer. To fight about whose turn it was was a part of the everyday ritual. To refuse to participate was an unheard-of breach. It was as though a child had turned its back on another child somewhere in the middle of the foreplay of life. "What's the matter with you?" Lillian said.

I said I was sleepy.

"You're not," she said, "you're just being perverse."

"I wouldn't call my shot on that one if I were you," I said, "nobody stands a chance of being perverse next to you. Nobody."

"I am not perverse," Lillian announced formally. She was lying, you could tell from her tone.

"You're the world's biggest brat, and the world's biggest liar and you goddamn well know it."

"That may be true," she said loftily, after a moment. "If it is, I humbly apologize."

The sudden admission left me to fume by myself. There is nothing more irritating than somebody giving up gracefully if somebody else wants a fight and she of all people knew it. Lillian was one of the great infighters of the twentieth century.

She had won the argument by refusing to take part in it and that was that. When we fought as two adults I stood a fair chance of winning but if you got in the ring with her as a child, God help you. God help any child who even sat down with her, unless he had his rule book in one hand and his balls in the other.

"Okay," I said, "you win. This is how it began."

"You don't have to tell it unless you want to," Lillian said sweetly, closing her eyes.

I swore at her and started.

The story she wanted was a story I had told her more than once, one I would go on telling her in some form until she died.

It happened the fall after my tenth birthday in my father's house in New Orleans, at one of those upper-class Southern dinners where little boys are told to come downstairs in pajamas and robe with their hair combed wet and say hello to the guests. I was an only child and I was used to performing good manners but the dinner-guest circuit was one I didn't like to play; I went around the room being introduced by my mother until we came to a woman with her back turned. Something about the back, an implied strength of tissue, came through the fragility of form and put me on guard. The woman turned, taking her time, and made a couple of remarks I no longer remember—in a tone I do remember. Lillian had a habit of speaking to everyone as an age peer. She did not curtsey with her voice to the elderly or stoop to the young.

"How old are you?" she said.

It was a stock question and I had the stock answer: "I'm only ten."

"I don't know what you mean by 'only,' " Lillian said. "Ten isn't so young." She turned her back and didn't look at me again.

I was hooked and the hook stayed in. I thought about her for what seemed like a longer stretch of time than any thought deserved—about a week—and decided at the end of it to write her a letter. It was a large decision: I had never written a letter before and I got her address from my mother and worried over what to say for several days. The idea of liking somebody enough to write them made me edgy, since it seemed to mean that the recipient owned a piece of you, and I wanted to say something snotty. What I wanted to say was that she was not the only writer I had met. My father was a writer and many of the writers who visited New Orleans came to his house and I had already spent an afternoon with a writer named Sherwood Anderson and one named William Faulkner, who took me on what he called a "nature walk" to the nearest bottle store. The last time my mother had picked me up at the Friday-night dancing school where my schoolfriends and I were forced to go, there was another writer in the car whose name turned out to be Henry Miller. So meeting a writer, I wanted to say, was no big deal, and if she thought I was impressed she could forget it.

What stopped me from writing that, or a version of that, was not the notion that it was an inappropriate thing to say but the fact that I didn't know how to spell Sherwood Anderson, William Faulkner and Henry Miller, and couldn't get into my father's study where their books were kept because he was at work with the door shut. I wrote a shorter note and a plainer one, though I no longer remember what it said. It was explained to me by my mother, who mailed the letter for me, that I wasn't to expect any answer to the letter because, she said, Miss Hellman received a lot of letters from a lot of people and wouldn't have time for anything else if she answered all of them. I didn't believe it but that was the year I joined a kids' radio program downtown and I had other things on my mind.

When Lillian didn't answer my letter immediately I forgot about her. A month later when a letter came in the mail addressed to me I was stunned and I walked around with it for days before I got up the nerve to open it. I kept it folded in two in a pants pocket and whenever anyone was looking at me I took it out and pretended that I had just received it. I spent hours trying to look nonchalant about it. The letter made me famous in school because it turned out that nobody in my class had ever received a letter from farther away than Baton Rouge and this letter—you could tell from the postmark—was from New York. I was pleased at my fame and when I finally opened the letter it was a terrible disappointment. It was typed, there were only three or four short sentences in it and it was very impersonal. It could have been written to anybody. I no longer remember what it said but I remember one sentence. The sentence was "I hope you're enjoying school." I thought it was without question one of the dumbest sentences I had ever heard in my life. From a woman who had written a play, a woman who had the sense to say "ten isn't so young," it was a huge mistake. It taught me that you can't trust adults no matter how good they sound, a lesson I have never forgotten and one I believe in as deeply today as I did the day I learned it.

I didn't see Lillian again till I was sixteen, in New York. My mother had moved there with me and Lillian came to dinner at our apartment a couple of times. Once, when she invited my mother back, Lilly included me in the invitation, but I didn't see her alone for the first time till I was eighteen and recognized her walking on the street. I remember that day because I stopped her and we went and had a cup of coffee together on the corner. Twice more that year we met because the coffee shop was on the way to a weekly appointment Lilly had somewhere and she liked to go early. By eighteen I'd had several years to practice being more interesting than I was at ten.

LILLIAN: *Interesting in your teens? —I thought you were the best-looking young man I'd ever seen and certainly the most boring.*
PETER: *Thanks.*

SOUND OF LILLIAN LAUGHING.

LILLIAN: *Well, you're not boring anymore and you're not silly-handsome anymore.*
PETER: *Thanks.*

SOUND OF LILLIAN LAUGHING.

The next part of the story—the next time I saw her—I was in my twenties. I had been living in Spain, making my living as I could and writing at night; when I came back to America I had a novel published but I knew almost nobody in New York anymore and a writer named Santha Rama Rau took pity on me and gave me a book party. Her apartment was small, she said, she could only manage six or eight people, and she asked me who I wanted. I had been told by somebody that Santha was one of the few people Greta Garbo liked, so I asked for Garbo. Santha said she'd invite her but she thought it unlikely, Garbo never went to parties, and what about somebody else. I asked for Lillian Hellman and Santha got them both.

On the night of the party the room seemed smaller than it was because Hellman and Garbo by themselves could have filled a football field. Lillian was at her most stoic—Garbo was gentle and quiet. She sat on the floor next to Santha with long straight hair that hung down on either side of her face so that you couldn't see her at all except, from time to time, when she tilted her head back to say something, and the hair fell away and the eyes and the low voice made you catch your breath.

Not many absolutes exist in this world, but here is one: all actresses think they're shy. It may seem contradictory for a woman to dress up and parade around in front of a camera and kiss men before millions of viewers and still think she's shy—but it was not contradictory with Garbo. By then she had long ago made her final press statement, "I want to be alone," a statement that kids of my generation used to go around mimicking with a Swedish accent, and a statement that turned out to be true. She did want to be alone. If she made an exception by coming to a small gathering for a young unknown writer it was partly out of curiosity, partly out of love for Santha. But when she glanced up politely and murmured: "So you have written a novel," my brain clanged shut and I froze and knew that I would never be able to speak easily again in my life—to her or anyone else. Even silent, Garbo shone—in fact, especially silent—she was the undisputed star of the evening.

Lillian took it for about an hour and then got up abruptly to leave. She was wearing a black lace veil pulled up tight around her face, a kind of veil she wore a lot, and Santha went with her to the door. I thanked her for coming and Santha made the requisite remark, how nice to have a successful novel come from such a *young* man. "How old are you?" Lillian said. I said I was twenty-eight.

"Twenty-eight's not so young," she said and swept slowly out of the room.

I was hooked all over again and I saw a lot more of Lillian in the next three years but I didn't see much of her alone. Hammett was on the scene and she was always busy. Once, when I gave a reading at Columbia University with Carson McCullers, Lillian came to hear us; afterward the three of us met Carson's sister Rita Smith and Tennessee Williams at the White Horse Tavern and sat around talking about nothing and drinking Wild Turkey and black coffee till Carson had to be driven back to Nyack and Tennessee and Rita went with her, and Lillian and I stumbled back uptown. Then one day when a play I had written was about to go into rehearsal for Broadway I called her to ask what to do about auditions; I hadn't ever been to an audition as a writer and didn't have a clue what to listen for.

"I don't know either," Lillian said, "I never did. All I can tell you is a good cold reading means a bad actor. Look for a quality. And show me your play if you like."

We made a date and at dinner I gave her my script and it came back a few days later with a note saying "You've done better than most novelists did in the theater but I'm not sure why you're writing about these people."

I tried calling her to find out what she meant but she was out of town with a play of her own and soon after that my first play—and Lillian's last play—both opened in the newspaper blackout of that year, a long strike that closed every legitimate thing on Broadway. I was broke and went out to the West Coast to do a movie script and didn't see Lilly again till she came out too, a few months later.

When I heard she was in Hollywood I drove over to find her straddling a heat vent in the floor of her hotel room in the Beverly Wilshire Hotel. "I've never been as cold in my life as I am in Los Angeles," she said. I muttered something about the city not being prepared for cold weather. "This isn't cold weather," Lillian said, "*I'm* cold. The sun's expensive here. It doesn't shine on just anybody."

We went for a drive and stopped somewhere for lunch and got back in the car and drove some more. I remember the sun on Lillian's hair and I remember taking her for a walk on the cliffs near the beach. Hammett had been dead for over a year and she talked about that for a while.

"You aren't planning to live here," she said at dinner that

night in a restaurant called Larue's. I hadn't made up my mind, so I shut up. "I'd watch it if I were you," Lillian said, "the only excuse for this place is a job and you'd better leave the day the job's done—I can't take the temptations of Hollywood and I have more character than you do. It's no place for a serious writer, you'll wind up with a swimming pool if you stay." I said I didn't want a swimming pool. "You'll want something," she said, "writing for movies is a sucker's game these days, it's not worth giving up your life no matter how much it pays. Just take the money and get out."

She acted on her own advice and left that week and a day later I got a letter from her.

> Beverly Wilshire Hotel
> 7:20 p.m.
> Wednesday
>
> DEAR PETER,
>
> I have had a fine, a rare, a desired and almost forgotten kind of voyage—the discovery of my feelings for an interesting man. I didn't remember the pleasure of the complexities, and maybe didn't want to. This isn't to say I know much about you, only to say that, after so many years, I want to find out.
>
> I am taking a ten o'clock plane. I'll try to explain that on the phone.
>
> Work well because . . .

I don't know what happened to the second page of the letter but I managed to keep the first page in a small pile of personal possessions that have survived twenty-five years of my otherwise disheveled way of life. It must have seemed important, I suppose, or I wouldn't still have it.

After that trip I saw Lillian whenever I went to New York. I thought of her by then as a kind of Southern blood relation and so the first Vineyard summer was to make us both feel a little incestuous, since she'd often made a point of saying I was the closest thing to a child she would have, a remark I took as a compliment though it seemed an odd thing to tell a new lover, even if the new lover is an old friend.

LILLIAN: *What'll you do when I die?*
PETER: *Throw myself on your funeral pyre like a decent respectable son.*
LILLIAN: *And then what?*
PETER: *Marry for money.*
LILLIAN: *Can I have some of it?*
PETER: *You'll be dead.*
LILLIAN: *What's that got to do with it?*

> SOUND OF COUGHING. SOUND OF COFFEE CUP ON SAUCER. SOUND OF SEAGULLS.

LILLIAN: *Will you want to live in my house when I'm dead?*
PETER: *No.*

"Why not?" Lillian said.

I had finished telling the story and the sun on the sea behind her was darker. The wind was suddenly cold. The Cape Poge lighthouse looked like a sailor with his hat on facing the water.

Lillian got up and began to put the things back in the picnic basket and I shook the towels out and put them into the Jeep. Between the spot where we had been lying and the lighthouse was the place where the dead swan was buried and I didn't go near it. I had no idea what the bird meant, why it had spoiled what otherwise might have been a nice afternoon—I didn't even know whether Lillian had noticed it or not. I thought so, but I wasn't sure.

A wind had come up and the sun was gone behind a layer of gray that sat like a shroud over the beach. Lillian put on a sweater and we got in the Jeep and drove back across the dunes, following the beach around Chappaquiddick to the mainland.

It took a while to drive to Vineyard Haven and by the time we got to her driveway a heavy rain had started. It rattled over the dirt road in big tropical drops that didn't belong in the New England landscape—one of those odd events that contradict their surroundings—like snow in New Orleans or an earthquake in New York or a literary movement in California.

⊱⊱⊱⊱⊱ III

A SMALL DINNER FOR THE CHINK

THE REST OF THAT autumn was taken up with Vineyard life after the tourist-shopping sharkfest of summer. Some of Lillian's friends had stayed on the island but most had gone and only those whose winter home was close enough came back for weekends. The Herseys were weekend people—John was Master of Pierson College at Yale—and the Styrons had stayed on. Lillian, who took a constant and affectionate delight in baiting the Styrons, came up with various theories about why they stayed, ranging in subject from Rose's money to Bill's sex life, though few of her theories had any basis in fact. But then she was not dependent on fact: a simple thing like lack of evidence was never a deterrent to a mind as open to speculation as Lilly's and there was always a certain grandeur to the guess even when it was wrong. When she got onto the subject of sex-and-money it was not the guess itself but the fecundity of the imagination which had produced it that was staggering. I wasn't, by now, as impressed as I had been on a street in New York, the day we passed a newspaper banner announcing the divorce of Arthur Miller and Marilyn Monroe and Lillian said, in a doomed tone: "Well, that's that—I always knew he married *her* for money."

The autumn mornings were spent working, as summer mornings had been, and Lilly was at her typewriter by six, finished by ten. That left her wondering how to fill the rest of the day—a problem that was largely responsible for changing her Pollyanna morning optimism into a Cassandra noon doom. Lilly had a habit of behaving, when she first woke up, as if a kind of wide-eyed brightness had taken her by the throat and affected her mind. You would think she had never seen a rose before, the way she carried on, until a noon whistle blew inside her brain and she began to think about how much money she'd spent on fertilizer for flowerbeds. This caused her to wonder how many hungry people she could have fed with the same amount of money. It was not a gentle transition—it was one thing and then it was another thing, rose to fertilizer, fertilizer to hunger, something like the movements of a freight train—and I never got used to it. At best it takes me several cups of coffee to wake up in the morning and I often found the wide-eyed Lillian harder to take than the gloom-filled Lillian, though I never knew which one was waiting for me till I got downstairs, and even then I couldn't be sure. Lilly's Southern nature was such that the sight of a six-foot man descending her staircase in the morning temporarily preempted any other emotion in her until the man sat down and she knew he was there to stay. Then look out.

One morning I came down late with a hangover and tried to wade through the blinding sunlight to the table where the coffee was. Lillian was busy scribbling on a pad, and I hadn't looked at the time, so I had no way of knowing whether she was thinking about the wonders of the acorn or anticipating a nuclear holocaust.

Lilly had one or two special ways of combating her morning boredom. Her favorite way was to call up a handful of friends on the phone and say, to each of them: "Do you realize how angry you sound?" This question generally succeeded in reducing the person she was talking to into a senseless seething rage, which soothed Lilly enough that she found the twelve o'clock transition from blossom to grave less jolting. But on this particular morning there was no one to call—no one to whom she could say "Do you realize how angry you sound?"—because almost everybody had left the Vineyard. She felt like chatting this morning, but the only person she seriously liked to chat with was Barbara Hersey, and Lillian was too deeply fond of Barbara to try a remark like that on her—and anyway Barbara was in New Haven. There was nobody around to help cheer a lady up. Nobody. Just me.

I sat down and gulped as much black coffee as I could manage. Then I remembered that it was the weekend and Lilly was planning a small dinner that night for a visitor whose name, let us say, was Mr. Johnson. I had met Mr. Johnson only once and had found him to be one of those sensitive souls who are too affected by what they have encountered in life. He was full of large-sounding ideas and his ideas shone like gold but he himself was an amalgam and the ideas were mostly alloy. Worse, Mr. Johnson was not a mean man, but he was a stupid man, and Lillian never saw stupidity for what it was—she always thought it was being done against her. All things considered I was not looking forward to the evening. Mr. Johnson's main claim to fame was that he was a very rich man who had come to the Vineyard on his own yacht and Lillian was hoping to get some money out of him for her Committee for Public Justice, a nonprofit organization she had formed to support liberal causes.

Mr. Johnson's only other claim was that he was half Chinese, half Western—by appearance as well as by ancestry—a mixture that often makes for good looks but had failed to do so in his case; in him the genes of Asia and America had not met in a happy way and he could not have been called a handsome man. He was, in fact, an ugly man, a thing which can happen to anybody, and which had. Lillian circumvented this unfortunate fact by referring to him delicately as "the Chink."

"I'm making the menu for the Chink," she said when she looked up from her pad, "he's coming to dinner. I can't think how I invited ten people to meet him, but I did. He's a nice man and you're to treat him like a nice man. I mean what I'm saying."

"Why wouldn't I treat him like a nice man?" I said without thinking.

"Don't get snappish," Lillian said.

"I'm not in the least snappish."

"And don't get your back up."

"My back's not up," I said irritably.

"Calm down."

"I'm perfectly calm."

Lillian leaned forward and stared at me, smiling. "Peter," she said softly, "do you realize how angry you sound?"

I may as well say here that I credit that particular remark with sowing the seed that will bear fruit the day I am put on medication for high blood pressure. (The remark first blossomed a few years later when a doctor told me for the first time that I had developed something known as labile pressure. Labile pressure is blood pressure that can shoot up from normal to twenty points above normal, with no known cause. No known *medical* cause.)

"Look, sugarpants," I said in a trembling voice, "I'm *not* angry, I'm *always* nice to your friends, and the Chink can come here or bugger off, as he chooses. I am not, I repeat, angry."

"Then why are you shouting?"

"I'M NOT SHOUTING."

"Is it something I've said?" Lillian asked, casting her eyes toward the floor in a demure way. "If it is, I humbly apologize."

That was the morning I threw my coffee cup at the ceiling. It was one of those things you don't know you're going to do till you do it: I had never done such a thing before, I wasn't aware of doing it then, and I have very little memory of it now. There is, happily, a kind of retroactive amnesia that sets in to help us through trying times.

When the dizziness began to ebb I found myself staring up at a wide black streak that appeared to begin at a crack in the ceiling and dance forward, as if it had been painted there by a demented, and extremely untalented, child. It took me a second or two to realize that it was only coffee. It looked like black blood. The shards of the cup were sprinkled around the living room and Lillian was kneeling in the middle of them patting my hand in a concerned way; having caused the explosion, she was now coming to my aid like Florence Nightingale on a battlefield, undaunted by flying shrapnel or by anything else. She looked at me understandingly.

"There, there," she said, "there, there."

I swallowed and tried to think of a way to get back at her; but cracking through Lillian's armor was no mean feat. She had cast her morning play with me as the devil, herself as the ministering angel, and only by taking her measure with extreme care could I hope to reverse the casting. Underestimating her wouldn't help.

I kept still.

"Can I get you some more coffee, darling?" Lillian said gently.

You had to give her credit, she was a real pro. My mouth went suddenly dry—a feeling hard to describe: it is possible that Ulysses felt a similar twang when confronted by his first Gorgon. It was silly of me to worry about underestimating Lillian: I had already underestimated Lillian. I tried to smile and couldn't.

"Feeling better?"

"Yes, thank you."

"Good," Lillian said. "Good."

I said nothing; but deep in the smithy of my soul, where the conscience of my race was being forged, I began to make the outline of a plan. . . .

I will draw a pair of merciful curtains on the rest of this scene, which I've been describing in detail only to demonstrate a point. If Lillian had a mind to, she could take a rational man and in about thirty seconds send him straight to wah-wah land. The rest of the morning did not go well for me, because, of course, my plan didn't work, and there was no way of getting back at her. Lillian countered every punch with kindness and didn't even seem to notice the murder in my heart.

I stayed upstairs for the rest of the day trying to work and poring over revenge fantasies—imaginary scenes in which I said something terse and scathing that wiped Lilly out. Around six o'clock I remembered that the Chink was coming and went downstairs to find her in a snit that had nothing whatever to do with me.

It was, yet again, due to what she called her nature, that whenever Lillian asked people to dinner she felt rejected if they refused and put-upon if they showed up. This phenomenon manifested itself in remarks ranging from "I wonder if they don't like my house" to "What in hell do they think this is, the Salvation Army?"

Guests for dinner meant that six o'clock marked the beginning of phase two and Lilly was already beginning to build up steam. "I worked four hours in the kitchen today," she said when I came in, "I hope the Chink is satisfied. I spent a great deal of money on this dinner. The price of food these days is frightening. I wonder how the poor manage to live."

I kept quiet.

"I hope the Chink's grateful for what I've done, he's not worth it—he's a silly man."

"A silly *rich* man," I said casually.

"Of course he's rich, what's that got to do with it?"

I kept still.

"It's unjust of you to accuse me of catering to the rich," Lillian said. "Nasty and unjust."

"I didn't accuse you of anything."

"It's what you meant."

"It's not what I meant," I said, "and you have no right to be angry."

"I'm not angry."

"Then why are you shouting?"

"I'm not shouting."

"Is it something I've said?" I said, looking down at the floor, "if it is, I humbly apologize."

Lillian threw her head back and laughed. "You are a shit," she said. "All writers are shits. Nobody should have anything to do with writers."

By seven-thirty most of the guests had arrived and she had begun to regroup them.

Credit ought to be given somewhere—here is as good a place as any—for Lilly's ability to choreograph a party. She managed it as if she were choreographing a group on a stage, only it was trickier than that, because she didn't have professionals to work with. Her behavior at parties was such an obvious talent that everyone took it for granted.

As a rule she started not long after all the guests were in the living room, when it occurred to her that some of them weren't sitting or standing in the right places. She would get up, walk over, take you abruptly by the hand, say "Come with me" and lead you off to another part of the room. The strongest-willed, bossiest guest went along with it without question, and even newcomers seemed to sense that they would be happier where she put them. People instinctively trusted Lillian when she took them by the hand, as a five-year-old will trust a parent—blindly, without question—with only the anticipation of pleasure.

What she knew about parties was that nobody has a good time unless the host has one, since guests are like children who take their cue from the parent. What she had noticed was that most people have a tendency to get stuck in one place, talking to one person, without knowing how they had got there or how to get away. Except for dyed-in-the-wool performers, nobody is ever relaxed at a big party, because the performance is all that matters, and so people who say they entertain a lot don't always know what the word means or how to do it.

Lilly knew how. She was, in the original sense of the term, a great entertainer. When she performed at her own dinners she

did it so naturally that you never caught her at it. There was
nothing robotic about her, and she was not one of those people
who shine their attentions on you like electric beams as soon as
you see them—the ones who are themselves absent, secretly out
to lunch. Most hosts think they've done well if they can seat
people correctly at a dinner table but Lilly's work started long
before dinner and went on for a long time after. She worked with
a kind of radar that told her when the guests in her living room
were having a good time and when they were not she felt responsible, if only because it was her living room; as a dinner guest
you never had a bad meal in her house and you never had a bad
time there if she could help it. She usually could.

People at dinner parties try to follow certain techniques for
survival, though the techniques don't always work as well as such
techniques do in the swamp or desert. In the end all you can do
at dinner is hope for the best: if you're seated below the salt you
make the best of that and if you're seated next to an evangelist
you make the best of that and if you're seated next to Roy Cohn
you leave. You decide early on what your limitations are—what
will sink you, what won't—and you try to steer a course that will
keep you afloat. I for instance have found that I can make do
next to just about anybody, as long as it isn't a doctor's wife. I
won't consciously sit next to a doctor's wife, any more than I
would pick up an alligator or sit down next to a snake, because
experience has taught me not to. Doctors' wives always have to
prove they know more about medicine than their husbands do,
and they always have to prove it at dinner. One day in the early
part of the summer when I asked Lilly if she would mind not
seating me next to a doctor's wife, she turned on me a look of
outrage and hurt. "What an awful thing to say," she said, "have
you ever known me to be disloyal?" I admitted that I had not.
"Have I done you some terrible harm I don't know about?" I
said she hadn't. "Then what possible right have you to speak to
me that way," she said, wringing her hands, "how dare you think
I would put you next to a doctor's wife? Just how dare you?"

I said I was sorry.

"It's not enough to be sorry," she said, "you can't say something like that and then walk away from it. You've upset me
now."

I said I would never say anything like it again.

But Lilly didn't seem to hear. "You thought *I* would do a

thing like that," she said over and over with a stunned expression. *"Me?* Put a man I love and respect next to a *doctor's wife?* It's a terrible thing you're accusing me of—I don't know whether I should have anything more to do with you . . ."

She went around grumbling and muttering under her breath for days. After a week of it I found myself thinking up little fun things to distract her. I never again made the same mistake and I never suffered in her hands because of it: Lillian's house was the only place I've ever been where you could sit down to dinner and leave your survival kit upstairs: you were safe and you knew it.

But safety didn't necessarily mean peace and calm—it certainly didn't mean boredom—and it often didn't mean, in a specific sense, security. Lilly was sometimes so busy protecting people from other people that she forgot to protect them from herself. Her perception of stupidity as something done against her was an attitude Hammett had often noticed but it was not an attitude he had done anything to correct.

The night of the small dinner for the Chink I forgot about this habit and I was busy holding up my end of the table when she blew.

There was a special quality in the sound of Lillian's temper. Once you heard her blow it was as familiar a sound as the foghorn that warned vessels in the harbor and I snapped to attention fast, only to hear her repeat, for the third consecutive time:

"I can't stand what you're saying."

A silence had descended on the table, and one look at Lilly told everybody what the trouble was. A desire to take the Chink's head off had crashed into the desire to make sure he was having a good time in her house—and Lillian's face looked as if the Battle of the Bulge were taking place in it. The other guests were sitting motionless, forks in midair, not unlike the corpses that are dug up from time to time in Pompeii, frozen in whatever attitudes they had been in when the eruption took place.

In that kind of emergency the Herseys were the only people in the neighborhood you could count on. I glanced at John, whose face had turned to amiable stone, then at Barbara, who was making an effort to circumvent disaster by distracting the Chink with questions about his travels.

". . . and where did you go *after* Haiti, Mr. Johnson?" Barbara said.

"I was in Haiti in June," the Chink said brightly, "I had a

fine opportunity to see the sights—Haiti is nothing but poverty—it was most enjoyable, Haiti."

"But where did you go *after* Haiti?" Barbara said pointedly, a hopeless sound creeping into her voice.

"In June I go to the beach," the Chink said. "In July I go on my yacht. In August I go to East Hampton. In September I go duck hunting."

"How do you kill October?" Lillian said.

"Lilly," John said quietly.

"I can't help it," Lillian said, "did you hear what he said *before*? He said the natives in Haiti *like* to be poor."

"Mr. Johnson probably meant the natives *make the best* of being poor," Barbara said. "Didn't you, Mr. Johnson?"

"No," the Chink said, pleased by all the attention, "no, my own belief is that they like to be poor." He smiled broadly at Lilly.

The other guests watched him the way people would watch a man who had skipped contentedly up to the rim of a volcano and was peering down into its mouth.

"That dessert was terrific, Lillian," Art Buchwald said in a small voice.

"Oh, shut up, Art," Lilly said.

"I don't blame you for being surprised, Miss Hellman," the Chink said, "I was surprised myself. But the truth is, the natives in Haiti won't even eat decent food. When I gave the maid lunch, she wrapped it up and took it home to her family. My goodness—I've never seen roses that big in my life," he added, looking out the window, "what do you put on your roses, Miss Hellman?"

"Ground-up money," Lillian said. "What else do the natives do?"

"Oh nothing much," the Chink said. "They weren't in physical shape to do much. Skin and bones, most of them. You ought to go to Haiti sometime and see them in their natural habitat, Miss Hellman. I think you'd be amused."

From somewhere inside her, Lilly produced a small sound like the distant bellow of a wounded buffalo.

Nobody else spoke. There comes a point at which a man who welcomes disaster too freely no longer seems touching to those around him and the Chink had passed it full speed ahead. People sat back with a sigh and averted their faces as they would have from a person who was busy trying to swallow handfuls of poison.

But you could never quite count on Lillian's temper: there was a perversity in her that showed up when you least expected it. If the Chink had tried to explain himself, she might have killed him. But if a man lay down in front of her and asked to be run over, she often wouldn't.

Her bellow turned into an acute coughing attack that lasted several minutes. When Lilly coughed she turned purple and her face looked as if all the thoughts inside her had run for cover.

After a while she stopped coughing long enough to light a cigarette and fill her lungs with hot soothing smoke. Then she got up from the table and led everybody back to the living-room sofas and chairs.

It had been quite a night and I remember thinking about it many years later at another dinner party in the same house when John Hersey arrived with a galley proof containing the dedication page of his new novel, a page that read: "For Lillian." He handed her the galley proof in silence as he walked in and Lillian kissed him and folded the galley quickly into a paper fan. She put one end of the fan like the stem of a flower between her breasts and kept it there all evening as she went back and forth from group to group. It was one of the most spontaneous and feminine gestures I had ever seen and I came to think of those two evenings— the small dinner for the Chink and the night John brought the galley—as a kind of antipodal definition of her behavior.

That night, after the Chink had gone, the Herseys stayed and listened to Lilly speculate upon the nature of a man who had come to his particular conclusions in life. She could not get it into her head that there's no explanation for the supply of plain stupidity you sometimes find in people, a supply tantamount in the Chink to a natural resource, and after a little while she gave up and the Herseys kissed her and went home.

Around six o'clock the next evening I mixed us a couple of dry martinis and Lilly settled back contentedly on the sofa with one of them and appeared, for the moment, lost in thought.

"Felicia Bernstein said something on the phone about Lennie coming to the Vineyard next weekend," she said thoughtfully after a while. "Is it your feeling I should give him a small dinner?"

$\succ\succ\succ\succ\succ$ IV

LILLIAN: This is one thousand percent for you . . . the plays aren't as good as I'd remembered . . . they're too on the nose— too airless. I pounded at things too much. They'll have a minor place in the end, the plays, but no complaints about that. A minor place is a good place, and I'm not a quitter . . . whatever's wrong with me, that's not. . . .

For a while now I've been writing Lilly's voice from memory rather than referring always to the tapes. I know the sound of her and I've come to trust that as much as a recording machine— more than perhaps I should, but no matter—I'm after finding out what Lillian meant by Lillian and I have no qualms about method.

Toward the end of October that year she had nothing to do in the afternoons. More and more people had left the island and there was no one to keep her company when I worked, though now and then Rose Styron played tennis with her and about once a week showed up for a game of Scrabble. Rose was, continued to be for years, attentive to Lilly—a sustained piece of thoughtful behavior that meant more in the end than Lilly's myriad complaint that Rose would do anything, go anywhere for a famous name—an observation nourished at least somewhat by envy in the presence of a pretty woman whose embarrassment of riches included her looks, her money and her husband. Often on a rainy afternoon you'd find the two ensconced in a corner of the living room staring down at the Scrabble board in silence. When Lilly was the loser she would walk around the house afterward muttering small dark things about Rose and when she won she was as happy as a child who had just slaughtered another child with an ax. The two of them were good at Scrabble and I made a point of leaving them alone with it because I am not good at word games: trying to compete with them made me feel foolish and the mere sight of all those loose letters paralyzed my mind.

One day I came down for a sandwich and found Lilly sitting in the kitchen looking like a six-year-old who has been abandoned—glum, despondent and moony. The rain was coming down out of an airless sky, falling without any wind, just falling, with the kind of dank hopeless sound that seeps into your soul. It was several hours past her work time and she had nothing to do. I asked what had happened to Rose.

"She went off-island for a few days," Lilly said. "She probably had a date. That or I'd better publish a book soon, I may not be a famous lady anymore. How's the work coming?" I said it was a slow day. "Why don't you take some time off once in a while," she said, "you always work as if something might happen if you stopped."

"Something might," I said. "Look what happens to you."

"Don't be silly—it's good for writing to stop now and then," she said, "even if you have to force yourself."

I asked what I would do with the rest of the day if I stopped.

Lillian looked as if she were considering the problem seriously. "I don't know," she said slowly, after a moment. "But I'll be glad to help any way I can . . . let's see . . . what can I think of to entertain you with? . . ."

There was a silence.

"*I* know," she said brightly, "what about a nice game of Scrabble?"

"You're full of it," I said. "I hate word games and you know it—I'm terrible at Scrabble. You haven't got anybody else to play with, that's all."

"Who've *you* got to play with? *You* know what it's like to be alone, you were an only child too."

"This only child's going back to work."

"Coward," Lilly said.

"Okay," I said, "okay. Get out the goddamn Scrabble board. Okay."

A NICE GAME OF SCRABBLE

A PLAY IN ONE ACT

The action takes place in the living room and dining area of Lillian Hellman's house on Martha's Vineyard on a late October afternoon in 1963.

The room is composed of deep yellows and whites. At curtain the sky outside is overcast and the swollen light falling in from the bank of windows facing the bay has a diffused bloated quality, like light without a source. Two bright reading lamps have been lit and placed on the dining table in such a way that they shine in concentrated yellow circles. The metallic glow of the lamp is condensed and made to look sharper by the surrounding gloom.

Lillian sits staring down at a Scrabble board with her back to the windows.

Her opponent sits in front of her looking lost.

The sound of rain is heard offstage.

PAUSE

LILLIAN
Take your time, Peter.

PAUSE

LILLIAN
I'm not in a hurry.

PAUSE

LILLIAN
A lot of people play with a time limit but I don't. So don't feel pressured.

PAUSE

LILLIAN

Is it something I can help with?

PAUSE

LILLIAN

Why don't you go ahead and put down any old word, darling. The main thing is to use the letters. Your mind will freeze if you just sit there.

PAUSE

LILLIAN

You can use your turn to throw your letters back if you want to.

PETER

I don't want to. And I don't want any rules made up for me.

LILLIAN

Don't be silly, it's a rule for everybody.

PETER

It's a rule for everybody?

LILLIAN

It's a rule for everybody.

PETER

Are you sure?

LILLIAN

Certainly I'm sure.

PETER

How many letters can I throw back?

LILLIAN

As many as you like.

> PETER

I'm throwing all my letters back.

> LILLIAN

Is that wise?

> PETER

I'm not going to sit here with seven vowels.

He throws seven letters back and takes seven new ones.

> LILLIAN

Okay, it's my turn . . . there . . . I'm just doing this to get rid of the letters. . . .

She puts down a six-letter word.

> LILLIAN

That's thirty-six points.

> PETER

Thirty-six points is huge. You can't say you're putting down thirty-six points, "just to get rid of the letters." It's an enormous score.

> LILLIAN

It's about average when I play with Rose.

> PETER

You're not playing with Rose.

> LILLIAN

I know that, honey.

> PETER

Rose can play word games—I can't play word games. I can't even do crossword puzzles, I never could.

LILLIAN
(soothingly)
You just have a block, that's all. You'll get over it.

PETER
"Just a block" is the same as not being able to. And I won't get over it.

LILLIAN
Not if you don't want to.

PETER
I hate it when you're smug.

LILLIAN
I'm not smug.

PETER
You are when you use that tone, you're the Jewish Mary Poppins.

LILLIAN
It's your turn.

PAUSE

LILLIAN
What's the matter now?

PETER
I've got seven consonants.

LILLIAN
Not one vowel?

PETER
Not one. I hate word games. I just hate them.

LILLIAN
There must be something you can do.

PETER
There's not.

LILLIAN
Can't you make some use of that *e*—the one
that's already on the board?

PAUSE

PETER
Okay, I'll use the *e*.
(putting two letters down)
There. *G—E—T*. That's six points.

He takes two new letters.

LILLIAN
Six points . . . good for you. Six points is considered a very decent score, Peter. Try being
pleased with yourself for a change—give yourself a pep talk. Everybody should say something
nice to themselves once in a while. Instead of
saying "I *only* made six points," try saying "I
made six points." Go on. Say it.

PETER
I made six points.

LILLIAN
There now, doesn't that make you feel better?
. . . Let's see, I've got a seven-letter word, that's
twenty-two, on a double word space, is forty-
four, plus fifty for using all my letters. That's
ninety-four.

PETER
Ninety-four?

Lillian writes it down and takes seven new letters.

PETER

Ninety-four?

LILLIAN

It's your turn, darling. Try to concentrate.

PETER

What's the score?

LILLIAN

One hundred and eighty-five to twenty-three.

PETER

You just made ninety-four points with one fucking word?

LILLIAN

Go on now—see what *you* can do.

PETER

I already know what I can do.
        (putting a word down)
This is ten points. Ten. That's all I can do.

LILLIAN

That's very good.

PETER

Lilly, how much money will you take not to use that tone?

LILLIAN

I don't know what you mean.

PETER

You know exactly what I mean, you're talking to me as if I were a defective child. You . . .

LILLIAN

I'm only doing this to get rid of these letters.
        (putting a word down)
That's forty-three.

PAUSE

LILLIAN
It's only a game, Peter.

PETER
(slowly and carefully)
Please don't say that. Please don't get me to play against my will, and wipe me out, and then say it's only a game. Please don't.

LILLIAN
Oh dear, you are in a snit.

PETER
Sure I'm in a snit—who wouldn't be in a snit? Ten minutes with you and Joan of Arc would have recanted.

LILLIAN
Funny you should mention Joan of Arc, I was thinking about her just the other day. You know what Dash said about Joan of Arc? He said she was the world's first career woman.

PETER
What did he say *you* were?

LILLIAN
If you'd rather not play with me, Peter, I will totally understand.

PETER
I hate it when you get understanding—whose turn is it?

LILLIAN
Yours, darling.

PAUSE

PETER

Okay, now listen: I've got one small word. It's very small. I'm going to put it down, and when I put it down, I want you not to tell me what a good score it is, okay?

LILLIAN

I won't say anything.

PETER
(putting the word down)
There. That's five.

LILLIAN

Five?

PETER

Five.

LILLIAN
(writing the score down)
Five points. I'm not saying anything.

PAUSE

LILLIAN

Well, this hardly seems worth it, but I do have to get rid of the *q*.
(putting a word down)
Thirty-eight.

PETER

Thirty-eight?

LILLIAN

Thirty-eight.

PETER

What's the score now?

LILLIAN
(gently)
You don't want to know, darling—it will only
upset you.

PETER
Tell me the score or I'll kill you.

LILLIAN
Two hundred sixty-six to thirty-eight.

PETER
I don't know what the fuck I'm sweating this
out for, I've already lost.

LILLIAN
I told you it would upset you.

PAUSE

LILLIAN
What's the matter now, are you stuck again?

PAUSE

LILLIAN
You mustn't feel there's any pressure about
time—just relax and take as long as you want.

PAUSE

LILLIAN
Why don't you let me try to help you, darling?
Come on—push your rack of letters over this
way so I can see . . .

PETER
Would you *mind* not looking at my letters?

LILLIAN

I only glanced at them to see if I could help.

PETER
(carefully)

Where I grew up we used to call that cheating.

LILLIAN
(angrily)

What an unjust thing to say. I am not a cheater
and you know it.

PETER

You are a cheater.

LILLIAN

I am not.

PETER

You're one of the worst cheaters I ever saw.

LILLIAN
(haughtily)

Take that back.

PETER

You want me to take back my honest opinion?

LILLIAN

Yes.

PETER

I will not cut my conscience to suit this year's
fashions.

LILLIAN

That's a disgusting thing to say.

PETER

I don't give a shit.

LILLIAN
Then I'm going to have to tell you something
I've been trying not to say all summer. There's
a large streak of cruelty in you.

PETER
That's it? That's all? That's what you've been
trying not to say all summer?

LILLIAN
And a large streak of dishonesty.

PETER
That's bullshit, you're only trying to change the
subject.

LILLIAN
I am not trying to change the subject.

PETER
Boy, are you ever a cheater.

LILLIAN
I am not a cheater.

PETER
You're worse than a cheater.

LILLIAN
I am not a cheater.

PETER
You are and shouting doesn't change it.

LILLIAN
I've always been afraid of this side of you.

PETER
Not afraid enough.

LILLIAN
I'm going to my room now.

PETER
I'm going to my room too.

LILLIAN
I don't want to play with you anymore.

PETER
I don't want to play with you either.

They exit. Sound of doors slamming offstage.

CURTAIN

In the afternoons when it didn't rain we drove to Lilly's shack in Gay Head, where she could swim in the nude. Gay Head had the island's most popular nude beach and once we got out there Lilly would lie down under a big towel and writhe and convulse while she took off all her clothes, then stand up naked and put on her bathing cap. She didn't feel naked, she said, as long as she had on a bathing cap. Modesty has its own rules even when preparing itself for nudity and clusters of naked people sitting around the beach watched the process with a certain bewilderment.

On the weekends when the Herseys showed up Lilly went swimming off John's boat. He still kept it anchored in Vineyard Haven harbor, protected by the breakwater off Lillian's beach, as he had done all summer. At four-thirty on almost any afternoon from June through Labor Day you could see John's head, topped by a white sailor's cap, bobbing up and down out of the dune grass, carrying a pair of oars to his dinghy and an empty pail for bringing home bluefish. You could set your watch by John: he left at the same time in most weather and he never came back late. At least once a week during the summer—and now every weekend he could manage—he made a point of asking Lilly out on the boat; Barbara and I went along and after an hour of fishing he anchored in a lagoon and we all went swimming and had lunch. The lagoon was usually deserted except for us, and

Lilly swam naked there too. John and Barbara knew her habits well, but Lilly's lack of embarrassment and sense of physical freedom were seldom what they appeared to be to others: she wasn't brash or exhibitionistic, she was aloof—disassociated—she liked the feel of the water and didn't give a damn about anything else.

Lillian's physicality, her relationship to her body, was, I think, the major clue to her life. It never seemed coherent for more than five minutes, an attitude that was not easy to fathom, but once you understood it you understood the woman.

Lilly had never been pretty, and in the South, in her generation, being pretty mattered almost as much as being rich. It sometimes takes a Southerner to get the point of another Southerner: my own guess is that she took a look in the mirror as a very young girl and decided her dance card was not going to be filled that way, she would have to go her own way, and she did. From then on, the two parts of her had nothing to do with one another: it was as if she had divorced herself from her physical self as a child and the divorce was complete and permanent—for the rest of her life she and her body occupied the same space, but they were two distinct people. In her declining years it was a shock to doctors that so distinguished a writer didn't know the simplest grammar-school facts about anatomy but she didn't. She did not know where her liver was or her kidneys or her spleen or even which side her heart was on. If she enjoyed being naked it was not because she liked her body, but because she didn't connect her body with herself. The imaginary separation was good in some ways, bad in others; if it was responsible for a certain freedom, it was also responsible for her inability to choose clothes and for her falling down, which happened with a kind of relentless regularity all over the world. Lillian fell on street corners—in traffic—in her living room—in other people's houses—inside or outside, wherever she happened to be; she never hurt herself badly by falling and she always blamed the fall on some part of her body, as though it had done something stupid without consulting her. Back in the late forties, when I was still in my teens, we had gone for walks in New York, and once Lillian fell six times on Madison Avenue between Fifty-fourth Street and Fifty-seventh. I thought she was drunk or doing it on purpose and I was wrong—she was doing one thing and her body was doing another.

The only place she never fell was on a boat and heavy waves that tumbled other people never upset her balance at all. She was by definition contradictory: a woman who sank on land but not at sea—who was shy about taking her clothes off but never shy about wearing none—who was at the same time timid and raunchy about sex, seductive and hostile with men. She was both painfully careful and pile-driving careless: she sometimes told the truth about herself in a more blunt way than anyone else and other times lied her head off. Lilly was given to opposite extremes but her perversity was on a grand scale and somehow at her best she made it all work.

On the boat she sat still watching John, who stood at the wheel with the understated elegance of all people who know what they're doing, and for hours after she got off, she remained a little in awe of him—as she was, from time to time, in awe of carpenters and house painters and bricklayers and others who could do things with their hands—as though the effective use of the body were some special privilege that had been denied her.

The truth is that Lilly's alienation from herself affected her view of everything. It wasn't just that she had trouble with east and west, north and south—she didn't know up from down or one continent from another continent. If you don't know your body you can't know the physical world: you have nothing to measure it by.

The worst fight we had that year took place on an afternoon when Lillian asked me to pick up the day's mail at Vineyard Haven. She gave me the combination of her post-office box: "Twice to the right to sixteen—twice to the left to ten—twice to the right to three—once to the left and open."

I walked to the post office, struggled with the lock a few minutes, walked back to the house and told her the combination didn't work.

"Of course it works," she said, "I've been using it for years. It's quite simple—a child could understand it. Now concentrate. Twice to the right, like this . . ."

"Look at your hand," I said.

"What's wrong with my hand?"

I said that she had moved her finger to the *left* when she told me to turn to the *right*.

"You mean like this?"

"Yes."

"No," she said.

"No what?"

"That's not left," she said. "That's right."

Half an hour later she said: "It's silly to stand here shouting at each other . . . let's draw it on a piece of paper." She got a pad and pencil and we sat down. "Now you draw what *you* mean—and I'll draw what *I* mean," she said. I said that was fine with me, and I drew this:

"See where the arrow is pointing?" I said. "It's pointing to the right. That's clockwise."

"Forgive me, but you're wrong," Lillian said. She drew this:

"Surely you can see where the arrow is pointing," she said, "it's pointing to the left. *That's* clockwise. You've got them backward, that's all—don't worry about it, darling, anybody can make a mistake. Is it so hard for you to admit you're wrong?"

Within minutes we had stopped speaking and the silence lasted all day. After that we stayed off the subject of compass directions.

During the afternoons when there was nothing else to do we took walks and in the early-October evenings we cooked dinner in the living-room fireplace and sat around the coals drinking wine or coffee. The ritual of story telling came into its own that fall. Lillian was becoming a better raconteuse than ever and the new version of an old tale always had a twist in the telling worth listening to. Often she would sit with her head back and her eyes half-closed like an ancient caster of spells, spinning yarns contentedly into the night. At such times there might have been a thousand listeners—the important thing was not the size, but holding the audience, since losing it made her feel dead, and in her own way Lilly was a little like Scheherazade, telling stories to keep herself alive. If she ran out of subject matter she could always rely on local gossip and if there was nothing new she could go back in time and reach for something that had happened long ago.

> *This is one thousand percent for you. A couple of years ago I guess it was, no wait a minute, it was three years ago—I remember because I have a diary entry— Frank Sinatra came to the Vineyard on his yacht and the Styrons had a party for him. I think it was when Sinatra was first going with Mia Farrow, or maybe they'd been going together for a while. . . . Anyway they arrived on the biggest and most vulgar yacht you ever saw and anchored it right off there, between the Styrons' house and mine. So, of course, the Styrons gave him a party—I knew Rose would call me sooner or later, and she did. God knows I don't care about being invited to a party or not being invited, whatever's wrong with me that's not, but Rose was at her most tactful that day. "Lilly," she said, "we're having a party, but I can't invite you." You have my solemn word of honor, that's exactly what she said. "And the reason I can't invite you is because of all those mean things you said about Frank, about his being a gangster and all that. But I did want you to know about the party from me*

rather than from somebody else"—she needn't have added that, I'd already heard about the party and she knew it, but nothing ever stops Rose, she's so convinced of her ability to charm—"so I thought I'd call you up, Lilly, and tell you how sorry I am you won't be here."

I said it was very kind and thoughtful of her to let me know, and that night I put my nightgown on and cooked myself a nice dinner and opened a bottle of wine.

I sat drinking the wine and looking out the kitchen window at the yacht. It was all lit up like a Christmas tree, with little boats carrying people back and forth. The party was half there and half at the Styrons' house and you could hear the laughter and the happy noises for hours—you can hear anything across water . . . I opened another bottle of wine and by the time I got halfway through the second bottle, all I could think about was how much fun everybody was having except me. So I got tired of it.

I put my fur coat on over my nightgown and took the second bottle of wine and walked a few blocks into town. I went into one of those phone booths on Main Street and I made the call from there, to the fire department.

"This is an anonymous caller," I said, "I wish to report a bomb under Mr. Sinatra's yacht." Then I hung up and started back to my house. I was good and tight by then and I had to walk slowly—I stopped every now and then to have a little sip of wine from the bottle . . . I must have been about halfway back when I heard the first siren. I guess the fire department called the police department because it wasn't only fire engines, it was squad cars too, and by the time I got back to the kitchen and sat down where I could see the water again, there were little Coast Guard boats running back and forth taking people off the yacht. It ruined the party, I'm afraid—absolutely ruined it. I was very pleased with myself. I watched the people scrambling off the yacht

*for a while and then went to bed and slept like a
baby. . . .*

Exactly how much of the Styron-Sinatra story was apocryphal I never knew and never cared enough to ask because it was
so much like Lilly to behave that way and then rat on herself by
telling about it, without trying to fancy up her motives, or do
anything at all to make them sound better than they were. Accurate or not, it was neither the first nor the last practical joke
she played on the Styrons for a multitude of reasons, not the least
of which was pure affection, however curiously expressed. Her
teasing of Bill often carried, I thought, a hint of sexuality in it,
and I sometimes had the feeling she was more attracted to him
than she cared to admit.

And then October was full blown and suddenly things were
different.

Autumn on the Vineyard brings about the island version of
the leaf change that takes place all over New England, when the
trees appear to tingle with a gaudy spectrum of reds, as if the
branches are reaching out for one last violent blush of life. It's
the best time of all to walk in the woods, and we went right on
walking and cooking and talking—but the time of living as a
couple was coming to an end and we knew it: the silences that
had been filled with fun began to be filled with something else, a
hollow feeling, as if what was real had turned without warning
to make-believe, like two children playing house.

For me, it was as though I had come to the island for the
summer and left my life behind. Early on I'd had the sense that
Lillian wasn't comfortable when I chatted on the phone with an
off-island friend, not because she minded the use of the phone
but because any invasion of a private world was perceived by her
as a kind of threat. So I'd stayed off the phone all summer. I
hadn't minded because I knew the situation was temporary and
the life I had left, such as it was, was there when I wanted it. But
now I didn't know how to put the two lives together.

I was thinking about that one evening, sharing a joint with
Lilly, who'd been given a lid of grass by a friend, when the feeling of emptiness became suddenly so acute I couldn't take it. I
wasn't used to smoking grass and I'd never had a bad trip before
so I didn't recognize this one for what it was—it felt at first as if

something inside had exploded: I had never been that afraid in my life. All I could think about was a set of butcher knives hanging in the kitchen, knowing I would have to pass them on the way to my room, wondering what would happen when I did. Just then I was afraid to breathe. I managed to mumble something about not feeling good and Lilly must have been listening because she heard more than the words, she heard the tone. "Go upstairs," she said, "lie down on my bed, I'll bring coffee."

I went up and before she came with the coffee the panic passed and I could breathe easier. When she handed me the cup I wanted to know how she had learned to act that fast.

"Dash," Lilly said. "Liquor, not grass. Drink the coffee, you'll be fine in a minute."

"I'm fine now."

"Drink it anyway."

"The summer's over, isn't it?"

"That's right," she said. "The summer's over."

After that we dropped the subject and spoke of other things. After dinner I had another joint and rambled on about growing up in New Orleans—about the first time my life had fallen apart and the price I had paid for being sexually molested as a child. I still felt bad about it and I talked about that, about the life of sexual freedom I had once taken up because of it, a time when I was driven to excesses of depravity and couldn't stop. It seemed a likely subject to discuss with an older woman if you're avoiding the real subject but after a while it didn't work. If I was expecting tea and sympathy what I got was coffee and antipathy.

"Frankly I don't care if you fucked snakes," she said, "I only care what you're going to do now. You don't want to go on living together, do you?"

I didn't know how to answer so I kept quiet.

"Okay," Lillian said.

There was a silence.

"Okay," she said. "Okay."

She said it like an announcement and there was another pause and then she got up and went to the door.

She stopped with her back to me and stared out at the water for a few seconds. I knew she was angry and the silence was heavy enough that I knew she was going to say something before she went out of the room but it was no use trying to second-guess her, so I waited. There were a lot of seagulls flying in a loose circle between the breakwater and the jetty as if the tide had washed in some minnows or baby blues. It was too dark to see the gulls but you could hear them.

"In every relationship there's a winner and a loser," Lillian said softly. "But the winner ought to be careful."

She opened the door and went upstairs to pack.

Wait Till I Die

>->->->->- I

IT WAS MONTHS after her funeral before I came back alone to
look at the Vineyard house and when I did it felt stranger than it
had the first time I saw it, only this time Lillian wasn't in it to
make me laugh. There was a musty smell on the upstairs floor,
dust all over, and the kitchen looked like something out of a
cheaply produced nightmare. Dishes and pots and pans and ta-
bleware from her funeral buffet were lying around where they'd
been left, food rotting on them. The smell was bad and I walked
through it and went out and sat on the beach.

I knew because she had left me the house that she'd expect
me to clean it up and set it right but I didn't know where I would
find the stomach for it. Or for the memories of Lilly at her best—
the boating trips—or the time we took to fooling around in her
bedroom and she said something that made me laugh harder than
is good for a man under those circumstances. And when I reminded her of it she laughed too but when I wanted to repeat it
to one other person who loved her—two other people—the
Herseys . . .

LILLIAN: *Oh, shut up. Wait till I die and write about it.*
PETER: *I don't want to write about it.*
LILLIAN: *Why not?*
PETER: *Because I don't want to sound like Alice B. Toklas is
why not.*
LILLIAN: *Can't you write about me without sounding like Alice
B. Toklas?*
PETER: *I doubt it.*

89

After a while the beach was cold. I walked back up the hill and found Melvin Pachico, the caretaker who had looked after the lawn and house as his father had her earlier house and lawn, and got started.

It was to take months to get things organized, more before the place would begin to be habitable again. For the last few years of her life Lillian had been legally blind and half-paralyzed, unable to supervise anything and in need of more attention herself than a housekeeper and trained nurses could provide: the place was a mess. It had to be gutted, walls sanded and painted, floors scraped and refinished and mouse droppings that had caked in corners and crevices cleaned with a chisel.

I took a bedroom up-island in a newly built bed-and-breakfast home for the first night so I could start lining up workmen the next day; but the new room was too unused, too empty of life or death, and I picked up my suitcase and went back to Lilly's. I cleaned a space around her bed with a mop and got on it with a blanket and slept there. I went to sleep right away.

Sometime after midnight I woke and lay still, wondering when someone dies at what age you remember them. Whether you picture them as they were just before they died or before that, and if so how long before that. Do you have different pictures of the person in your mind, like a photograph album, at all ages? Do you remember the whole time of the person or just one time of the person? I had known Lillian for forty-three years.

On a sunny afternoon, over a year later—after the workmen had finished and I'd moved in—I fell asleep on the beach and something large licked me. It was a dog, a female about the size of a German shepherd or a little bigger, with long black hair like a chow and a sweet face and ears like a mule. I took her up to the house, gave her some water and phoned around the island but nobody knew her. Then someone stopped by who did know her; her name was Sadie and she belonged to one of the trained nurses who had taken care of Lillian.

I called the nurse but she didn't want the dog anymore: Sadie was thin and suffering from malnutrition and mange and heartworm and you-name-it, but after a few weeks of steady meals and trips back and forth to the vet she was fine.

So Sadie moved in with me and things settled down; I began the job of sifting through transcripts and papers and journals, still not sure which age of Lillian was the right age for memory, what was the real point of her, or what, after it was all over, I remembered best. In the mornings I worked and Sadie slept. In the afternoons we sat out on the deck watching the birds and the boats.

That was when I saw the osprey. I was thinking about that first summer and there it was. I liked it better than Sadie did but she didn't mind watching it with me. We were sitting together waiting for the osprey to dive when John Hersey called from his house to say that a hurricane had come out of the Gulf around Florida and was headed north along the coast, according to the latest weather report, straight for Martha's Vineyard.

The hurricane's name was Gloria and its approach was, I thought, well past the last straw or the unkindest cut—out in the land of whatever. Fixing up the house had not been simple: people who aren't aware of their own hostility often cause more trouble than people who are, and Vineyard workmen, dependent on rich summer visitors for a living, are hostile without knowing it. The population goes up from twelve thousand to eighty-five thousand in summer, beaches are privately owned down to the low-tide mark, and land is so expensive many of the natives can no longer afford access to the best beaches in season, yet all are expected to attend to the whims and needs of outsiders who can.

On top of that there was another problem. During the last years of Lillian's life she had been dependent on nurses and so had been out of control: blindness and paralysis in a managerial nature caused a sense of helplessness that soon turned to fury and she'd whipped up a storm around her. Word travels fast on an island and there wasn't a plumber or electrician or carpenter who would come near the house if he knew it was the Hellman house— Lilly had alienated all of them. In trying to fix the place up, I'd cajoled and wheedled and overpaid for months: I was tired of asking favors that cost too much when they were granted, tired of the plumber who made an appointment to come on Friday and showed up a week later on a Monday if he showed up at all. It had been an endless Rube Goldberg series of problems and now that the house was at last ready to live in, a hurricane named Gloria was going to come and take it away.

By the time the weather report upgraded the hurricane warning to a hurricane alert, I was walking around in a rage that would have done credit to Lillian. I knew about tropical storms from New Orleans but the knowledge did me no good. What I wanted was to make an announcement. Look here, I wanted to say, a hurricane is not a Jewish event: pestilence, plague, famine are Jewish events, but not a hundred-and-fifty-mile-per-hour wind going around in circles. Jews don't need that outside—we have that inside: take your hurricane and shove it, I wanted to say, but there was no one to say it to, so I went into town and bought a dozen rolls of masking tape from the hardware store.

It took me four hours to tape all the windows because the side of the house that faced the sea was three quarters glass. By then some radio announcer was advising Vineyard Haven residents who lived within two hundred yards of the water on sea-level land to prepare to evacuate their homes right away. I was not about to do that and I told him so; it made no difference that I was only talking to a radio, and I went ahead with what else had to be done.

With the sense that Lilly was standing behind me commenting on every move I filled the bathtubs and sinks with water, opened a couple of windows an inch on the lee side of the house, moved everything portable from the ground floor to the upstairs floor in case of a flood and sat down to wait. I remembered then Lillian telling me about a neighbor who had once complained that the toilets in his house didn't flush after a hurricane, and Hammett's contempt for a man so ignorant of how a house works that he expected toilets to go on as usual. I knew that toilets wouldn't work, and so I knew if the house survived Gloria I would be back at the mercy of the plumber again.

Rage has the virtue of eliminating fear and when the first wisp of wind hit the island I was in a state Lillian would have called rocking-chair crazy. The beach was a solid mass of sea-birds standing shoulder to shoulder—the osprey not among them—all of them facing the storm. Just then I felt a wave of sleep so strong I couldn't keep my eyes open, and when the wind increased I heard a voice say out loud: "Screw you, Gloria."

Sadie whined and Lillian's spirit, perched boredly next to me on the arm of the sofa, dangled one delicate foot and said:

"That's right, Gloria. You heard him. Screw you."

⊱⊱⊱⊱⊱ II

MY MEMORY OF that October ends with a picture—or a series of pictures—of Lilly walking slowly down the hall from her bedroom to an open suitcase in the larger guest room, holding on to one shoe. Almost nobody likes to pack, since packing tends to remind us of death (that's what the pyramids are: big suitcases) but Lilly went into a kind of trance when she had to do it. She would disappear into the guest room for a minute or so, come out empty-handed, and walk just as slowly back to her room. After a while she would reappear with the second shoe, amble down the hall again in a somnambulant way, drift back into the guest room and come out with the shoe she had just wrapped and packed, together with its mate, having decided she didn't want to take that pair with her in the first place. Lillian had in common with Lizzie Borden that she did not do things in a hurry. To my knowledge she never ran anywhere in her life and if she attempted to speed up she fell down.

After she left for New York, I stayed, to finish a chapter: I went on working and watching the leaves sift out of the trees that formed a spring-summer barrier between two houses—hers and the house next door known as the Mill House where she had lived with Hammett. The Mill House was owned by some people named Snow who had bought it from Lilly when Hammett died but the Snows only used it in summer. Before I left, all the leaves were gone and you could see it, stark and high and rambling, with that odd stuck-up quality houses get when they have been lived in and deserted.

When the chapter was finished I went to New York for a

day, long enough to have a couple of meals with Lilly, then went down to New Orleans to finish my novel.

In my memory the next few months tilt into a long sludge of time, the first of a period of years that feels more remarkable today than it probably was. Single events or systems of events or small galaxies of them glow in what otherwise is darkness so that memory is like space travel, a trip through the leftover fancy of some fumbling interstellar being trying to recall by the night-lights of childhood what happened before the first big explosion.

Settling down in New Orleans was easy and natural. Like many people hell-bent on going back to their private lives, I didn't have much of a life to go back to—it's always harder to leave home if you don't have a home than it is if you do. For the next few weeks work kept me busy; I had taken two rooms in a small residential motel in the French Quarter called the Richelieu, a comfortable and faintly squalid place with a nice rambling family air. But I hadn't been in New Orleans for years and I felt like an alien walking the same streets I'd walked as a child—streets Lillian had walked in a different childhood, an earlier generation. I missed her a lot and we spoke on the phone a couple of times a week and wrote random affectionate notes.

DEAR LILLIAN:

My toothache is worse. I am dying, Israel, dying.

Peter

3 A.M. Friday

DEAR PETER:

So sorry, really sorry, to have your death letter of this morning. Your death probably accounts for the phone call of last night and for the fact that I couldn't reach you, although before "going" you should have had sense enough to tell the switchboard not to say you were out. But I don't mean to correct your manners across the sacred places. I want only to say: 1) I do not feel guilty. 2) You wrote, before passing on, very funny letters. 3) I would have wanted a few love letters to carry with me, but I should have known they would never be written, could not be written, and when Morisot-Levi-de-Guinzberg gets to your biography I have promised to tell him why. 4) I am sorry that you didn't come back to see me in New York before you died, but then, of course, you always knew you weren't coming and 5) Dr. de Guinzberg thinks it might have contributed to what he calls your "dental-depth-death-desire" and 6) there will never be another man because it is all just too much trouble and therefore I will never do our things,* there being plenty of other things for those foolish enough to want them and 7) I have this morning refused a dinner invitation with a twenty-five-year-old swinger because I don't want them and 8) because I intend to spend the rest of my life staring at a ceiling wondering what world brought us forth, you and I, or the you that was and the I that could have been, and so I send you love, wherever you are, and wish that something else had happened between us.

Lillian

P.S. Did you leave me any money?

By the third week I was edgy, by the fourth a monumental lonesomeness had set in that was so empty I sometimes mistook it for something else. The week after that Lillian called to say she had some free time and did I want her to come for a visit. I booked an adjoining suite at the Richelieu and went to the airport half an hour before her arrival time and sat down to wait near the gate.

Lilly was never the first off a plane because she never, visibly, acted in haste; she came walking off slowly after most of the other hurrying passengers—taking her time and looking straight in front, head high. One of the reasons she fell down so much was the fact that she never looked down, and I pushed through the crowd fast and stood directly in her path where I couldn't be missed. She altered her course by a few degrees, like a ship, and sailed slowly past me like someone standing on a Mardi Gras float, still looking ahead, serene and regal, impervious and im-

---

* Reference to the end of Hemingway's *A Farewell to Arms* and the goodbye words spoken by the dying heroine to her lover: "You won't do our things with another girl . . . will you?"

placable. It was more than her usual unseeing walk and I wondered for a second if something was wrong with her eyes and then forgot it and circled around and stood in front of her again. This time her face lit up and she stopped.

"Hello, darling," she said, "I was beginning to think you weren't here."

I reminded her that she had told me not to come to the airport.

"I'm glad you didn't pay attention," she said, "I'd never have spoken to you again if you did. Are you glad to see me?"

Back at the Richelieu she lit a cigarette and said: "This is a nice little place—I like it—the rooms are bright and large. But I don't think it's for me." She was staring out the window and I asked what the matter was.

"Nothing. It's fine for a couple of nights," she said, "I'll move tomorrow or the next day." I pointed out that the price of a suite of rooms in a big hotel would be twice as much. "I don't want a suite," she said, "I never liked suites—not even when a movie company paid for it—I was always too afraid I'd get used to it and find myself working for that."

I asked what she disliked about the Richelieu.

"It's a pleasant place."

"What is it, Lilly?"

"It's honestly nothing," she said, "it's foolishness, I know it is. But I saw so many of them in the Quarter when I was young. I'm scared of rats, I always was."

"There aren't any rats," I said.

"Probably not, but it looks like it in the courtyard and I wouldn't be able to sleep for thinking about it."

I remembered then my mother's sudden stillness one afternoon when we lived in the Quarter on St. Peter Street and she came home to find the butler holding a spade over a large gray rat he'd cornered in the hall. It seemed best not to press the issue and I took a single room for Lilly in the anonymous-looking marble-foyered Royal Sonesta for the next night. The Sonesta was in a much better part of the Quarter, a big mausoleum of a hotel, too antiseptic for cockroaches and much too expensive for rats.

We spent the next few afternoons walking the city, the places she knew and the places I knew. We strolled by the big green plants called elephant ears, the honeysuckle and steaming bitter coffee, the snarled tangle of smells in the Garden District. We both liked the azalea bushes that lined the cracked sidewalks, the camphor trees and the faint odor of camphor rising from berries that popped underfoot when you walked.

We went the length of Prytania Street looking for the narrow shotgun house where Lillian had been born, then found it—and after that I took her to a place high on the levee where I used to go and sit when I was little. In the dawn the mist unfolded gently like tissue paper from the river below. It began to burn off as the sun rose, the brown water sliding forward, heavy with silt like a vein in the earth to the Gulf. There were other things we liked, the white clamshell roads and the tar-streaked pilings in the port, the great rotten gulps of river smells in the air, and the air itself—always the air—the insinuating air, soft and warm and damp on the skin.

There was a place we both knew about from childhood by the lakeside where you could sit for hours with a string and a piece of meat, waiting for blue crabs, and we bought a couple of oyster poorboys and went there on a city bus. The trip seemed to take forever and the winter sky looked hollow and gray and cold, the way I remembered it from my childhood. That was the day I felt so empty I ran out of words.

We sat for a while on some cement steps looking out at the lake water and the odd bits of animal waste and junk that lapped at the rim of the lake, the filthy garbage flirting with the shore. A few scrawny-looking birds stood next to us hoping for something better.

"Were you lonesome growing up?" Lillian said abruptly.

I said I guessed I had been.

"Me too," she said, "the trouble about being an only child is very simple-minded—it's just having nobody whose measure you can take. Nobody the right size to take yours. We had nobody to play with."

"We do now."

"That's right," she said. "We do now. Maybe we'd better not lose each other."

I said I wasn't planning on it.

"Okay," Lillian said.

We sat for a while and then she said: "You'll have to get a place to live till you finish the book. A hotel won't do. Even a cheap hotel. Hotels cost too much."

We took the bus back to the Quarter and that night some

old friends, Ella and Adelaide Brennan, the owners of a fine old restaurant called Commander's Palace, asked us for dinner. We set out to get rip-roaring drunk but because we had set out to do it we didn't even get high. After dinner we went dancing in a nightclub and stopped on the way back at Preservation Hall to listen to some jazz.

Lilly had a key to my rooms at the Richelieu and the next day when I finished work I found her sitting in the living room with the real estate section of the morning paper and a pencil. She had the paper folded at APARTMENTS FOR RENT, FURNISHED. "I've marked five," she said, "but only one looks good—I called the owner—I said you'd be coming around after work."

I asked where it was.

"Bourbon Street," she said. "The loudest block. Let's go."

I got dressed and we walked over together. Bourbon runs from Canal Street all the way across the Quarter to Esplanade, and the first few blocks in from Canal were solid wall-to-wall sleaze: stripper joints and barkers and bars and lewd underwear shops and people whooping it up. At night it was turned into a mall, with neon lights. Throngs of tourists and locals drifted together from bar to bar, drinking beer from paper cups or chatting, most of them looking for company; the noises and lights and the crowds mixed to make an effect of nonstop, nonspecific raunch, and I had always liked that and so had Lilly. But I didn't see how I could do any work in it.

She led the way to a tall door set into a high metal wall and pushed the buzzer. An answering buzzer rang. The door opened onto a kind of private alley between two buildings and the alley onto a courtyard. Inside, the place was muted in shadow, a city oasis: there was a sense of green silence, a couple of banana trees and a magnolia tree and some bushes—you couldn't hear the sounds of the street at all. It was as if the little courtyard had come here on tiptoe, holding up its green skirts, and dropped them inside the locked gate, barricading itself against the noise and sleaze of the outside world; it might have been a brothel or a nunnery. Water was dripping very slowly from a rusted pipe into a goldfish pond and you could hear each separate drop. There were two floors in the building and the apartment was on the second, a living room and kitchen, bedroom and bath, furnished, for $275 a month, with a small balcony over the courtyard.

I took it right away and we went to the Richelieu and packed my things and brought them over. On the way back we picked up some groceries and wine and cooked dinner together as we were used to doing on the Vineyard. That night we didn't mean to get drunk, so we did. I forgot about the emptiness of growing up and Lilly forgot about her rats and dozed off quietly on the sofa. I figured she wouldn't mind just this once waking up in a part of the Quarter that wasn't exactly antiseptic and I was still asleep in the morning when she sat up and said:

"Well, that's that. Is it your feeling I should make coffee?"

That was on a Friday and I rented a car for the weekend and drove her out of the city, around the Atchafalaya River-basin swamp into Cajun country, and we spent Friday night in Lafayette. In the morning we had breakfast in a Cajun diner on the edge of the swamp. After the heat of summer the water was very low and you could see the cypress trees with their naked knees sticking out of the water and the Spanish moss and tupelo gums and glistening elegant mud. It was the wrong time of year to take a skiff into it but we made a pact to come back in spring. We had dinner that evening in Abbeville, spent the night in Lafayette again, drove down to Morgan City to look at the shrimp fleets on the Gulf, then drove back to New Orleans.

LILLIAN: *Tell me where we went that first trip.*
PETER: *I just did.*
LILLIAN: *Tell me again.*
PETER: *Lafayette.*
LILLIAN: *Is Lafayette where we had the stuffed shrimp?*
PETER: *No. Morgan City.*
LILLIAN: *Then what did we do in Lafayette?*
PETER: *Never mind.*
LILLIAN: *We did?*

PAUSE.

LILLIAN: *What about that nice little duck restaurant?*
PETER: *Opelousas. We went there on the second trip.*
LILLIAN: *I wish you didn't always sound so patient with me.*
PETER: *"You always," "you never"—we talk like an old married couple.*
LILLIAN: *We are an old married couple.*

SOUND OF LILLIAN COUGHING. SOUND OF SEAGULLS.

LILLIAN: *Wouldn't it be nice to go back to Lafayette? And Ope-lousas . . . I liked that little duck restaurant.*

PAUSE.

LILLIAN: *I wish I could see it now. My poor eyes.*

PAUSE.

LILLIAN: *I wonder if it's normal to feel sorry for your eyes.*

Lilly lingered on in New Orleans for a couple more days and just to keep things familiar and reassuring we had a fight. We were walking along Dauphine Street and I saw a stray dog snarfing in an empty food container. It looked thin and hungry and I asked Lilly to wait while I ran into a grocery store on the corner for a can of dog food but she went on walking with her usual slow pace down the street. I called to her but she wouldn't stop or look back. When I caught up with her she spoke.

"It's disgusting to feel that much for animals, it's sentimental crap. You and Dottie Parker."

"You can't be jealous of a dog," I said.

"I can if I want to, who made that rule? And you can put everything I say down to jealousy if you like. But I don't think you should *always* reduce people to their lowest motive—it's a dangerous habit."

"Since when do I reduce people?"

"I don't want to talk about it," Lilly said.

We had dinner in unrelenting silence. We both knew it was because Lillian was leaving and angry about it but I was angry too.

After dinner, as if by unspoken agreement, we left the anger in the restaurant and walked away from it. We went and sat on a bench overlooking the river near Jackson Square and Lilly said: "Tell me about Dottie in Los Angeles."

I asked if she meant like a story.

"I always mean like a story," Lillian said.

It was an old story, one she was familiar with, and she sounded as if she were looking for something new in it, though I couldn't figure what; but I told it to her all the same. When I first went to Los Angeles I had lived on a small street called Norma

Place a couple of houses down from Dorothy Parker and after work I would sometimes walk over and have a drink with her.

Dorothy and Lillian had been friends for a very long time by then. They were a perfectly matched pair, a kind of intellectual vaudeville team, though in many ways they were opposites: Dorothy was a prim mouselike little thing with a soft voice—a pretty woman who could blush at will. If a good-looking man walked into the room she turned all pink and dimply and batted her eyes and gave every indication of being at a loss for words; but inside her something yawned and I always had the feeling she didn't like men much. Lillian's response went the other way. She had anything but a soft voice and when an attractive man appeared her tone would go down, her shoulders up and her back would stiffen in an almost hostile way. But inside her something had fainted. Lillian liked men a lot.

Often it seemed as if the two of them were working the same street selling different wares. There's a secret place where everybody wants to be insulted and Lilly knew how to find it. She was a master at the kind of insult that carries with it a concealed compliment ("It's foolish and ignorant of you to work as hard as you do, it's stupid past belief, you'd be a distinguished man even if you did nothing!") and she used it whenever she could. While Dorothy was busy flattering men Lillian was insulting them and the teamwork was remarkable: seated face to face in the presence of a member of the opposite sex they were like internal mirror images—each embodied what the other was feeling.

Apart from that, they often amused and observed each other with affection. I no longer remember where it was that a few friends had gathered for the weekend, including the two of them and a married couple I didn't know, when Lilly came in to announce that a party was being given in honor of Helen Keller. She herself was going and everybody was welcome to come with her. Dorothy was busy reading a book; the couple I didn't know was out somewhere; Hammett, who didn't like Dorothy, had gone away for the day, and I was on the sofa with a cold, being fed soup by a girlfriend. Lilly put her coat on and left.

I still don't know who gave the party but Lillian said afterward that a lot of famous people had been there: Leonard Bernstein had played the piano and Helen Keller had held Lennie's hands while he played; then Lennie had cried and the other famous guests had cried and Helen Keller had cried, and Lillian, who hated displays of sentimentality, had got sick of the whole thing and walked out.

When Lillian came back from the party Dorothy was still absorbed in reading, eyes glued to her book. Lilly made herself a drink and sat down in silence; after a moment she lit a cigarette and heaved a very loud sigh.

"It's your own fault, dear," Dorothy said quietly, without looking up, "didn't I tell you she was a conwoman and a dyke?"

Lillian laughed so hard she choked and had to be whacked on the back and Dorothy put a finger in her book to mark the place and glanced up sadly for an instant.

"I have something terrible to tell you about myself, Lilly," she said. "I hate the blind."

My memory isn't all that good about Dorothy but I think it was the same winter the two of them took to fighting about which one had slept with the lowest-down men. It was an argument that was to make them sound like a pair of giddy gay boys and it went on for most of an afternoon while Barbara Hersey and other people walked in and out of the room. Dorothy, who always posed as the lowliest and most unworthy person anywhere, claimed that there was no contest, since she'd slept with far worse men than Lillian would have looked at; and Lilly kept claiming that Dorothy was boasting. They went through the names of advertising men and gangsters and movie producers and other lowlife. After several hours of it Lillian was ahead by one PR man and a gangster when Dorothy leaned forward with an expression of dark finality—fixed her eyes on Lillian—and softly, carefully pronounced the words: "Elmer . . . Rice." I never met Mr. Rice, a distinguished playwright of his day, but I gather he was not a nice-looking man because Lillian had the same response she'd had over the Helen Keller episode. She was still spluttering and gasping for breath when Dorothy turned to the maid and said gently: "It was wrong of her to compete with me— I *told* her she'd fall in a well. Do anything you can for her, dear," and wandered off to the bar.

Recently, in the sixties, Dorothy had moved from Los Angeles to the Hotel Volney in New York and for some reason Lillian had taken to feeling guilty about her. She had never gone to visit her in California, not because she was angry at her but because she couldn't take the now almost constant drinking; but for a while now she'd been asking what Dorothy was up to—a loaded question because she already knew the answer.

Dorothy's world had collapsed around her and all she was up to was surviving—as Lillian was to survive much later—the best she could. She was older than Lilly, one of Hammett's generation of writers and so part of a crowd that drank too much and fought too much and lived by a kind of nose-thumbing attitude that had been on its way out since the hippies were on their way in. You couldn't poke fun at the same things now: *épater le bourgeois* was a way of life for many writers who came to the end of their road when the middle class no longer gave a damn about being baited, having thrown its own rules out the window. The new middle class had interpreted free love to mean gang bangs, as their children had swapped fancy cocktails for coke and pot; Dorothy had gone on drinking as Hammett had gone on drinking, but epataying wasn't fun anymore, it was a way of death, not life.

On the park bench near Jackson Square, Lillian leaned forward and said: "Is Dottie all right for money?"

I said she lived on a shoestring but the shoestring was okay as far as I knew.

"Let me know if she's not," Lillian said, "*she* won't."

She didn't, and the two were never to see each other again. It was a curious fact that Dorothy, who was aware that Lillian had dropped her and who bad-mouthed so many of her former acquaintances, never had a bad word to say about Lillian until she died. She died penniless and after her funeral a couple of large checks Lillian had sent her showed up uncashed in a drawer. Some time after that Lilly gave me a worn-looking Viking Portable Library edition of Dorothy's work that Dorothy had inscribed to her. The inscription is written with an old-fashioned fountain pen, in dark blue ink.

FOR MISS HELLMAN—The most beautiful, the most rich, the most chic, the most dashing, the most mysterious, the most fragrant, the most nobly-born, the most elegant, the most cryptic, the most startling, the most glorious, the most lovely—
In short, for Miss Hellman
From Miss Parker

LILLIAN: *Remember the last time I asked you to tell me a story about Dottie? I didn't want the story. I wanted to see her.*
PETER: *I know.*
LILLIAN: *I couldn't, I'm not sure why.*
PETER: *You didn't want to be a Fillalloo Bird,* I guess.
LILLIAN: *But I am a Fillalloo Bird, I can't help it. I miss Dottie.*
PETER: *Me too.*
LILLIAN: *You? I didn't think you missed anybody.*
PETER: *I don't as a rule—I figure you either miss people so much you can't stand it or you don't miss them at all.*
LILLIAN: *I wonder if you'll ever miss me.*
PETER: *Not if I can help it.*
LILLIAN: *Not while I'm alive, you mean. Wait till I die.*
PETER: *Go to hell, Lilly.*

SOUND OF LILLIAN LAUGHING.

LILLIAN: *Wait, honey, wait . . . wait till I die . . .*

The story Lillian asked me to tell that day on the park bench was short. It happened one evening in Los Angeles when I walked over to have a drink with Dorothy. A friend of Dorothy's, a well-known actress living in the neighborhood, had just come to visit with her little boy, who was six.

The actress kept her son in a viselike grip on her lap and played with him while she talked. She could not let the child alone: her hands wandered over his mouth and face and chest and crotch and legs and feet and toes and then started all over again, while the child squirmed and wriggled to get off her lap. At last he slipped out of his mother's grip, jumped to the floor and ran into the next room to be alone and play.

"I *know* I'm prejudiced," the actress said, smiling, "after all, he's only six . . . but he *is* a beautiful little boy, isn't he?"

"Yes, he is," Dorothy said. "Strange he never married."

---

* The Fillalloo Bird, once sold in New Orleans drugstores, was a small wooden bird with feathers and a plaque underneath that read: "I am the Fillalloo Bird. I fly backwards because I don't care where I'm going but I like to see where I've been."

⊱⊱⊱⊱⊱ III

AFTER LILLIAN WENT back to New York I settled into the furnished apartment on Bourbon Street and for a time we spoke daily on the phone and wrote each other once or twice a week. Lilly had begun to perceive my absence as a form of rejection and her resentment grew from week to week.

3 A.M. Friday

DEAREST PETER,

I called you back a few hours ago. It's the second time this week I've done that and my only explanation—it's an odd thing for me to do—is that I do not say what I think the first time, then do not say what I think the second time, put it away only to find it breaks out a few days or a week later. But what is it I want to say? Some fumbling, too-fast explanation of what I am capable of, incapable of, what pleases me or reminds; what, I guess, is the neurosis—a hateful word. Do I want also to say that I have glimpses into your difficulties, and that because they are different from mine, I don't always feel connected to them, often do feel that they have stood in your way in some manner I as yet don't understand?

God damn all these vague words. I think you are saying that of course we must meet, and often, and that of course that will be good, but that when we meet and how often is not in your hands, but is controlled by many other things—a home, work, whim, money, your

105

nature, an unpacked valise—and that up to now I have been saying, in some over youthful fashion, that I have never lived that way, have trouble with it . . . Well, I will try it your way. I am not sure that I won't slip, maybe never get up, but I'll try . . . I don't want a mess, or a loss or even sadness that doesn't have to be: I am sick of the troubles of the lucky. I never liked them, really have tried to live without them—they have no true seriousness.

What is serious is that I love you, and hope to love you, and would like to be around all the niceness and fun that is in you.

Lillian

And accompanied by a chain with a small Fabergé eagle she had once given to Hammett:

DEAR KNIGHT FEIBLEMAN,

May this take you through the Crusades in safety. May it guard my honor, be worthy of your honor and your queen, prove to the miserable infidels your famous prowess on the field or fields or Fieldston School.

Certainly it brings you my love and, I am sorry to say, all that I have now in this world. May God bring you back to me.

Saint Lilliana of Prague,
Queen of Bohemia, Lithuania and the
southern half of the Holy Roman Empire
through marriage to Charles V who
died yesterday.

(My dear, think what his death could mean to you, *us!*)

And by itself, like an afterthought:

DEAR PETER:

Please teach me to speak with a New Orleans accent again.

Love,
Lillian

DEAR LILLIAN:

I will teach what I can. The following is the first thing I wish to correct in your speech. (The Jewishness we can't do anything about, but certain of your Southern roots seem to have been covered over by your ethnic persuasion.) For general reference:

Yawl is a term referring to one person.

Both yawl refers to two people.

All yawl refers to three or more people.

Yawl and all yawl is a term to be used when addressing members of two different generations, generally out of respect. For instance if you are standing in a room with a grandfather surrounded by his children and/or grandchildren and you wish to extend an invitation to the entire family, "Will yawl and all yawl come to supper?" is the proper thing to say.

Thus we arrive at our current and popular Southern usage:

Yawl go obscenity yourself.   (City talk)

Yawl go obscenity yawl's self.   (Country)

Both yawl go obscenity yourselves.   (City)

Both yawl go obscenity both yawl's selves.
(Country)

All yawl go obscenity yourselves.   (Rural)

All yawl go obscenity all yawl's selves.   (Urban
middle class)

Yawl and all yawl go obscenity yourselves.
(Pretentious, generally the mark of a social
climber)

Yawl and yawl go obscenity all yawl's selves.
(Aristocracy)

I hope you learn to keep these distinctions clear, as the pitifully small group who care about such things decreases every day. Sad, sad. The South isn't what it used to be. Up to us, I think, to maintain certain standards.

For what it's worth, I love yawl. For better or worse, in sickness and I suppose in health, yawl hear?

Professor Feibleman

DEAR PETER,

I was right: the [black] desk clerk has sold your letters [instead of mailing them] and neither one of us will like it when they come up at auction. I needed to hear from you this morning and I'm in a bad humor about niggers and maybe about Jews.

I swing: how lucky it's all been, how it almost didn't happen, how pleased, happy, amused—and how good it is bound to be; then—time for me is not time for you, and that isn't only a question of age. It is temper and training and a different way of life and I would like to know about that, but at this minute, I don't, and find myself late at night wondering if there is a solution that will work for both of us. A way of living, I mean, that does not hold you down where you don't want to be held and still allows for my nervousness about jobs or work or travel. (These words, that paragraph, are too vague. To hell with it for now.) . . .

How much of it all is my surprise at the sudden, unexpected, unwanted dependence? So forceful now that it seems to me my days are spent waiting to speak to you on the phone. How did that come about? Just answer me that and do it fast and mail the letter yourself because I need to know and in the meantime send you a great deal of a great many of a great lot.

L.

DEAR LILLIAN:

Yes, I want to live together and, no, I don't. Two thoughts with but a single mind. I don't have a problem, Lilly, I am a problem, I'll feel more like a wall-to-wall person when I finish the novel. For now, I'm too rocky to trust what I feel on most subjects, let alone the subject of you, with one exception:

I needn't send you my love, you have that.

P.

DEAREST PETER,

It seems to me that I start out O.K. to say what I mean and then find myself on other paths wandering around in the past. In any case, I hope that nothing I said could deny my true, I mean true, gratitude for what you did for me in the past—book, sickness, pleasure, all the nice things . . .

I love you very much, indeed, and I have proved it this last year and a half. More than anything I could want would be a long, close friendship, good and helpful for us both. If I can do, or stop doing, anything to help that, you must tell me. But it is you who have taken the actions and I think it is you on whom the mending depends.

I send you a very great deal of love for just everything: the book, other books, breakfast.

Lillian

5 P.M.

We have spoken on the phone [about taking a trip together] and if you can spare a few minutes from the poetry, you have promised me an answer.

Miss H.

It was, I think, a month or so after she left New Orleans that Lilly called to ask if I wanted to meet her in Puerto Vallarta for a week's holiday. Vallarta was an unexpected choice because neither of us had ever liked Mexico much but there was a nice hotel on a beach facing west, with the sound of surf, gaudy Technicolor sunsets, and a great many palm trees of the sort Mark Twain once described as feather dusters struck by lightning. The hotel was called the Camino Real and I started to make reservations there but Lilly decided she wanted more space and she found a rental agent who had a list of full-service houses available by the week; I flew from New Orleans, she flew from New York and we met in Vallarta. A few days before we went, she said, like an excited romantic child: "Let's not use the phone tomorrow. Let's not talk again till we see each other . . ."

My flight landed later than hers and when I got out of customs I saw Lilly standing on the other side of a glass wall wearing a straw beach hat she had just bought and a bright pink dress. She looked like a lollipop. She was smiling and waving, jumping up and down like a little girl, and it made you feel good just to see her. I went and stood with her in the steamy air and the dust and flies. Lilly said she had been to the rented house, hadn't liked it, had had a fight with the rental agent and moved over to the Camino Real. The hotel was fully booked but she had managed to get us space—two adjoining rooms on the twelfth floor. She had accomplished that by telling the general manager that she was the private secretary of an important executive in the CIA who was bilingual and arriving on the afternoon plane.

When we got to the the hotel we spent the rest of the day settling into our rooms. Lillian went out by herself to a grocery store and came back with a paper bag containing a tin of sardines and one of tuna and a piece of cheese, some tired-looking tea bags and a jazzy wire thing that was guaranteed to boil water and didn't. She arranged all her possessions carefully on a shelf in the closet of her room while I set up a portable typewriter and a stack of pencils in mine. When we were finished she had a makeshift kitchen, I had a work area, and we sat down and complimented each other on what we had done. What we had done was to mark out our territory with the pride of discoverers and the instinct of deer urinating on trees. It was a ritual we were to practice from then on in hotels all over the world, and afterward we went downstairs and had a Mexican tourist drink and watched the candy sunset.

The next afternoons passed quickly: we swam in front of the hotel or hired a car and drove down the coast into the jungle fringe. In the mornings I worked and Lilly had thunderous one-sided arguments with the room-service waiter and once she knocked on my door and asked me to have a talk with him right away. She had ordered a three-minute soft-boiled egg, she said, but the egg the waiter had brought her was not cooked for three minutes. She had sent it back several times from the twelfth floor to the kitchen; but each time the waiter returned with a new egg, the new egg was either hard-boiled or raw. Would I please tell him to stop it—would I tell him in Spanish that it wasn't nice to treat decent people this way.

The room-service waiter was a boy of thirteen or fourteen who looked as if he were trying to go deaf. He understood a little of the Señora's English, he said, but he didn't understand the Señora. He had taken the egg back to the kitchen four times. The last time he had taken the egg back to the kitchen, the cook had said bad things about his ancestors. After that he had come up-stairs again and the Señora said some things about the egg he didn't understand but he could tell from her tone that she was not pleased. So could everyone on the beach.

But what the Señora didn't know, he said, was that he, the waiter, could not take the egg back again.

"What's he saying?" Lillian said.

"If I take the egg back," the waiter said slowly, in Spanish, "the cook will shoot me."

"I have something to tell you," Lillian said, staring at him.

"I'll take the egg back," the waiter said.

"He's doing his best," I said when the waiter had gone, "why give him such hell—he probably can't afford to lose his job."

"It's unpleasant of you to take his side," Lillian said.

Later, at lunch on the terrace, she put her fork down and said: "I must tell you, I was very offended by your standing up for that waiter. Did you really think he needed protection from me?"

"He needed protection from the cook," I said.

"Why?"

I said that the cook had threatened to fire him.

"Why didn't you say so?" Lillian said. "Don't let them take my salad."

She got up and walked away. I ate the rest of my lunch and fifteen minutes later she came back. "It certainly takes you a long time to make things clear, Peter," she said, sitting down, "if you have something to say, you ought to be simple about it. You know I can't stand it when people are unjust to other people."

"Who was unjust, the waiter?"

"No," she said, "the cook. You were right about the waiter, the room-service captain says he supports a family of six. The cook almost fired him twice this morning, but it won't happen again—I had a little talk with the cook just now."

"In what language?"

"You know I don't speak Spanish."

"The cook speaks English?"

"He does now. I hit him in the face with a pizza," she said. "I didn't know they had Italian food here, I wonder if they can make a decent marinara."

On the way out to a taxi we passed the general manager of

the hotel, a serious-looking gray-haired man. "You had a little problem in the kitchen, Mr. Sanchez," Lillian said, "but I straightened it out. This is my boss, Mr. Feibleman. I've been his secretary for twenty years, and he's extremely grateful to you for arranging our rooms."

Mr. Sanchez bowed formally.

In the hotel taxi on the way down the coast to look at the jungle, Lillian said:

"Life would be so much simpler for everybody if people just said what they meant."

A few days after that I worked from ten o'clock one morning till eleven the next and went into Lillian's room feeling shaky and hollow and nauseated. I had finished.

When I told her, Lilly pushed me back into a chair and sat in my lap. When I looked at her she was crying.

"It's just the first draft," I said.

"The rest is clean-up work," she said. "This is the real one, finished is finished. I want to do something. What can I do?"

I asked what she would like to do.

"I'd like to smell this place in your neck," she said.

I said I wished she wouldn't go sniffing men like a dog all the time.

"What an ungrateful person you are," Lillian said. "I don't sniff men all the time. I only sniff men I respect. You can't go around smelling people you have no respect for, are you crazy? I used to sniff Hammett every morning."

I asked what he'd done about it.

"Nothing," Lillian said. "He was a gentleman."

We had lunch in a beach restaurant and then had a swim and took a walk on the sand. For an hour or so we searched the edge of the water for lucky stones. Lucky stones, Lillian had explained to me on the Vineyard, are stones that have a single unbroken ring of another color around them. I found two and Lillian said she had never known anyone who found two lucky stones on the same day and for the rest of that day I felt luckier than I had ever felt before in my life.

A little later we climbed up a cliff and found a place that hung out over the ocean. We sat down on a piece of granite and watched it.

"There's something wrong with the Pacific," Lilly said after a moment, "it doesn't look right. What's the matter with the Pacific?"

"It's the bus-and-truck Atlantic," I said. "It's only a road-company ocean, but it's okay."

"It's only okay if you haven't seen the original," Lillian said.

The next morning I found a note under my door.

> Friday 6 A.M.
> I have been lying awake, miserable with your insult. I do not sniff people like or as a dog. I sniff only those people I like very much. When I cease to sniff you, it will be my way of saying goodbye.
> Miss Hellman

LILLIAN: *Maybe I'll be buried right here on the Vineyard.*
PETER: *Could we please for chrissake talk about something else?*
LILLIAN: *I wonder how many people will come to my funeral.*
PETER: *Oh, shit.*
LILLIAN: *I don't want one of those little good-taste funerals—I want a big one. I like big funerals. I think people should sit up and say "Something large has left us." Some kind of acknowledgment should be made. Are you listening to me?*
PETER: *No.*
LILLIAN: *Somebody should listen to me.*

PAUSE.

LILLIAN: *I have a right to be listened to, I have a perfect right.*

PAUSE.

LILLIAN: *I don't want a good-taste funeral.*

The next event I remember is going to New York for the publication of *An Unfinished Woman* and reading the good reviews. Lillian had been keeping her first book of memoirs finished in a drawer "to let it settle," and when it came out she announced that she wanted my company, but apart from that I don't remember her making a fuss about any book of her own, not with me, though she made a great deal of fuss with other people.

She was teaching that year at MIT, a course she'd named "Stealing 1." Taking off from a line of T. S. Eliot ("immature poets imitate; mature poets steal") she taught beginning writers to take ideas from other writers openly but with certain well-defined limits. The story she'd been using to teach was Melville's "Bartleby the Scrivener" and the students' job was to steal it by careful reading—by digesting and knowing it inside out—then by resetting it in a different time and place with different characters. Once when she came down with the flu I took over the course for a little and it wasn't easy, but it was fun. Teaching students to steal made you begin to see stories in other stories: Balzac's *Eugénie Grandet* in Henry James' *Washington Square;* something of Tolstoy's *Anna Karenina* in Faulkner's *The Wild Palms;* Henry James' theme of the innocent American corrupted by Europe, reversed, in Hellman's *Watch on the Rhine.* That year one or two of her MIT students balked, as had some students at Berkeley, and when a couple of them walked out on the course, she seemed pleased. "They missed the point, but they're nice honest kids," she said happily, "they don't approve of stealing."

She came to see me in New Orleans again that spring. By then I'd reworked my novel and sent it in and I remember Lilly sitting by the swimming pool of the Royal Sonesta listening to my gloomy predictions for the future of the manuscript. It was a crazy time for me—a time she was to write about one day:*

> I have lived around writers all my life and have never seen anything to match Peter's frantic nervousness as he finishes a book . . . I flew down to New Orleans to see what I could do. There was, of course, very little I could do except to listen, and to listen was a horror: What, for example, should happen if the publishers (who had always published him) decided not to publish him? What, for example, would happen if he were shot the next day? (Although who besides myself would have done the shooting, I don't know.)
>
> At the end of two or three days, I began to cry. This evidently touched Peter, who invited me to go to Brennan's for dinner. I was in such a state of nerves by this time from answering his numbskull questions, that three vodkas and half a bottle of wine went to my head. I was off to the ladies'

---

* Quotes from *Eating Together,* published by Little, Brown, in 1984.

room and on my way out afterward, I fell on a stone step, cut my knee very badly and was knocked unconscious for a minute or two . . .

The captain came running across the restaurant to the table with a concerned look. "Something's happened to Miss Hellman," he said, "she seems to have fallen."

I got up and followed him back into the foyer. Lillian was wearing a sparkly black dress and she was lying on the marble floor in front of the ladies' room with an expression that was made up of three quarters peace and one quarter boredom. "I hurt my knee," she said. "I hope you're worried."

A small crowd had gathered and the captain had sent for the manager. "Stand up, Lilly," I said, "the headwaiter's having a fit."

"Who cares about the headwaiter?"

"All right, damn it, I'm worried," I said, "*I'm* worried. Now will you get up?"

"I don't want to," she said dreamily.

"You can't just lie there on your back on the floor in front of the ladies' room."

"Apparently I can," she said, "what's the difference? Nobody cares."

It took three minutes of wheedling to maneuver her to her feet—three more to get her past the hatcheck woman, who applied mercurochrome and a Band-Aid to her knee. Then we went back to the table, where Lilly arranged herself on a chair, asked for another glass of wine and said:

"How can I convince you not to worry so much about your book, darling?"

"You're doing fine," I said. "You could upstage God."

Lillian laughed.

The headwaiter came back and hovered over her. "Is Madame all right?"

"Madam's fine," she said, "but the chicken's cold. I didn't know it was cooked in cream sauce or I wouldn't have ordered it."

The captain took her plate way, gave her a menu and began suggesting other dishes while I stared a hole through Lilly. She knew what I meant and avoided the look.

For most of her life Lillian had displayed an unfortunate tendency to separate all food that didn't please her into one of two categories: goy drek and kike drek. Baked Alaska was the epitome of goy drek, beef Wellington was kike drek. All canapés were goy drek, so was all food cooked in cream sauce, but well-done meat was kike drek. The only food that crossed all barriers was nouvelle cuisine. Nouvelle cuisine was generic drek.

Given her freewheeling use of cultural terminology, which also included chink, jap, nigger, wop, spic, gringo, frog, kraut, mick, wog, limey and dago, it was a little tricky in public when she began talking about food, especially around people who didn't know her. The truth was that she had almost no prejudice, unlike the people she was out to tease: the well-heeled butter-wouldn't-melt liberals who were shocked and horrified by her use of such words—shocked at hearing them—horrified because they were thinking them. Lilly had, I believe, sensed something about such people without quite knowing what it was. Just as dedicated hand washers often seem possessed of a secret desire to immerse themselves in their private filth, so people who relentlessly cleanse their vocabulary of all possible prejudice sometimes appear to be scrubbing away at their own dark thoughts: the world is full of good-hearted souls who wish to take care of other people's poverty because they can't cope with their own. (I once saw a lady, one of a group of rich liberals visiting tenements in Harlem, walk up to a poor black woman whose baby had been bitten by a rat. The baby had died and the black woman was sitting in a chair staring at nothing when the rich lady approached and tried to console her. "I can't stand to see things like this," she said, "it's terrifying that people should be forced to live with rats, and I intend to help put a stop to it." The black woman raised her face and looked at her with blank haggard eyes. "Lady," she said, "please don't put your emptiness on top of my emptiness.") If Lillian liked to bait the rich and the genteel it was the natural result of an epatayism she had inherited from Hammett and Dorothy Parker, but go explain that to a headwaiter.

"Would Madame like a nice veal cordon bleu, or a slice of beef Wellington?"

"No," Lillian said, "Madam wouldn't. What have you got that isn't fancy frog drek, or kiked-up goy drek?"

"Madame?"

"She means she likes plain New Orleans food," I said, loud.

"Ah-hah," the captain said. "Allow me." He flipped back in the gold-embossed menu Lillian was holding and pointed at a page.

Lilly stared at it and pretended to read. You could tell from the way she was holding the menu that she was pretending and it was the second time I'd had the impression that something was wrong with her eyes. When the captain went away I asked her about it.

"It's only when I go into a very dark room like this—or a room full of blazing light. My eyes take too long to adjust. It's why I tripped over that step just now, but it's not very serious—they call it preincipient glaucoma."

I asked who had called it that and when.

"Some doctor in New York a couple of years ago," Lilly said.

"A couple?"

"Four or five," she said evasively, "six maybe—please don't chivy me about it, darling, eye trouble is exactly the sort of thing that throws me."

I said it didn't throw her enough.

"Okay, okay, I promise to do something about it when I get back—now leave it alone," she said peevishly, and I went along with that and let her change the subject because I wanted to believe her and because I had in common with her doctors that I was stupid enough to believe her. It was her body again, acting up on her, and if she had done something about it then, it would, they said later, have been all right. But she didn't, and by the time she was able to face it it was too late.

The next day we drove north to Baton Rouge and crossed the Mississippi, then took the causeway west over the Atchafalaya River-basin swamp and south to Opelousas. The duck restaurant was at the edge of a wood outside town. It was run by a black family from New Roads and it had the comfortable rank smell of all small family restaurants, a smell indigenous to all countries all over the world. The food was wonderful. You could have duck any way you wanted it and in the space of two days we ordered roast duck and duck jambalaya and stewed duck and duck étouffé and duck salad: we had full orders and half orders and side orders and duck coming out of our ears. The second day, Lilly made friends with the family, and the last day they prepared us a lunch box with six more pieces of duck for the drive. "A sane woman wouldn't want any more," she told the manager from the car window, "I'm not a sane woman. Tell your son to call me if he ever comes to New York."

The son did, a gawky nineteen-year-old with a ravenous mind and glassy intelligent eyes, and Lillian found him a place to live and a job, providing him with extra cash when he needed it. She managed to do that without his knowing whose money it was (explaining that it had been sent him by his family and asking the family to stick to her story for the son's sake, so he wouldn't lose country roots in the city) and she went on with it for several years. One day when the son flew home for Christmas, by then a store manager on vacation, he was welcomed like a king, then erased like a mistake in one of those unnecessary and sick-making flukes of whatever is unnatural in nature (a car crash, not predictable, not his fault, not even his car) and when that happened she wrote the family endless letters, believing by then that they were her family, not because of money but because of death, as though she had lost a son.

Driving away from the restaurant she said: "I like poor people like that—they're not for sale."

"They're not poor," I said, "they own a restaurant."

"They run it—I doubt they own it."

"You like your poverty pure."

"Do I?"

"Evidently," I said. I was sour and dyspeptic from too much duck.

Lillian glanced at me. "I may be a romantic," she said, "but sentimental I'm not. I still think people come before animals. I'm surprised you can bring yourself to eat a poor little defenseless thing like a duck. A sensitive nature like yours."

I asked if she wanted me to take the time and the trouble to guide her into the Atchafalaya River-basin swamp or if she would prefer to go fuck herself.

"Oh, shut up, grumpy," Lillian said.

We tried getting into the swamp from that side but the encampment I was familiar with was closed and we drove back along the causeway to Baton Rouge and made arrangements on the other side.

We went in by skiff along the Atchafalaya River bordering

the swamp. We took one of its smaller tributaries, then a spin-off of the tributary and a turn-off from there. At that point a man piloting a plane high over the swamp might think he was looking down on a monumental mistake—one of those disagreeable messes made by an obsessive Creator whose intent had been to draw one perfect waterway. If you put a piece of green glass flat on the floor and took a hammer to it in a random and infinite series of small meaningless whacks you would know what South Louisiana looks like from the air.

From inside the river basin, creeping along in a skiff, it looked at first as if we had come upon a bottomless supply of a nameless substance composed of three parts water, two parts earth and one part air—a recipe for some primordial glup brought into being before God created the blender. The substance appeared to have no purpose beyond its own existence, as firmament might have appeared before anybody took to mucking around with it. It takes you a while to comprehend that much firmament; I once had a childhood friend, a Cajun boy of ten, who closed his copy of the Bible one day in tears, feeling sorry for God. Faced with a universe full of firmament, he said, the poor Son of a Bitch did the best He could.

Lilly sat in the prow of the boat and after a little I turned the motor off in the stern and drifted. The flow of bayou water was as pervasive as it was directionless—going west in the morning, east in the afternoon—the myriad motion dependent on the water level of all the lakes and streams around it. Floating through the stinging-green leaves in the heat of the sun gives a sense of impenetrable quiet—a hush at the center of the world. There is no silence like the silence of a cypress swamp. The big trees pass in weightless shadow over the surface of the water, countless vines and creepers writhing up out of the earth, growing, always growing, without a sound. Now and then the water roils without breaking as a catfish or an alligator gar or maybe something waiting to be born swims under the surface, pushing up and sinking back into that dumb and importunate and timeless place beyond the first grunt. Then the silence breaks and all the insects hum as one, millions of them starting at the same instant, angry and neglected, like the buzzing of possibilities, as though sound itself had been suspended inanimate and somnolent before the cry of birth or tick of time.

"Where in hell is it coming from?" Lillian said.

"There, maybe. Hell."

"Don't be silly," she said after a moment. "There is no hell but here."

We drifted past a white heron standing on one leg in the water near the shore, motionless, like a sentinel. About a foot behind it were two very small herons facing the same direction, each on one leg, in imperturbable and profound imitation of the older one.

"I'm the one on the left," Lilly said. The one on the left had shinier feathers. "I don't want to be the drab one."

"I think your feathers are fine."

"Of course you do, darling," Lillian said, "that's what lovers are—people who like each other's feathers." She kept her eyes on the water.

"I'm sorry I was mean to you about poor people," I said suddenly, for no reason.

"I had it coming," Lillian said. "I have an awful habit of making symbols of things. Like that duck restaurant. It wasn't anything but a duck restaurant. And you're right about the family, they're not poor. It's the others—the poor who don't get enough to eat that I . . ."

She didn't finish and I didn't try to help. I knew by then that Lilly was the fiercest romantic in any town. It was her clinging to the shining ideals of feeding the poor and changing the world— the ideals of the twenties and thirties—that had led to her being blacklisted in the fifties, not out of fealty to any political system but because of a stubbornness that could not so easily or so publicly give up so nice a dream. Despite Lillian's monumental perversity, a rebel makes a lousy revolutionary, which is probably why she had never joined the Communist party. That was the day I asked if Hammett had.

"Everybody knew he had," Lillian said, "it's no secret. And they can't prove I didn't, I wouldn't want them to think I got mad at Dash and finked out."

"Was that why you didn't?"

"No. I don't know why. I had reservations and I got lazy. Look at that thing swimming."

There was something moving in the water, shiny and soundless. By then the crickets had quit and a drowsy heat was taking over the river basin like a distant humming you were never quite sure was there.

"Hammett said I don't have any stamina," Lillian said.

She said it like a child tattling on another child to an adult—it was my turn to be the adult.

"I'm sure he didn't mean it."

"He meant it," Lillian said.

There was never any point in answering that kind of hurt and I kept quiet. After a few minutes we settled down in the skiff; I pulled the string on the outboard motor and it turned over and caught; Lilly took the tiller and we began to move slowly in the stream back toward the river.

She lay back against the gunwale. In the distance a great blue heron swooped up and sat on the wind like a shadow of something torn out of the swamp.

Lillian didn't talk anymore and I knew why: I had been listening to every word she said and it made her nervous. You can often hear the past in the present if you listen to people, and sometimes the future. But you have to listen. You can't just hear.

›››››IV

THE SLUDGE OF TIME keeps me from knowing now whether another summer passed before I went to join her in New York; but I was still in New Orleans when the publishers called to say a book club had taken my novel and that same week a paperback sale came through for more money than I had ever seen at one time in my adult life. Up to then I had lived on good reviews: the idea that people would pay you that much to write what you wanted to write was a piece of luck I hadn't dared to imagine and I called Lilly in New York to tell her the news, planning to chat about something else and then mention it offhand, just to get a rise out of her. But as soon as I heard her voice I blurted it out. Lilly blossomed so fast I could hear her flush: "Look at you—well look, just look at you—high-born and rich."

I asked why she had forgotten to mention mysterious and cryptic.

"You're right. It's not nice of me to skip things," she said, "I'd like to apologize. And I'd like to add elegant. Oh I'm glad—oh I'm so glad . . ."

There's something about the sound of another person affected enough by you to feel misery at your misery, joy at your joy, that stays in your ears, and I felt as tender about Lillian that day as I am capable of feeling, which may not be much, but still. If you pin down what you truly feel outside of pain and anger and sex and fear and triumph and gratitude, it is never much, but if you know you feel love when you feel it, you are grateful no matter the amount. That's when words disappear—you have nothing to say.

"Hello?" Lillian asked.

"I'm here. My mind wandered."

"Oh, let's not have your mind today," she said, "not your mind, darling. Let's have fun today. Let's think how we can celebrate when we're together."

I said I wasn't going to wait, I was going out and buy her a very expensive present.

"No, you're not," she said fast, "that's what *he* did when *he* got a check. Even his Social Security check and his pension, it was all he had to live on after the government took all his copyrights, but he used to go out and buy me a piece of god-awful primitive African art—little ebony figures and baskets and things I hated—you're not to do that. You're to save this money to live on, are you listening to me?"

"No."

"You've got to listen . . ."

I forgot what I spent on her, but that was the day she told me about Hammett and the Spanish lace. It happened when they were nearly broke and she was walking with him one day in New York. It was a fall afternoon, she said, and they were strolling down Madison Avenue when Lillian stopped to look at an antique lace altarpiece spread out lengthwise in a shop window— well preserved, dense, delicate. The lace was eight feet by three feet, an elongated rectangle depicting the famous Spanish Catholic royalty, Ferdinand and Isabella, with their court around them. Lillian stood admiring it a few moments and after they walked home, Hammett went back alone and bought the lace with the last money he had in the bank for them to live on. When he gave it to her, Lilly blew up at him and threw it in his face. She ran back to return it but the lace had cost a lot and the shop wouldn't take it back. She never used it or adverted to it or even looked at it after that, she kept the lace folded up in an old plastic bag on the top of a walk-in closet with some hats and when she thought about it she got mad at Hammett all over again.

The present I sent her was not nearly so extravagant, a carved silver necklace from Taxco that she seemed to like, and later that month I went to New York and took a sublet apartment on West Ninth Street for twelve months. I thought we were close enough by now that we could make a go of it in the same city with a little effort, a little sense.

I was wrong. Lilly took the move to mean that I was willing to give up a possible life with people my own age and it wasn't true. I needed friends who were age peers and I was open about it, reticent only about introducing new friends to her. The thrust toward random sexuality I had grown up with was on the wane but even if it had not been it wouldn't have disturbed Lilly on those grounds, since she had once faced the same problems herself. She had taken to deflating any new relationship I found, not for its thrust but because she wanted things to be like the Vineyard, and I wanted things in a combination that wasn't possible: the Vineyard and the easy close friendship we'd had before.

New York was heavy going and for almost a year we wasted time and ourselves with the same drumming weekly jabber.

"I called you twice last night."

"I was out with friends."

"Out with friends is always the answer."

"What's always the question?"

"We'll talk about it Friday."

"And ruin Friday?"

"We're having dinner Friday."

"That won't ruin it, Lilly, talking will."

"I'm sorry if my questions upset you . . ."

In spring I packed again and went to Los Angeles, to a house I had decided to buy with a small down payment. The house was high on a hill with a view of the town and the ocean. Things between us seemed easier from there and the problems of jealousy receded and were replaced by a kind of desperate attempt to hold things together.

Sunday

DEAREST PETER,

Nothing in this note will be new to you and I am going to try saying it once more on the phone . . .

We love each other and there is no question of that. It is my deepest hope that we can make the past even better. (Once in a while trouble does pay off.) But this time, because I think it will be the last chance we will ever have, you must know not only what you want but what you are capable of doing and I must know exactly the same. Then we must live it out and not in words but in actions. If you feel that the past cannot be improved or even revived, you must say that. It is possible that I might be hurt or angry, but I tell you, going on my own past, that honesty will impress me and the pain or anger will go away fast and we can come out friends, if nothing else. But if you seem to promise, or wish, out of kindness to yourself and to me, to pass over what cannot be passed over . . . I will not forgive you. More important, I will not forgive myself because I will feel a fool . . . That may not be your nature, but it is mine, and when that happens there is never again any hope, which is a nice, self-flattering way of putting it. Therefore, if there is a chance we can understand each other and ourselves, please come because I deeply want to see you. But if there is any doubt, then it is best not to come. There are many levels on which we can stand together, some close, some not so close. But the platform on which I cannot stand, will not, is the one of the last 14 months. As I have said before, you have every right to any life you want, but it is only plain, simple justice that I know about it and that you allow me my choice. There has been enough bitterness about that: I don't want anymore. And you can't want anymore, either.

Much, much love,
Lillian

DEAR LILLIAN:

Your letter is strange, it's written as if things had never been discussed between us. But they have, and often. You ask me to be clear about what I want or don't want—but I've made myself clear over and over again. The problem is not that I haven't been blunt, but that I have.

Here it is once more: I don't want to live together, Lilly, not on a permanent basis. I need other people too much and I need to make a life. Remember the facts: I went to Spain at twenty-one and came back at twenty-eight with one novel published and another on the way—I haven't stopped working since. I can share my time with you, but I can't give it to you, I haven't enough for myself.

Travel together is wonderful, so is visiting each other here and on the Vineyard in summers: part of a life together is wonderful but the prospect of a whole life together is not, not for me, I need what the kiddies call my own space, my own time. Maybe I'm one of those tired characters in soap operas who can't make a commitment—or maybe I'm still a philanderer at heart with adolescent sexual fantasies and the need to act them out. Maybe I have a touch of the satyr, maybe I'm uncertain of my own masculinity and still need to prove it. Maybe I'm my age, or younger, or no age, but whatever I am, it must be taken into account. I don't want to run the risk of losing it in order to soften the truth because in the end I would lose you anyway— and I'd come to hate myself for it. We have a shot at a new kind of friendship now, let's not muck around with it, Lilly. If we can't go back to what we were before that summer, we can go on to something better and take with us some of the pleasures found along the way. This ought to be a time of happiness, not sadness: I don't feel gloomy, I feel only that I care about you and that we live across a necessary time and space. How about enjoying what we have, not regretting what we don't, and how about getting together soon.

How about I love you.

P.

Thursday, 5 A.M.

DEAREST PETER,

I have tried this letter, off and on, for the last two weeks, maybe the last two years. I have no hope now that I can say what I mean, but this time I will finish the letter and send it off.

I am deeply, deeply sad that I cannot say—maybe because it's me and I don't always believe in me—what I mean. To repeat: I do not want to live with you any-more than you want to live with me; I do not even believe any longer in the need for the same city because it didn't work, in my sense, even when you were here: you were too worried about intrusion and freedom and such worries send my back up and pride going strong. I do believe, however, that life cannot be lived on a telephone, or by letter, unless the reason for the distance has some realistic emergency. Nor do I believe in meetings of two weeks at a time: they are marks of love and devotion but they don't teach me anything, give me very much, or allow me to give very much . . . The best times we ever had together were your months in the Vineyard that summer, best for you as well as for me . . . But, of course, I want no such times unless you do—they wouldn't be any good any other way. My own belief, mistaken or not, is that people, to come to their best, need to share time, air, space, dawdling, foolishness, and so on. This is not your belief and I can no longer argue with it, although I deeply believe that your way leads to winning the battles and losing the war. (But then I have, in my way, also lost the war: I envy ladies who have sense enough to take what they can get—even realize that at my age that is more than sense—but I tell myself that if I knew what they know I could not know what I know, although that doesn't make me feel much better.)

The difference between what we need for life . . . is that I meant the speech in *Autumn Garden**: I have known that I must live by a pile of small things, can only learn and feel that way. You have lived by more dramatic decisions and see solutions in more dramatic forms: Spain, the turn you said you almost took last winter, even people, often places. Someday I will write about that in me and maybe then it will be clearer to you. Now it comes down only to time going slower.

And then, too, no matter my age, I think love, desire, even friendship, should have more spontaneity: we have enough money to meet for a few days just because we want to and because most grown people know a little trouble is worth the possible pleasure and gain . . .

* See page 343.

Lillian and Peter at various ages during their
forty-three-year friendship

Halsman

Ferencz Gorog

Inscription written to Peter reads:
"This only child sends a great deal
of love to that only child from
Audubon Park."

Bender

C. Brewster Dedelow

Lillian as a young woman

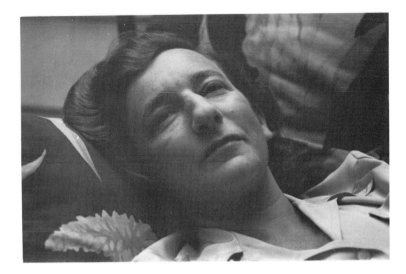

Lillian on the sofa made for the original production of *The Little Foxes*

Dashiell Hammett taking a
photograph of Lillian

Lillian in her late teens
De Barron Studio

Dashiell Hammett and Dorothy Parker at world peace conference

Dorothy Parker

Robert Coates, Dashiell Hammett, Nathanael West, Laura and Sidney Perelman on the Perelman farm in Bucks County, Pennsylvania

Mike Nichols

Mary Ellen Mark

Maureen Stapleton

Elaine May

Jules Feiffer, without his cigar

John Hersey
C. Brewster Dedelow

Lillian with Barbara Hersey
C. Brewster Dedelow

William Styron and Robert Penn Warren

C. Brewster Dedelow

Lillian, Warren Buffet, Barbara Hersey,
and William Styron

Rose Styron

Annabel Davis-Goff Nichols

Ann and Art Buchwald

Diana Walker

Lillian with Richard Poirier in living room of Vineyard house

Courtesy of Cornell Capa

Lillian with Dr. Milton Wexler

Lillian with Dr. Jonathan LaPook

Lillian with Leonard Bernstein

Christina Burton

Following page: Lillian posing for the Blackglama mink campaign
Bill King

For me, for myself, I do not have to tell you this: the agony will be that I have not taken what is serious with seriousness. To that end, I would cross Asia and Africa with typhus, I think, to make this straight between us. If you think there is any hope of that, no matter how we fail, it will, in the end, comfort me to come to L.A. for a few days. Far from being a sacrifice, fail or succeed, it must be done as well as I can do it . . .

No declarations of love, except to comfort, are needed between us. We have both proved what we felt and neither of us has any doubts. I love you very, very much. Maybe more than I have ever done before, although, as you know, the ties of a younger life are strong because they made me and I haven't much else to fall back on. But we must, if we can, find a way to live with the love we have: for me, it must have vigor, and the face-to-face problems and pleasures of daily mess, at least part of the time.

I know that I should be satisfied, worldly satisfied, with what there is. But I guess the hope of something else, no matter how unrealistic, frail, silly, is what has carried me and will have to do that until the end of me.

Please don't hesitate about a trip to the Coast. I will now and in the future suffer if I think I didn't take the chance, make the try. It will be no sacrifice: it will be done for me.

> Much love to you,
> Lillian

> Monday morning

DEAR LILLIAN:

For God's sake forget crossing Asia and Africa with typhus, you don't even know what typhus is. Just come, Lilly, we'll have fun. And in the spring I'll come to you in New York and in the summer to the Vineyard.

The only trip I can't make is the new one you mentioned on the phone—the trip to St. Maarten—I have a deadline to meet then, but I could meet you

somewhere afterwards. How about Spain or France?
How about Mars?

My love,
P.

The Caravanserai
Saint Maarten, N.W.I.
Thursday

DEAREST PETER,

People look glum at the idea of the phone which
exists only in the hotel office and in the main town,
ten-twelve miles away, and then very doubtful under
four or five hours. I'll try tomorrow when I'll rent a
car for a few hours and will probably never be heard
of again since a few hours ago I had to be led to the
dining room and back again. Back again are two fine
rooms, two baths—a favor, it seems, of the Ford-Vizelli
owners—and you could have had your own bath and
even your own necessary bed.

Maybe I'll feel better in a few days. Now I have a
sore throat—bugs appear in a new place every day—
and am sick of the Nazi anti-Nazi fight that's going on
somewhere in [my] blood cells.

Conroy met me yesterday and last night I dined
with his groupies. The house is owned by a very rich
Chink * . . . who told me that although he was born
here his pa sent him back to China to be educated and
that the Chun King Chinks had two favorite plays—
Foxes and *Cyrano*. The only trouble with that compliment was that *Foxes* was not as yet written in his
education days, but I nodded with the charm that came
from good red wine. The house seems to be run by the
beautiful China Machado—see the cover of *Harper's
Bazaar* this month—and her beau called Sven something and her two young children. Barbara Harris . . .
is staying at another hotel and there was the usual
tropical tall pair who earn a living at real estate or

* Not the Chinese man at the small dinner. Reference is to a new acquain-
tance, a Mr. Casey.

something and used to be radicals. Swingers, as you
know, are often earnest, and when that got too much
we all went off to the casino where I coughed so much
they gave me free brandy and I won $56 and left the
others for my lonely bed and fell down on a concrete
walk and have a bruised knee and am now going to
disappear in a small sailboat and never come back because you wanted this separation and aren't even going
to dedicate the book to me because, of course, you had
previously promised it to Kitty, and who can blame
you. If I ever see you again I will certainly love you.

L.

I did go to see her when she came back and Lilly came to
see me and we had a good time. We spent two weeks in Paris
that year and a week in Madrid; from then on, with one of us
ensconced on either coast, we batted back and forth like badminton birds across the States when work permitted, spent summers
on the Vineyard, winters in Los Angeles and New York, and odd
times traveling. In between visits there were other affairs, other
people.

For a while the distance between our homes worked, but
then one day it too failed, or maybe we failed it—or failure was
built in. Just when everything was going better than ever, the
trouble I'd sensed that first Vineyard summer—the trouble we'd
tried to avoid—the stubborn idiot trouble that dogs the lives of
those who fear it, as doom is the exclusive nightmare of people
foolish enough to believe in it, surfaced, and nearly wiped us out.

The stage was set when Lilly called to say she was going to
rent a house with some friends in Sarasota for part of the winter
and I said I'd join the party for a couple of weeks. The Sarasota
rent was being shared equally among Lillian, Sid Perelman and
Albert and Frances Hackett. The Hacketts were a nice couple
who were older than Lilly, a witty pair of screenwriters who had
done the movie script of *The Thin Man* and the play of *The
Diary of Anne Frank*. Lillian had helped them with that and they
were grateful and fond of her.

The four of them had hired a local cook and the Sarasota
house had the comforting feel of a writer's dormitory, a rambling
one-story green-and-white affair built around a central patio, with
a great many walls of little windows.

I liked being the dorm's youngest writer by twenty-five years, I liked the Hacketts and Sid, and when they asked why I lived in Los Angeles—all four had gone there at one time or another for work and hated it—I said I liked the weather and had a lot of close friends. It was true about the weather but it wasn't true about the close friends and while the others listened, Lillian looked down intently and pressed the cuff of her blouse with two fingers. Almost any talk of what I did on my own—just seeing or getting close to people—could still lead to trouble, because of what she called her jealous nature, coupled with my own tendency to be private, especially about sexual matters, though it was well established between us that we each had our freedom. If the need for privacy was the reason I lived alone it was also the reason Hammett had never lived with Lilly for more than a short time in the same city—had never lived with her at all except on a perennially transient basis—until the end of his life, when he was sick and needed nursing. We were all three problem people and problem people are better off by themselves.

The rules we lived by now left us plenty of room. Lilly had three or four friends she dated in New York, I had three or four in Los Angeles—and then I had two . . . then one.

That broke the rules and I knew it. Four was all right—four hundred was all right—but one was not all right. Not unless I wanted to break off relations with Lilly and I didn't. *In every relationship there's a winner and a loser, but the winner ought to be careful.* It sounded fine, but I didn't want to be the winner and I didn't want to be careful: I wanted Lilly, but I also wanted more and more people my age.

In Sarasota I forgot about everything but the pleasure of seeing her again in a steady humdrum boardinghouse life where everybody met for meals. The Hacketts were spry and crackly and fun to be with; Sid Perelman was dour even for a humorist, a good-natured man with a kind of cheerful gloom who was famously careful about money. He insisted on dividing the weekly food bill into five while I was there, over the protests of the other three, who claimed that a guest of one was a guest of all. Since I was not the only guest they were expecting Sid stuck to his guns and when he asked me to go to dinner with him on the cook's night off, the others stared in amazement.

"He must want something," Lilly said, "Sid hasn't invited

anybody to dinner since he quit writing for the Marx Brothers."

We drove to a place he'd found, a small neon-lit diner on the highway, and talked about travel. Sid was planning a trip west around the world and wanted to know how to prevent a geyser of dirty laundry every time he opened his suitcase in a new city. I didn't know any solution but we talked about that and then about life, and then with two beers about love. I didn't know any solution to that either but we went plodding on like teenagers to another subject—favorite writers; Sid wanted to know if I had a personal God among them, and when I said Dostoevsky he bristled and said Dostoevsky depressed him and we argued about that for a while.

After that we jumped from subject to subject till Sid got around to his reason for asking me to dinner. Then he looked embarrassed.

"Lilly gets in too deep. She can't find her way," he said after a moment, examining a stain on the tablecloth. "She's like me, she can't help it. She loves you a lot, I know the signs, but she's a heavyweight. If she loves you too much, she'll never forgive you for it. Then she'll have to pay you back."

I started to ask what he meant exactly but Sid ordered another cup of coffee and changed the subject again. He still looked embarrassed and I remembered then an incident Lilly had mentioned once about Sid's wife, Laura—Laura Perelman was Nathanael West's sister—and Hammett. It was something about Hammett and Laura having a fling one weekend. Though Lilly hadn't gone into details, neither she nor Sid had ever forgiven Hammett for it, that much she said, and I tried to steer the conversation back but it was no use—Sid was on to other things; we stayed about an hour more and had a good time, and when we got back to the house everyone else had gone to bed.

I went to my room and read for a few minutes, a book I'd brought with me, but my mind was glazed and when I'd gone over the same sentence a dozen times without knowing what it meant I put the book down and went out to look at the night.

There weren't any stars, the air was sluggish and tinged with heat, the darkness full of the sound of tree frogs. On the way back I passed a telephone that was sitting on a low stool next to a wall of windows. Through the little glass panes you could see the central patio, then another wall of windows, then the empty sitting room outside Lillian's bedroom. There was a second phone there, a third in the kitchen, a fourth in the entryway: there were only four phones in the house. None of the bedrooms had one, so it was safe to talk at this hour, and I made a credit-card call to the person I'd been seeing in Los Angeles, a woman several years younger than I was. I felt like a skulky child sneaking a call after the grown-ups were asleep but I reasoned, as children do, that I wasn't doing anybody any harm, and after talking a few minutes I hung up and went to bed.

I don't remember how I explained the calls to myself for the next few nights but I managed: I had the usual excuses and I didn't take Sid's warning very seriously, since I already knew that Lillian's relationship with Hammett had been full of what they hadn't even bothered to call infidelity. Casual sex is more urgently casual than casual anything else and one night when my friend in Los Angeles said she was planning to be in New York the following week, I made a date to meet her there on my way back. It was past two in the morning Sarasota time before we agreed on a hotel and we went on chatting for five minutes more before I turned without thinking to face the wall of windows; across the patio Lillian was standing in the sitting room with the phone in her hand.

It took me a second to realize from her stillness that she'd been standing there for some time. When I did, I had to rein myself in. There is no more self-righteous feeling than the outraged virtue of a man caught doing something he thinks is shabby. I said in a stiff voice: "I'm on the phone, Lillian."

"Sorry," she said and hung up. I could tell from the look of her back how angry she was and I got off the phone and walked around to her sitting room.

"Maybe no civilization ever found a solution to the problems of men and women that suited all of us," she said as I came in. "But some have done better than others, and I think your way stinks."

"My way isn't eavesdropping."

"I was trying to use the phone."

"At two o'clock in the morning?"

"That didn't stop *you.*"

"It's only eleven at night in Los Angeles."

"It's only a lot of things at night in Los Angeles," Lillian said.

"I was making a credit-card call, do I need permission to pick up the phone?"

"Ask the little lady."

"She's not a little lady."

"Whatever she is."

"Somebody I met, nobody important," I said, "and nothing to do with us."

Lillian laughed. "It's a good thing you're lying," she said. "I wouldn't like to think you believed that."

There was a polite cough in the next room and we broke apart like fighters when the bell rings and went to our respective ends of the house.

It wasn't till late afternoon the next day that the Hacketts and Sid, made nervous by the silences, went into town to do some shopping. I found Lilly sitting outside in a lawn chair with an unopened book in her lap.

"Next thing," she said without looking up, her voice low and droning as if there had been no break in the conversation, "next thing you'll be asking if it's possible to love two people at the same time. The answer is no. You don't mean any harm. You never . . . you always . . ."

Her voice rose and broke and her tone changed. Then she got up suddenly and faced the tree line at the end of the lawn, as if it had just occurred to her that the world didn't stop there.

"You go about your business trying not to hurt people," she said, "and now you've got a virago on your hands."

"Do I?"

"Oh, boy," she said.

LILLIAN: *How long did your affair last, do you remember?*
PETER: *What affair?*
LILLIAN: *Our lady of Los Angeles.*
PETER: *Oh, that. A few years.*
LILLIAN: *And the one after that, the young man?*
PETER: *That wasn't an affair, it was an afternoon. I was seeing Joan what's-her-name at the time.*
LILLIAN: *Forgive me, but whatever it was, you clung to it past belief. You clung to all of them.*

PAUSE

LILLIAN: *All your silly jabber about obsessions nearly put me under the ground, if you don't mind my saying so.*
PETER: *I wouldn't like to take all the credit.*
LILLIAN: *We nearly put each other under the ground, is that better?*

PAUSE.

LILLIAN: *Well, we got through it, that's the main thing, didn't we? We came out fine in the end, didn't we, darling?*

PAUSE. CLINK OF COFFEE CUP.

LILLIAN: *Didn't we?*

Years after Sarasota, in a café in Lyons, sitting at an outdoor table watching the stream of faces move by, it seemed as though the intervening time had not existed. As if the whole thing had been a dream, something concocted, wholly fabricated out of de-

137

sire to camouflage an emptiness harder to face than anything it might contain—as if we'd been dead a while.

"Peter."

"Yes."

Lillian said: "What are we doing in Lyons?"

"I don't know, but it's nice. How do you feel?"

"Older. I am older."

"Me too, I'm in my forties, Lilly."

"Let's for God's sake not go on about how old we are."

"What'll we go on about?"

"Anything," Lillian said. "Or nothing. Why can't we just sit here?"

The café in Lyons was dusty and hot. It was the end of the line after years of fuss and laceration and it was a pleasant way to end it—a late summer and the lazy dispossessed feeling that comes with dimming battle sounds, when the gut settles down and life goes back to whatever it was before. But it had taken us too long.

It had taken much too long. . . .

When I left Sarasota I began immediately to flaunt a life of my own while Lillian began methodically to tell her friends, one thousand percent for each, that I was going crazy. It was, I think, true that I was a little off-balance, but nothing new; I'd long been given to passionate, short-lived crushes that colored and took over my life, a familiar problem and one in which I had always felt helpless, as though sex were my only outlet for feeling, like a sickness that stops your world for a while, and there had been times in my life when I'd wondered whether falling in love was caused by a virus. Over clumps of years, then and in the past, a Jane had become a Fred had become an Emily had become a Jane again, and much of my life had been a series of erotic acrobatics that Lillian had occasion to ask about one day in New York when she found herself inexplicably drawn to a friendly orangutan in the Central Park Zoo.

I flew from Sarasota to New York, made a trip to Central America for a magazine piece, and flew back to Los Angeles. I was not traveling alone and for a long time after that I was seldom by myself. There were endless weeks of angry phone calls from Lillian, violent calls, threatening everything from my career to my way of living; her explosion lasted for months at one level—

years at another—and I should have known from the beginning
where she was headed but I didn't. I wasn't even surprised the
morning she called to say she'd had an "anonymous phone call"
about me and a "certain nameless party," warning her that she
was "in danger" and ought to be careful. I figured someone she
knew had taken to embroidering upon the rich tapestry of vividly
colored imaginings that she herself had begun to weave, a tapestry in which anyone I was close to, no matter in what degree,
was secretly out to destroy her. It was a long time before I took
the anonymous calls seriously, longer before I began to suspect
who was behind them. Then one September day, about six months
after Sarasota, something odd happened.

It began with Lillian's sudden concern about her godchild,
Fiona Field. Fiona was the daughter of Ruth and Marshall Field
III, who had been good friends to Lilly during her first career and
on through the McCarthy years when she was blacklisted. Marshall was dead now but Ruth was very much alive: a nice woman,
warm and very direct, one of the people Lillian had drawn upon
in writing the upper-class elderly lady who appeared so often in
her plays.* For years Lilly had both courted and broadsided Ruth,
liking the friendship sometimes and fighting it at others, as she
was both drawn to and resented the power of money. Ruth had
put up with her occasional tantrums for decades, allowing her to
rant without patronizing her, hitting back when the going got
rough. She seemed to know that Lilly was amused by her and at
the same time a little envious, not so much of her fortune as of
her children, in particular Fiona, who was the same sort of rebel
Lilly had been at the same age. In those days Fiona gave most of
her vast annual income to charity and lived a simple life on a
farm, in the humorless plodding heavy way the rich assume when
they take to living simply. She was third-generation rich—the
generation between an American princess and an American aris-
tocrat—and it showed in almost everything she did. From time
to time she would disappear—drop out of sight without any
warning—and Ruth sometimes called Lilly to complain about it.
This time, it seemed, Fiona had not been heard from in weeks,
and Ruth was worried.

*Mrs. Tilford in *The Children's Hour;* Fanny Farrelly in *Watch on the
Rhine;* Mrs. Eillis in *The Autumn Garden.*

"Not worried enough," Lilly told me irritably on the phone, "I'm going to have to do something about this—Fiona may be in trouble, with nobody to turn to."

I started to say that young people who have no one to turn to usually turn to their mothers but I thought better of it and changed the subject. Lilly didn't bring up Fiona's disappearance again and after a while I forgot about it.

One morning during the next week Lillian mentioned on the phone that she didn't understand my having gone, the night before, to a dinner given by the Smiths—a smug reactionary couple who traced their origins back to New Orleans. The remark caught me off-guard because I'd gone to the Smiths only to accompany a friend and had kept it from Lilly in order to keep my friend's name out of the conversation: the only way she could have known was from someone else. But the Smiths' party had been a big one, anybody might have mentioned it, and I shrugged it off and turned the talk to other things. Lilly allowed the turn and I might have been suspicious of her letting me off the hook that easily, but I wasn't—I was too busy with work.

The next time she phoned was to report another of the anonymous calls. "I know you don't take them seriously, but I do. Calls like that are frightening and I'm very pained by your lack of interest. What if I were being threatened in some way— what then?"

"Are you?"

"No," she said, "not overtly. Only by inference. But I don't like the tone of the caller. There's something unpleasant about him, and about the woman who sometimes calls for him. It seems to have escaped your attention that they only call to talk about you—the warnings are always the same."

I asked what they were warning her about now.

"I'm not sure. Someone you've been seeing doesn't wish me well," Lillian said, "that I'm sure of, but I can't be more specific than that—it's all I've been told. Someone you know hates me."

"I wonder who."

"I don't want to talk about it," Lillian said angrily, "I know your tone when you're not interested. It's a hateful attitude, Peter—let's change the subject—you've upset me now. . . . Talk to me about something else—anything else. How did your business meeting go at MGM?"

I said I'd had no business meeting at MGM.

"Haven't you?" she said after a moment. "I thought you were there yesterday."

I explained that I'd gone to MGM the day before to have lunch with a friend, but it wasn't a business meeting. "How did you know?"

There was a silence.

"You must have said something about it," Lillian said evasively, "I'd better go now, I've a lunch myself."

After she hung up I sat for a moment wondering if I'd somehow taken to giving Lilly a more detailed schedule of my daily life than I meant to. Then I shrugged it off and went upstairs to work.

The next morning when I went out to the mailbox I noticed a car on the street outside my house. It had been parked there on and off for several days and I'd seen it before and stored it away in that warehouse of memory where people keep small no-count observations they have no immediate use for, like the crack in the flagstone that needs fixing or the azalea bush that ought to be watered soon. In the front seat of the car was a man reading a newspaper, and his face seemed familiar, but then I realized it was only because he'd been there all week. He was probably a friend of my neighbor's, I decided—then remembered that my neighbor was in Europe and had been for several months.

One of the letters in the mailbox caught my attention and I pushed the thought back onto another shelf in the memory warehouse.

But the shelf I pushed it onto was already full of trivia—things I'd decided to think about tomorrow: the Scarlett O'Hara shelf—and when Lillian called toward evening, the shelf fell down. I can't remember precisely what she called to say but it was another instance of her knowing some minor fact about my life that she had no way of learning, and suddenly in the middle of the conversation the pile of trivia tumbled and kaleidoscoped into a different order—and then all at once I got it. The anonymous calls and Fiona's disappearance and the Smiths' dinner and the MGM lunch. At first I thought it couldn't be true and then knew immediately that it was.

I asked for news of Fiona.

"She's fine," Lilly said without thinking, "he found Fiona the second day, didn't I tell you?"

"Who found Fiona the second day?"

There was a very slight pause.

"The detective I hired," Lilly said, "Fiona was in San Francisco, she'd never disappeared at all, she just forgot to call her mother for a while . . . how's the book coming—did you work today?"

I knew from her voice that she'd heard the slip at the same time I heard it and done the only thing Lillian would do—finish the sentence as if nothing had happened, and change the subject.

For a few seconds I was too full of anger to speak.

"Hello?" she said.

"Jesus Christ, Lilly," I said after a while.

"What's the matter?"

"Jesus Christ."

"Don't keep saying that, what is it?"

"I thought you were supposed to stand for freedom . . . cutting your conscience and all that."

"I don't know what you're talking about," Lillian said. "Why are you breathing so hard?"

"Look, Lady Liberty," I said as quietly as I could, "call off your dog. He's been sitting in front of my house in an old Chevy since Monday reading the *Herald Examiner* and if he's there tomorrow . . ." I couldn't think of anything large enough and I fell into silence.

"There's no point carrying on about it," Lillian said after a moment. "If you don't take the anonymous calls seriously, I do. Using a detective is perfectly natural under the circumstances."

I asked her where the detective was from.

"Interpol," she said. "I couldn't very well go to Pinkerton, could I—Pinkerton's where Dash used to work."

"You hired a detective to spy on me?"

"Certainly not," she said in a voice filled with indignation, "how dare you think I would hire a detective to spy on you? Just how dare you?"

I waited.

"I hired a detective to find Fiona," she said, "but you can't hire them by the day. Not the good ones. You have to hire them by the week. He found Fiona in two days—I had five days left over."

I kept quiet.

"So I sent him to you. Why waste a perfectly good detective?" Lillian said. "Why are you breathing that way?"

I said nothing.

"You've upset me terribly," Lillian said, her voice rising, "I'd better tell you that and be simple about it—imagine your accusing me of such a thing—of *hiring a detective to spy on you.* Just imagine. I think you should examine the contempt in that accusation one day—it's unspeakable of you. . . ."

She went on in the same vein for a while and just then I didn't know whether to burst out laughing or never see her again—or both—or possibly neither. I still couldn't think of any words and after a few minutes Lilly began to wind down, having by then talked herself into an attitude of outrage—the moral pique of the misunderstood. She said she'd call me back when she got over the pain I'd caused her and hung up.

That was the afternoon it occurred to me for the first time that Lillian would have made a great politician.

It was also the day I realized that Lilly's almost legendary sense of justice, the justice upon which so much of her life was based, was the justice of a child. If she believed a man had betrayed her with another woman, then she believed she had a right to do something about it and she balanced the weight of what she did against the weight of the hurt. It didn't matter whether the man had truly broken the rules of the relationship any more than it mattered what those rules were, as long as she felt that something had been done against her. It was sandbox thinking, neither the highfalutin justice of Athena nor the gutbucket law of the jungle, but something so young it was hard to acknowledge in an adult.

The biggest difference between Lillian as a grown-up and Lillian as a child was that she was taller.

⊱⊱⊱⊱VI

HOW WE GOT THROUGH the winter I don't remember. For a while we stayed off the phone—I didn't want to talk to her till my mind had stopped reeling—but little by little hurt feelings were repaired and eventually a kind of armed truce began to take effect. It was beginning to seem as if, outside of perversity and spite, nothing could happen that was large enough to spoil a certain ritual of friendship. There would be no way of explaining that to anybody except to say we had made a commitment to each other and that wasn't quite the truth—it never is. People don't make commitments. They wake up one day to find them made.

What kept me from making too large an issue of the detective was the threat of the anonymous phone calls, which never ceased. Summer on the Vineyard began in a stiff way, with that tinged and stilted and excessively polite tone people use when they're trying not to strangle each other ("Please pass the salt, would you?" "Yes, of course, sorry to be hogging it." "You weren't." "Thank you." "You're welcome." "I should have put two saltcellars on the table." "No, it's my fault, really . . .") and whenever the phone rang I leaped to answer it; but when I picked it up it was always a friend, never the ominous and shadowy stranger who was beginning to become such a threat.

For a while it seemed as if we had to learn how to live together in the same house all over again, and the awkward days passed slowly: I spent a lot of time alone and so did she. About once a week I'd come back from a walk to find Lillian sitting or pacing in tense silence and I knew there had been another call—

she was getting four or five a month by then—but I still had no
definite idea who was behind them. What scared Lilly most, she
said, was not the calls themselves but the man. It was always the
same voice, or the voice of the woman who called for him, and
the pair appeared to alternate between an attitude of warning
and one of jeering: they warned her of possible malice from my
friends and jeered at her loyalty to me. Though I hadn't heard
the caller's voice I began to feel as if I knew him and every night
I ran over the list of people who might be responsible. It was
hard to imagine anyone I knew wanting to harm Lillian but it
kept me wondering and one night I suspected my friend Ann, the
next night my old friend George, the next my new friend Sally,
though I never came up with any suspicion that lasted more than
a few days.

But there were other things to keep me occupied and after a
while I quit thinking about it. That was the summer Lillian worked
long hours on what she had been referring to as a book of portraits—the book she was later to call *Pentimento*. Because we
had spent so many months cheerleading each other through our
last books she expected the same with the portraits, a surprising
attitude under the cold-war circumstances of our truce. But writing was a constant with Lilly, its ebb and flow no more meaning-
ful than the waxing and waning of the moon: she took her work
routine so seriously you didn't notice it any more than you would
the beating of someone else's heart, and she'd been trained by
Hammett to accept help as she had trained herself to give it.

She had once, many years before, told me the story of a
girlhood friend, the daughter of some rich Americans—a woman
who'd been sent to school in England in the twenties and stayed
on in Europe in the thirties to help fight the then flowering Nazi
movement in Europe. The friend had eventually died in that effort and Lilly had cried when she first told me the story—cried
in hurt and cried hard—so that her decision to include it in a
book seemed a good sign: the only way a certain kind of writer
can cope with a certain kind of pain is to make a story of it and
Lillian was above all else a storyteller. She had mentioned her
friend's name once in talking about her but now she needed a
made-up name and she went through several before she found
one she liked. When she brought the first few pages downstairs
on a hot muggy morning in June and began to read them aloud

they were the sketchy beginnings of a portrait of a woman named after her mother: Julia.

Lilly didn't often get stuck in work but when she did it threw her for a loop: early on in the portrait of Julia she bogged down in a swamp of detail that threatened to drown the small story. In tone, the opening pages had the resonance of a longer piece, the first notes of a symphony rather than a sonata, and I asked why she wouldn't do it as a novel but Lilly made a gesture of dismissal. "I can't write novels, you ought to know that."

I wanted to know why not.

"Because I can only sustain as long as I can sustain," she said. "It's not a question of form—I'm stuck, that's all—maybe getting drunk will help."

I said I didn't see how.

"It used to," Lilly said.

"Before what?"

"Before I was cured," she said. "You remember when I was an alcoholic—Zilboorg said he wouldn't treat me unless I quit drinking—I quit for ten years."

I said the fact that she was able to drink in moderation now proved that she'd never been an alcoholic, since by definition alcoholics can't.

"I was," Lilly said, "and I can. I can do what I have to."

The next morning she came down with several more pages of Julia's portrait but she still hadn't licked the problem. The quagmire of detail now engulfed the little story and made it seem petty and overblown. I couldn't think of a way to help, except the way I might have taken myself—tell it straight and fast to a place where the reader will keep turning pages to find out what happens, then stop and loop back for detail: she could go without preamble until the place where she got into trouble on a train headed for Germany, then leave herself in trouble and go back for explanations. It was a kindergarten solution for a writer and I was awkward and embarrassed but Lilly listened to it and lit up.

After a moment she trotted upstairs and when she came down with new pages the next morning the bones of the story were formed and clear. "I didn't like to make too much of the train," she said, "suspense kills drama, I had to flatten it. But it works, you're nobody's fool."

To be able to help would have been enough but to be called nobody's fool was the largest compliment I'd ever received about writing and I walked around glowing for days.

The portrait of Julia took Lillian another few weeks and she spent much of her time talking about what knickknacks might have been on what bookshelves, what wallpaper in a Berlin café, how the entrance to a London funeral parlor had looked, what boat she might have taken to bring Julia's body back to the States so long ago, when it was over. Choice of detail tells the story, as any writer knows, and Lillian went after it with the skill of a great set decorator. There is something satisfying about seeing an old pro at work when early training shows best and she had always worked the same way. Long before she started *The Little Foxes* she'd paid a graduate student to research the period and type all the facts into a loose-leaf notebook: the notebook was divided into sections, each section tagged in an all-inclusive spectrum of detail ranging from economy to table manners. Now she dredged up a similar if shorter list for "Julia," a little like an anthropologist working with some artifacts found in the river-bottom of memory, making up what she had to, inventing or reconstructing the past, spreading out her findings every morning and arranging and changing and diminishing and polishing every day.

Lillian was in the process of dramatizing her life. She brought to the business of memory the art of fiction and she was beginning to forge for herself a new form. Because I was interested in what she was doing it never occurred to me at the time that people would take all the details of the story for literal truth, since it seemed so clear that she was fusing fact with fiction. Lillian wrote about that in the last of the four memoirs, *Maybe,* whose title carries the meaning of the whole. Shortly after *Maybe* was published and not long before she died, Lilly remarked to a friend* that she'd discovered a new form for herself in writing, a form that was neither fiction nor memory but a combination of both, which is probably what most recollection is. "I've been over-praised for the books," she said, "I'll be attacked too hard to make up for it—but maybe one day they'll be read for what they are."

*Dr. Milton Wexler, a California-based psychoanalyst and head of the Hereditary Disease Foundation, which Lillian admired and helped support.

Maybe.

The first of the memoirs, *An Unfinished Woman*, was officially about Lillian, actually about other people; the second, *Pentimento*, was officially about other people, actually about Lillian.
The difference between them was not so much purposeful as
probing—their balance, like all balance in writing, so necessary
that it seemed haphazard. But it was not haphazard and for a
writer like Lillian the fabric of story is never accidental. At worst
it is mistaken, at best it is rooted in the subconscious, that un-
charted place where things become other things—a man walking
turns into a woman running, a grunt becomes an aria, a song is
a scream. When the book of portraits was done, the week before
she turned it in, Lillian wrote a prefatory note: *

> Old paint on canvas, as it ages, sometimes becomes
> transparent. When that happens, it is possible, in some pic-
> tures, to see the original lines: a tree will show through a
> woman's dress, a child makes way for a dog, a large boat is
> no longer on an open sea. That is called pentimento because
> the painter "repented," changed his mind. Perhaps it would
> be as well to say that the old conception, replaced by a later
> choice, is a way of seeing and then seeing again. . . .

Strange that the special fabric of longing she worked so hard
to weave would one day be examined thread by thread, picked
bare by all those nimble writers whose finest tools are a magni-
fying glass and a pair of tweezers, until the impact of the whole
was lost to them because of it.

When "Julia" was finished, Lillian went on to other portraits
and then one evening over an after-dinner bottle of wine she told
the story of a snapping turtle she had found on her farm in New
York State and been unable to kill. Hammett had killed it, taken
its head off, and the turtle had walked out of the house without
a head.

In the McCarthy days, Hammett had pleaded with Lillian
not to buck the House Un-American Activities Committee; given
the sharpness of her temper, he said, she'd be cited for contempt
of court and sent to jail. The worst of that was not the possible
confinement, but the fact that jail was filled with rats: Lillian had
strength but she had no stamina—she could not live for long in

---

* From *Pentimento*, published by Little, Brown, 1973

a place that had rats. Hammett himself had not her strength, he said, but he did have stamina—he was like the turtle—he could go on walking if they killed him. He went to jail and, though the experience broke him, he did not die for several years.

Lillian was good at survival themes and when she finished telling the story of the snapping turtle—and the wine bottle was empty—I made a long-winded and fatuous and impassioned plea, begging her to make use of the turtle as one of the portraits in the book. When I'd done I had the hiccups and Lillian came over and kissed me. "I knew it would pay off in the end," she said, "it's nice to have a writer around the house." She began the story called "Turtle" the next morning.

Work that summer, like every summer, alternated with horseplay, though there was often a desperate quality just under horseplay or so it appeared, since Lilly was one of those people whose lives demand a certain amount of silliness and fun no matter what. Having brought to the outraged heart of childhood the cold intellect of a vengeful adult, she was given to coasting along until the cheerful nature and stubborn playfulness of the child demanded to be heard.

Whenever Lilly got too bored with herself on the Vineyard she took to baiting friends like the Styrons but it was a while since she had pulled off a successful practical joke. The most recent attempt was one she'd fumbled some years before, upon the imminent arrival of the Styrons' most impressive and famous house guest to date—a personage referred to diplomatically by Lillian as "the widow Kennedy"—who was invited for a weekend. Mrs. Kennedy was without question the most famous woman in the world and Lilly had mused over her impending presence for days, convinced that Rose Styron, in staking out the widow as her private property for a weekend, could now claim a corner on the celebrity market for life.

"I can't let Rose get away with it," she muttered to herself over and over as the day approached, "it's too much."

Nobody in the world is quite as impressed by famous people as other famous people, and the Thursday before Mrs. Kennedy's arrival the air around the little circle of summer celebrities quivered with anticipation. By then Lilly was a bundle of nerves and she still hadn't come up with a solution. On Friday morning, in a last-ditch and somewhat lame attempt to save the day, she spread

a rumor that Elizabeth Taylor and Richard Burton had unex-
pectedly arrived at her own house for the weekend, begging sanctuary. "Rose will have to invite the Burtons to dinner—she won't
be able to stop herself—and I'll say they're busy, and it will ruin
her weekend."

She was talking on the phone to Sue Marquand, a close friend;
but Sue, who generally went along with Lillian's plans without
question, was not convinced. "How would the Burtons get on
the island without being seen?"

"By private plane, of course," Lilly said, regarding the telephone with a look of dreamy patience—the look Don Quixote
turned on Sancho Panza after hearing that windmills were windmills, not giants—"it's a perfect plan, there's nothing wrong
with it."

Within two days, half the population of Edgartown and
Vineyard Haven thought the Burtons were staying with Lillian,
and the plan seemed to be working. Then Barbara Hersey called
to report, in a hollow voice, that there was a bulletin in *The
Boston Globe* announcing that Elizabeth Taylor had just broken
her ankle in Capri.

"You're lying," Lillian said in the calm tone she reserved for
national disasters and other emergencies, "please say you're lying,
dear. We all lie once in a while—it's no great admission."

But Barbara wasn't and Lilly's joke fell flat. Ever since then
she had lain in wait daily for Bill and Rose, seeing them often
around the island, always hoping to catch one of them off-guard.
One evening I took her out to a restaurant in Oak Bluffs for
dinner and she spotted Bill sitting at a booth with a female friend.
Rose, who worked for Amnesty International, had gone to Rome
for a couple of weeks and the friend was a woman Lilly didn't
know, which led her to believe, inaccurately as it happens, that
she was witnessing the first night of an affair, and she decided to
go into a phone booth in the corner and dial the restaurant we
were in.

I asked why.

"Novelists have no imagination," she said in a tired voice,
"it's a thing I've noticed before. Outside of work, you're dead-
heads, all of you. The reason I'm going to call the restaurant
from the phone booth is simple: I'm going to say I'm Rose, of
course—why else, dopey . . . I'll say I'm phoning long-distance

from Rome and I want to speak to my husband, and whoever answers the phone will page Bill, or go to his table and get him, and either way it will scare hell out of him."

I asked how Lilly was planning to get to the phone booth and back without being seen, when she had to pass directly by Bill's table in order to do it.

Lilly sighed. "Have you no sense of adventure?" she said after a moment, "is life for you just one day after the next? Why don't you have a little courage, darling. Things have a way of working out."

I didn't think so and I was wrong again. In one of the most remarkable of her performances, Lilly got up—shielded her nose with one hand—and tiptoed like a cartoon mouse straight across the restaurant, passing within inches of Bill and calling more attention to herself by tiptoeing than she would have by walking normally. When Lilly got subtle, it was like a rhinoceros hiding behind one blade of grass.

She got away with it cold. Bill was absorbed in conversation and failed to see her pass—nor did he notice anything out of the ordinary when the cashier trotted over to say that there was a long-distance phone call for Mr. Styron from his wife in Rome and please to hurry because Mrs. Styron sounded very upset.

But when he went to the phone all he heard was a dial tone. The plan worked but there was little satisfaction in it for Lilly because there was no real payoff—Bill never spoke about it and neither did Rose. The search for the perfect joke went on.

Some months after that, during a week when I was off-island, Lilly went to the Styrons' for dinner and called me to say that she'd met "an international society lady" there. The society lady, she said, was staying the weekend with the Styrons and was a sitting duck. Early the next morning Lilly took the ferry to Woods Hole, registered at a local inn, asked for some extra stationery and went to her room; she spent the rest of that day writing lyrical love letters to Bill—signed with the society lady's name and dated two weeks apart. Then she got a friend in Boston, another in New York and a third in Los Angeles to mail the letters for her at two-week intervals, as if the society lady were traveling. After that she settled down on the beach at the Vineyard Haven Yacht Club with a pair of binoculars to watch Bill walking on the sand as he read them.

"He was trying not to look excited," she reported later, "but he can't fool me. If he's so calm, why doesn't he read his letters at home? No," she said, happily, "no. If you go for long walks on the sand in moony solitude, you're a cooked goose."

It was some years since the incident of the love letters and I had by now come to the conclusion that her teasing of Bill carried an even more obvious sexual undertone than I'd thought at first. One morning I came down to find Lilly bent over a grimy little piece of paper in intense silence, making up a guest list. She'd decided, she said, to give a beach picnic on Sunday, and spread a rumor that Marlon Brando was locked in her bedroom.

I asked why.

"You know perfectly well why," she said, "I want to see what Rose will do."

"I know this will sound silly of me," I said, "but why would Marlon Brando lock himself in your bedroom if you're having a beach party?"

Lilly heaved a deep breath and raised her eyes to heaven. "You worry your life away, Peter," she said. "There could be any number of reasons. Brando could be sick, for instance."

"In your bedroom?"

"What's wrong with his getting sick in my bedroom?"

"Nothing," I said, "who's sick in his?"

"I see what you mean," Lilly said thoughtfully.

I asked why the man couldn't be sick in his own bedroom.

"The lock on the guest-room door is broken."

"So what? Nobody's going to open the door and walk in on him."

"You don't know Rose," Lilly said.

She settled for announcing that Brando was ensconced somewhere in her house, too upset over a broken love affair to come to her beach picnic. As soon as people started arriving she spread the story, making sure she told it to the guests she knew would repeat it, in each case whispering "This is one thousand percent for you." By five-thirty a reporter from *The Vineyard Gazette* had called to ask for an interview with Brando and by six o'clock a few of Lillian's New York guests had made a pact to save the sensitive actor from the tasteless mercies of her Los Angeles guests. After the picnic she found two notes pushed under her bedroom door, but neither one was from Rose.

"I'll catch her yet," Lilly said, "see if I don't. If she thinks she can outsmart me, she's got about fourteen more thinks coming."

That night she lay down and asked me to massage her neck for a few minutes. Rubbing Lilly's neck was one of those small affectionately private customs that exist between people and it always started with the same request: "Pat me."

"Do what?"

"*Pat* me," Lilly said irritably, "it's comforting to be patted, for God's sake. Don't tell me you've never patted anyone before."

Patting her inevitably led to rubbing her neck, and rubbing her neck caused her to produce a sound not unlike purring. "If *I* could make someone feel that good," she said in a shamelessly innocent tone when I was getting ready to quit, "I'd keep it up twenty-four hours a day."

LILLIAN: *Whose neck will you rub when it's over?*
PETER: *What's over?*
LILLIAN: *When I'm gone.*
PETER: *Unhappily you won't be.*
LILLIAN: *Dead isn't gone?*
PETER: *Not in your case.*
LILLIAN: *What will I be when I'm dead?*
PETER: *Just as much of a pain in the ass as you are now.*
LILLIAN (laughing): *Darling . . . oh, darling, what a lovely thing to say . . .*

In September I made the usual arrangements to go back to Los Angeles and Lilly wanted to know who was waiting for me there. As it happened no one was but rather than be put on the defensive I ducked the question. Instead of going on with it Lilly dropped the subject and toted up the money she was owed. Ever since the first summer she'd been charging me for certain favors, with a price list that covered all acts of a sensual nature. This summer the going rate was $1.75 for a kiss, $2.75 for anything more than a kiss and $3.00 for anything that went on for longer than ten minutes. Her fees, she explained, were in accordance with the cost of living, and it was to be expected that there would be an occasional hike in price to accommodate inflation. She toted up the summer's pleasures carefully and found she had made

$11.75 between June and Labor Day, a sum that made her very happy.

But while I was packing the phone rang and Lilly came out of her bedroom a minute later with a grim expression. "It's another one of those goddamn anonymous calls," she said, "one of your West Coast friends has been saying unpleasant things about me again."

I said I'd do anything I could to put a stop to it and Lilly seemed pleased; we spent the last weekend on the Vineyard having a good time, though the good time was guarded. When I got on the plane the threat of the anonymous caller still hung in the air like a nightmare on hold.

How Do You Kill October?

>>>>>I

> The storm's eye missed the island but the wind is bad
> and the lightning still comes every few seconds. Sadie's afraid
> of lightning—like my father. When I was little my father used
> to keep an easy chair and a lamp and bookshelf in his closet
> so he could shut himself in and read when there was an
> electrical storm. I think Sadie would crawl under the bed if
> she could, but she's too big, so she crawls under me.
>
> We haven't gone outside yet—won't till this is over—
> the sea is only halfway up to the house but the house seems
> to be holding. Full of leaks and creak-crazy, but holding.
>
> I wonder what the osprey is doing out there in that wind.

I had been thinking about Lilly and watching the seabirds
when the storm hit. By then according to the transistor radio the
hurricane was headed northeast so we wouldn't get the worst of
it, only the heavy periphery—a lot of rain and a whipping wind.
But the birds knew something, they must have sensed the power
of it high in the air: they weren't flying. They were huddled
shoulder to shoulder on the beach with no pecking order—big
birds next to little ones—sandpipers and gulls and terns all facing
the wind. The osprey wasn't there but a black-backed gull stood
out because it was the biggest and there were so many seabirds
you couldn't see the sand.

When the first spew of rain hit it covered the birds from
view and the sea grass exploded. The worst was the sea itself.
There was always a chance it would rise, pushed by the wind,

159

cross the space between the house and the beach and take the house. It was pure luck, the radio said, that the storm had struck at low tide: if it had come a few hours later, when the tide was in, it might have pushed the sea into the town.

The rain came hard and Sadie whined and we sat on the floor against the back wall of the living room and watched it. There's something voluptuous about pitting yourself against a hurricane, something sensual and almost lazy. It didn't last long, two hours maybe, half an hour at peak, and most of the time we stayed where we were. I thought if it got too bad we would go upstairs and if it flooded the house we could continue on up the hill into the car, and get out. I didn't yet know there was a tree down in the driveway.

After a few lashes the rain thinned and we saw a small bush gouged up by the wind. Lilly would have liked watching that and for a moment I wondered how she was making out in the grave-yard. Branches and sand and loose debris sailed hissing out over the earth in streaks and the sky seemed to roll down fast.

A few boats were left in the harbor and one of them looked as though it were floating over the dune grass toward the house; by then the big stone breakwater was covered with water and the jetty too. Just then a bird hit one of the windows and fell, bro-ken, into the bushes, and it wasn't long afterward that the tran-sistor battery gave out and the radio quit.

I don't remember much after that. By the time the storm began to ebb we were upstairs and Sadie wasn't whining any-more. We stayed there together till the storm was gone.

Honey, look in my book and get me Maureen Sta-
pleton's phone number, will you? Or even better, dial
it for me. Goddamn my eyes. And damn eye doctors,
they're so smug. I hate the light in this room, is this a
decent light to your eyes? . . . Oh, hello, Maureen, I
haven't heard from you in weeks. . . . I don't care
how busy you've been, don't you think the rest of us
are busy? . . . You're doing what play, Maureen? . . .
Who? . . . Oh, him. He's a nice man and a terrible
actor. Who else is in it? . . . Oy. Who? Oy. That's a
fine mess you've got yourself into, you can act both
those kiddies off the stage, and they'll both make you
pay for it—I wish you wouldn't tell me things like that,
Maureen, it just upsets me, and there's nothing I can
do about it. Now what did I call you about? . . . Well,
if you don't know, who does? . . .

Wait a minute, I know what it was, I called to ask
you for the weekend. The nineteenth, that's a week from
Friday, I'm having a dinner. No, a smallish dinner. Well,
a medium-sized dinner . . . it's Jackie Onassis, Kay
Graham, Carly Simon and James Taylor, Felicia and
Lennie Bernstein, Mia Farrow and André Previn, the
Styrons, Annabel and Mike Nichols, Jules and whoever
he's in love with by Friday, and the Cronkites and the
Buchwalds and . . . what? . . .

Maureen, don't just go on repeating "no-ne-no-no"
over and over again, it's a silly thing to say even once.

*Well, why can't you come, you must have a reason.
. . . Maureen, you can't be rehearsing all weekend, who
do you think you're talking to—I've been in the theater
all my life—nobody rehearses on weekends, it's unheard of. Actors can't stay awake that long. What? . . .
Well, just tell him you're busy, that's all, he won't know
the difference. He's a terrible, terrible actor, Maureen,
the only reason he wants you to stay in the city and go
over his scenes is so you can teach him how to do them.
What? It doesn't matter whether you agree with me, I
don't want to hear your side of it. Look. If you don't
want to come and see me, you don't, that's all. Be simple about it. Please don't go on with that jabber, you're
upsetting me now. . . . I only thought you'd like to
see me. All right, talk to him, then, and call me back.*

SOUND OF PHONE HANGING UP.
PAUSE.

*I wonder what's the matter with Maureen, she
sounds nuttier than usual.*

>>>>> III

IT WAS IN THE beginning of the next year that I first got to know three of Lilly's off-island friends—three who were closer to her than most: Hannah Weinstein, Dick Poirier and Rita Wade. Hannah was a small woman with an infectious laugh and electric eyes, a kind of generic mommola you would not expect to see outside the kitchen, a happy and talented cook, a feeder of people, a gentle mother to her three children and, when she took the saber out from under her knitting, one of the best executives and producers in the movie industry. Dick Poirier, who lived in New York and taught at Rutgers, was a witty man with a kind of attractive irascibility, a scholar who started as the son of a fisherman in Gloucester, Massachusetts, and wound up as a distinguished literary critic in New York. Rita Wade was Lillian's secretary, an Irish woman from Newfoundland with a fierce sense of loyalty, who had the intelligence, and the humor, to help run Lilly's life. The three of them served different needs and there appeared to be a kind of unspoken agreement among them, a tacit understanding that was odd in three people with such different backgrounds.

Besides them there were one or two others who were close to Lilly and stayed outside the circle of friends, maintaining a sort of intimate and separate system with her that was unique in her life and theirs, like Mike Nichols.

Her friendship with Mike was a good example of Lilly's way of bonding. They had met in the sixties, when he was on Broadway with Elaine May, and Lillian was dazzled by their humor and went backstage to congratulate them; but the bonding took place a month later at a party given by Felicia Bernstein for her husband, Leonard Bernstein.

The Bernsteins loved Lilly and she went alone to the party, given to celebrate the unveiling of a portrait someone had painted of Lennie: it was a select group and when the painting was unwrapped the guests spoke up politely as people will at a vernissage, saying things by rote—how perceptive the painting was —how delicate—how extraordinary. The flow of complimentary jabber went on for a while and was broken by Lillian's voice, silent up to then, deep and harsh and helpless when it exploded: "What in hell is everybody talking about, it's an awful painting— it makes Lennie look like a middle-aged fag—I think it's the worst mess I've ever seen in my life."

A silence followed, then Felicia led the other guests gracefully away while Lillian stayed where she was, clapped her hands over her eyes and said—quietly—to no one: "Now look what I've done." And Mike, who had been watching her, stepped forward and put his arms around her and said: "Will you marry me?" and from then on they were friends.

It was often that way with Lilly, people were attracted to what was uncontrolled in her and a few of them tried to control it, others allowing themselves to be controlled. Once in a while somebody as special as Mike swam through all her fuss like a lonesome sperm looking for an egg to fertilize and made contact with her and that was the conception of a friendship. Once it was conceived that way it usually went on for life because Lilly didn't like to let her friendships go.

She did not like to be left, for any reason.

LILLIAN: *Are you going now?*
PETER: *Not quite.*
LILLIAN: *Oh, the hell with it—leave if you're going to. Go ahead, please don't worry about me. I'm much too dependent on you and you know it—I went hats-over-the-windmill about you twenty-five years ago. No, thirty years ago—whenever it was, I should have known better. Don't have any consideration for me, darling, what do women matter in the end?*

PAUSE.

LILLIAN: *I thought you said you were leaving.*
PETER: *I can stay for a little.*

LILLIAN: *Then stay. Do what you want, but don't for God's sake announce your departure every ten minutes.*
PETER: *I haven't announced anything.*
LILLIAN: *Then why are we talking about it? If you can stay half an hour, stay half an hour, don't let's waste the time discussing it, all right?*
PETER: *All right.*
LILLIAN: *All right then. Try to enjoy yourself. Stand not upon the order of your going. Go, darling, if you have to. Just go. . . .*

The most important friend Lilly ever had was and always would be Dashiell Hammett: he had been the coupling force behind the thrust of her early ambition and he had guided and trained her as she went. Lilly sometimes saw him in a more romantic light than was necessary, as Isak Dinesen saw Denys Finch Hatton or George Sand saw Chopin, the way we all prefer to see those who love us, though the truth was made of tougher stuff than romance, with none of its gossamer quality. Lilly's second most favorite form of loving was fighting and sometimes when she spoke of Hammett it sounded like the admiration of an admiral for a five-star general.

Hammett's name came up that winter when I went to see her in New York. She had some travel brochures spread out on the coffee table—we were planning a trip to Europe in February or March—and when I hedged about fixing a definite time for the trip she blew her stack. One of our running problems was anything that involved a schedule, since I had a congenital aversion to making definite plans and Lilly was happiest knowing she had an appointment twelve weeks from Wednesday.

"Travel is fine—I like to travel," she said, "but I have problems with it you don't understand. You speak too many languages too easily—travel is a special thing to me. It was to him, too. It was an outlandish thing to him."

"Him?"

"Hammett," Lilly said and fell silent. You could tell when she wanted to talk about him and I settled back to listen.

Instead of speaking Lilly went over and opened the window. The sounds of New York traffic swam up from the street, urgent and shimmering, and a pigeon flapped off the sill into the night.

"Dash wouldn't leave the continental United States," she said, "not with me, not with anybody. He didn't trust foreigners." She lit a cigarette and held off for a moment. "He never even went to Europe—he hated the idea of going anywhere outside America—you remember the contempt he had for people who lived in France or Spain as you did—Dash was a very provincial man. I begged him, but he wouldn't go away with me. I always had to travel alone."

Her voice diminished and she sat down suddenly. "It wasn't just foreigners he was suspicious of, Dash didn't trust anybody. He especially didn't trust women—the women in his books were always the villains. And he liked being alone . . ."

She went on for a while in the same vein and I knew she had embarked on one of those memories that come over people when they get a sudden violent whiff of the past and sink back into it. The memory of Hammett was heady stuff for Lillian and I was thinking about that when I came to and realized I hadn't been listening for a while.

When I tuned in again, she was saying something about tenderness.

"Say it again," I said.

"I said," Lillian said, "you can feel tender about somebody's defects—more than their strengths. Like the way he put up with me when I wanted to travel. Or his legs—he was ashamed of them . . . I used to feel very tender about his legs. . . ."

She lit a cigarette off the old one and went on.

"It happened when he went to Lenox Hill Hospital for those treatments . . . it was called the fever treatment. They put you under very hot lights and lowered the lights to within an inch or so of your body for half an hour. You got a flash fever from it and that was said to kill the syphilis, and when Dash went in they put him in a room with a nurse and she turned on the lights and lowered them and then she left the room for some reason. The nurse wasn't ever supposed to leave the room in case the patient fell asleep but Dash's nurse did. And he turned over in his sleep and his legs stuck to the lights. It took most of the flesh off."

She got up and stood facing the windows with her back pressed against the empty room. "I loved his legs, I used to want to hold them, but he wouldn't let me, it embarrassed him. He thought it was pity, he never understood the reason. It can make you feel so gentle and tender, a thing like that, and it's nice to feel tender. I wish you felt tender about me."

I did and she knew I did so I shut up. Lilly stayed with her back to the room for a while.

"Dash said I had one of the most beautiful Renaissance faces he ever saw," she said in a low voice, "he was a very withdrawn man, but sometimes . . ."

When she turned around her face was red and she altered her tone. "Sometimes when I couldn't make a decision, it amused him . . . that always amused him, I think. Once in Pleasantville I went into his room and asked him whether I should take a two o'clock flight or a three-thirty flight. I was having trouble deciding which one I wanted and Dash was reading a book. He said very firmly: 'Go out of the room and come back in an hour.' I went out and sat in the kitchen stewing about it, and went back in exactly an hour and knocked on his door and went in. 'The three-thirty flight,' he said without looking up. He hadn't moved and I started to laugh and then swore at him, but I was grateful. He was affectionate with me that day. He trusted me a little, I think, that day. . . ."

She went back to her chair and sat down. In a lighter voice she said: "He had such enormous contempt for lying—Dash wouldn't lie about anything. He didn't always tell the truth but he wouldn't lie. Not even the day he disappeared with Laura— Laura Perelman. They were in Los Angeles, the four of them, Dash and the Wests and Sid Perelman, and when Laura didn't show up one night Sid called me in New York in a panic . . . he said he couldn't find her anywhere and Dash was gone too, and he wanted to know if I'd heard anything. I hadn't, but I had a pretty good idea . . . it turned out Dash and Laura had rented a car and gone up to San Francisco for the weekend. I cut up about it badly when I found out. I think it was probably the reason I never married him. He kept the truth from me because he'd given Laura his word not to tell anybody—given *Laura* his word, can you imagine? I wish he were alive, I could kill him for that . . . even now, after all this time . . . I could still kill him. Loyalty was large stuff to me, it still is—I was hipped on the subject of loyalty . . . so was he. But he was loyal to Laura and I found out from Sid . . . Sid never spoke to Dash again and I . . ." She mashed her cigarette out and shrugged. "Dash didn't lie about it. He wouldn't discuss it when I confronted him but he didn't bother denying it. . . ."

Lilly's voice changed again, one of those flicked tones she

used when she was probing the past. "I don't remember how much later it was but I remember we were on the Turnpike, about an hour out of New York. It came absolutely in space. I was thinking about something or other and Dash said: 'Let's go home and mix a pitcher of martinis and take it to bed like we used to . . .' and without knowing what I was going to say, I said: 'No, I don't ever want to again.' He had a hand on my knee and he just took the hand off and that was the end of that. It was such a simple thing for such a complex feeling. But we never did again. We often slept in the same bed after that, cuddled up like kids. I would wake up kissing the back of his neck but we never . . . it was over then—things changed. Or maybe they didn't change so much. . . .

She lit another cigarette and puffed. "It's true we'd only lived together when we were in the same place, like his visits to the farm or the Vineyard—Dash always kept his own apartment. Always. Till he called that day from Katonah to say he was going into a veterans' hospital and I couldn't stand it. . . ."

She coughed for a moment. "That was the beginning of the end, I guess. He'd been broke since he got out of jail and the government had taken over all his royalties and when he got sick he had nothing to pay medical bills, the only place he could go was the veterans' hospital. He didn't have any feeling about that one way or the other . . . he was a strange man, Dash. If the government had taken away my royalties forever I'd have been angry and bitter about it, but not him—he never hoped for more from any world. He just figured it was the price he paid for standing up for what he believed in. So when I begged him on the phone to come live with me till he got well, he wouldn't. I got so desperate I called Gregory Zilboorg—I didn't know what else to do . . . I was crying so hard I couldn't stop and Zilboorg said to go see Dash . . . to stop crying here and go cry there. And to say I needed him—he said it was the only thing that would work—if I needed him—not if he needed me. So I drove upstate and found him and said it. I didn't have to pretend to cry, I was already crying when I got there. I was a mess. But Dash just seemed surprised. 'Oh,' he said, 'I didn't know. Sure I'll come.' "

She flicked the ash from her cigarette and took to coughing again. The traffic outside wasn't as loud anymore and she opened another window and sat down.

"That's when I put him in bed on the library floor of the Eighty-second Street house. He stayed there almost five years— the longest we'd ever lived together. It took him that long to die. He'd long since quit drinking, but toward the end I knew he wanted a drink . . . the trouble was, I couldn't think of a way to offer him one without letting him know he was dying—I tried once, but he only looked at me. I'd been so against it for so long—I'd told him once if he went on drinking I'd never see him again . . . so that night, when I asked if he'd like a martini before supper . . . he turned his head and looked at me. About a week after that he started to fail and they came for him with an ambulance. I was putting on my coat and Dash said: 'Oh, are you coming too?'—just like that, in a surprised voice, 'Oh, are you coming too?'—it was the angriest he ever made me. In all the time I knew him. I was shaking with anger. I said: 'How dare you think I wouldn't come with you to the hospital? Just how dare you, you son of a bitch, who in hell do you think you are . . .' And he grinned like a baby. But he trusted me then . . . I'm pretty sure he did—that was when he finally trusted me. . . ."

Lilly snuffed her cigarette and lit another one and smoked through her cough for a while.

"All I remember after that is waiting outside the hospital room. He was in coma for days and about eight o'clock one night the nurse came out and signaled to me . . . I went running in fast and called his name—I called 'Hammett' very loud. He turned his head like this and opened his eyes and stared at me a second . . . I don't know if he saw me . . . I don't even know if he knew I was in the room. And a few minutes after that they said he was dead."

She put her head back on the chair and kept still. There was a breeze coming up in the street outside and the traffic noises were getting louder again. Somewhere an angry driver was leaning on his horn.

"I was relieved when he died," she said. "That was the winter I went to teach at Harvard. Suddenly I could do anything I wanted . . . I was free; as if a thousand-pound weight had been lifted—I thought, I can travel, I can go when I want—I don't have to worry about his meals, or whether he's eating . . . I can do anything in the world, I'm all by myself now . . . I didn't start to miss him for over a year—almost two—and then it was so sudden and so bad I . . ."

She got up and opened another pack of cigarettes.

"We were talking about travel. All right," she said, "travel. Where shall we go?"

⤳⤳⤳⤳ IV

WE WENT TO LONDON for a day and the Normandy coast of France for two weeks, then back to London for a weekend on the town. There was a play I wanted to see that Lilly didn't. "It can't be news to you that I hate the theater," she said.

I said it was.

"Nobody believes me about it . . . I keep having to use that thing Prokofiev said. I went to a state dinner in Moscow once and they seated me next to him; there was a small orchestra playing in the next room and he sat still for maybe half an hour and then punched me with his elbow and said: 'Let's go have a drink.' I said I wanted to listen to the music and asked why he didn't and he said: 'I hate music.' There's an old American joke with a line like that but he couldn't have heard it—he really meant it—he got up and left the room. Later he said he was telling the truth and I know what he meant. He hated music the way you hate something you might love too much. He didn't like sitting down at dinner and listening to it. That's how I feel about the theater . . . I don't want to go unless I know I'll be crazy about it and who can make that guarantee?"

It was a play that had both the Oliviers and I asked somebody else to go with me, an old friend living in London, so when Lilly changed her mind at the last minute and wanted to go it was too late. I couldn't uninvite my friend and Lilly couldn't see why I couldn't and when I took a tough position about it we had a knock-down-drag-out fight all over the lobby of the Connaught. Mostly it was a shouting match, since Lilly managed to resist the notion of throwing scones or tea sandwiches, and we

171

didn't make up till Sunday when it was time go to home.

On the flight back we planned another trip and I dropped her in New York and went on to Los Angeles. Later that day she phoned me to say there was a message on her answering machine—another of the anonymous calls—and the man must have known the date of her return because he'd called again just now, and got her. He was full of the usual information about which of my friends had been staying in my house during my absence, which friends I'd been seeing, why Lilly ought to be careful.

"Careful of what?" I said.

LILLIAN: *I don't know. I keep telling you, I never did know who it was.*

PETER: *Is that true, Lilly?*

LILLIAN: *I'm going to be very, very angry in a minute. It's not nice of you to talk like that—it's unjust. I'm hipped on the subject of justice, and it's indecent of you to be so cynical . . . this was something that affected my life, for God's sake. I'm not given to exaggeration—whatever's wrong with me, that's not. I was being warned of possible danger. You were living with somebody I didn't know.*

PETER: *I was sleeping with somebody you didn't know, I often was, and I told you about it.*

LILLIAN: *What's that got to do with anything? Being straightforward about what you want is just another way of getting what you want. Grown-up people make choices, they give up one thing for another thing. I couldn't possibly have written* Children's Hour *without Hammett's support, not just his advice—I didn't have any money in the beginning. You make a choice and you take your chances.*

PETER: *I've made a choice or I wouldn't be here . . .*

LILLIAN: *That's not enough to say—it's me as well as you. It doesn't explain things.*

PETER: *I can't explain things, Lilly.*

LILLIAN: *Well, you'd better try. It's not my job to explain things— not anymore—I've done the best I can. It's you. You. You will have to explain the past. . . .*

We never settled the argument, but after the trip we settled down again to a habit of living that had already lasted, was to last, for years. We put up with each other when putting up with each other became necessary, spending more time together than apart because, I suppose, we liked it better that way.

Sometimes we both did magazine pieces that forced us to travel and one day in the early seventies we took writing assignments at the same time in different parts of the world. Lillian's took her to Alsace-Lorraine—mine to Cabo San Lucas—and we planned to meet somewhere in neutral territory when we were done, but the meeting never took place. When Lilly finished I was still working and she met her editor, Billy Abrahams, and his friend and co-author, Peter Stansky, in Strasbourg and drove to an inn in Avallon. That night something took place at the inn, something that was never quite explained, an episode I was to think of years later as the precursor to a whole series of unexplained happenings. The first I knew of it was a call from Paris.

"I'm in the American Hospital," Lilly said, "I can't tell you why and I don't want you to come. If you come I'll think I'm dying and I'm not. I don't know what's the matter with me and neither does anyone else."

I asked what had happened.

"I'm not sure, I woke up in my hotel room. It was morning and there was broken glass around me and a lot of blood. But I hadn't had anything to drink the night before—not more than a glass of wine—and I hadn't taken a sleeping pill . . . I hadn't done anything but go to sleep . . ."

The story, pieced together later, made her description accurate, but it didn't clear it up. The first night at the inn in Avallon Lilly had gone to her room, and in the morning she didn't answer her door, which was locked from the inside. When no one could rouse her a member of the staff climbed through a window and found her lying down, asleep or unconscious, with a cut on her forehead and the heavy bedside table overturned. Billy asked her to see a doctor, Lillian refused, the next day she felt worse. The doctor who came to examine her recommended that she go to a hospital. Later, much later, Lillian wrote about the experience.*

> I said I didn't want to go to a local hospital, and so a younger doctor was brought in. He did some more tests, whatever they were, and finally concluded that I should go to the American Hospital in Paris, by ambulance. I think it

---

* From *Eating Together*, published by Little, Brown, 1984

was the longest ride of my life—semiconscious, not knowing what had happened to me and being, most of the time, unable to communicate with the drivers, who talked the Alsace-Lorraine French-German that I once knew (because I grew up with it) but had long ago lost and was too sick to remember.

I landed in the American Hospital in Paris, to see my old friends, Gold and Fizdale, the pianists, sitting in the room waiting for me. I still do not know how they knew I was arriving, except that Billy probably called them before he and Stansky drove to Paris.

I don't remember the next two or three days very well, except that a good many tests were done on me. I was in a room with a very nice lady, who gave me a large bottle of perfume for a present when she got up to leave. On my fifth day in the hospital, I began to grow very nervous about the hospital itself, and on the sixth day, I decided to leave.

I packed my bag and carried it downstairs, waiting for somebody to stop me. Nobody did. I went by taxi to Air France and from Air France back to New York. Nothing more was ever discovered about this incident, no cause, I mean, although Robert Lowell, who heard about it and offered to help, thought it was a stroke. Peter, who thought the same thing, met me at Kennedy Airport and was all for transporting me immediately to another hospital. I was all for not going, so we had a royal battle in the airport. (Peter is convinced that any action he does is a piece of giant nobility and entitles him to boss you around, forever.)

I didn't go to another hospital, and I have no idea to this day what caused this episode, although it may have been the beginnings of all that has happened since. But no doctor seems to be interested in it, so it's very possible that Mr. Peter Feibleman is the best doctor of all. . . .

I wasn't a doctor but I was a confirmed and dedicated hypochondriac and people like me often pick up what doctors miss. Lillian's initial response to the episode was anger at Billy for abandoning her but she had no right to the anger and I told her so by phone and by letter. She kept on with it as people do when they're scared, looking for distraction, and when I told her I thought the fuss was diversionary she left off chewing Billy out and turned the anger on me. That at least was familiar and we fought for a couple of days before Lillian dropped it and dismissed the whole episode as inexplicable and not worth thinking about—one of those mysterious and now not infrequent occasions when her body took to cutting up without her. It was the first time I'd been aware that the imaginary separation could do her any harm and I should have given it more importance than I did. The final danger of Lilly's temper was not that it diverted her fear but that it took everybody else's attention along with it.

Over the rest of those years, the early seventies, a lot of notes and letters were written and some still have Lilly's voice in them. Her complaints about me never changed much. Because of her jealousy, and the steady drumming of the anonymous calls, I was both stubborn and open about sustaining whatever life I happened to have when she came to stay with me in Los Angeles and we made a rule that each of us was to come and go in the house freely, without explanation. Since we didn't always like each other's friends we often kept them separate and one night I went out to meet someone for dinner and came back quite late to find Lillian asleep on the living-room sofa with a note on a table beside her.

Dear Vronsky,
    I am off to the railroad tracks—the measure of my bitter love. May the Greek Church reach out and take you back.

Anna

The next week there was another note:

    I did not throw myself onto the railroad tracks. I knew I had to live only for my son, my poor, darling son.
    I did not know then that you would be my son. May God prove you worthy of my sacrifice.

Warm regards
Anna

There followed a flurry of amiable scribblings left on a table or the kitchen counter.

11 p.m.
I am in what we call my bed.

Warmest regards,
L.

Dear Tolstoi—

For reasons too complicated to a non-boasting Jew, it may be necessary for me to call you about 3:30 for a ride home. To that end, I have put the phone in the hall. My regrets to your majesty and disciples.

Your admirer
Mrs. Tolstoi,
Countess

In those days I was given to occasional midnight food binges, a habit she accepted with her usual delicacy and aplomb.

Yes. So Elaine woke you up. Then your mother. Then you took a sleeping pill. Then you worked for three hours, then you went back to sleep. Then Mrs. San Francisco woke you up. Then you vomited. Then, to settle yourself, you ate a can of red beans mixed with Pepsi and mayonnaise. Now you are dozing lightly. Goodbye and I thank you for everything.

Miss Hellman

On a piece of torn and soiled notepaper, written to the Herseys, who were in Cambridge:

DEAR JOHN AND BARBARA.

Thank you for the letter . . .

Mr. Peter rises late and then can never find his stationery: hence this. But Mr. Peter is a fine host except when you have to watch the terrible junk he eats. For example: I rose at 5 a.m., for some reason sleepless, and found Peter eating a piece of cheese cake, followed by cereal, followed by a sandwich made of peanut butter, mayo, catsup, bacon and something green . . .

I go this Sunday to Tucson for an appearance, chiefly because I feel guilty for canceling the teaching course. I'll come back here for a short time and then go to San Francisco for another round with the eye doctor. Perhaps because he had a firmer opinion than the others, I had more comfort from him which, of course, does not mean that he was right or wrong. I will come home, I think, about March 22 or 24.

I can give you only one small present from the wonder land of rich silliness. There is a lady agent here, high powered, young, earning $400,000 a year. At a party last Saturday night she said: "I get tired of working. I wish I was a rich man's Pasha."

Much love to you both
Lillian

And on odd, small, no-count bits of paper left here and there around the house:

. . . I am upstairs. If you come home alone, or bearing gifts, do come and tell me because I may wish to descend for a snack. If, however, I am asleep, cry for an hour and then have a sweet sleep.

L. H.

A car just drove up. Nobody seemed to get out. But it stayed for three or four minutes and then took off. Unpleasant.

Elaine May called. But no Emma, no Anne, no Jill (?). Sorry.

Miss Gooheim [a reporter] will interview me at 10:30. Whatever happens please interrupt by 12:30 by asking if I am coming with you or any forceful suggestions that will get Miss Gooheim out of here.

Most sincerely,
Your Admirer

Sweet dreams, sweet prince.

Clarissa

DEAR WIDE-ALWAYS-AWAKE—
I have gone off and possibly, probably, will return, but who knows where, how, or why under the laws of "freedom" and "liberty." If I do not return, my warmest personal regards and thanks.
The following: 1) Emma called. 2) A man came to the door. I was in a brown bathtowel. He said his name.

I do not remember it, but it was something like Jerry. He said he came to find out if the house was O.K. I explained the bathtowel and asked him to return. 3) Your sainted mother called to speak only to me, although I literally begged to wake you. I will save that conversation in case we meet again, but it had mainly to do with the disaster of the storm here in Laurel Canyon and, obviously, I was giving the wrong non-disaster answers. And so she supplied some of her own about her grandchildren. God bless you.

Please—I cannot see anything in the room—return to the dining table the papers you put away yesterday, the typewriter, Donne's poems, and all other evidence of human existence that you find so disturbing to your guests.

My warmest personal regards and so on.
L.H.

The message about my mother was, had been for years, tinged with a certain malice, since my mother was still beautiful, educated and seven years younger than Lilly. They had known each other since I was six and a polite cold war now existed between them due to Lilly's rivalry about who had the most serious illness and my mother's withheld criticism of Lilly's memoirs. *Pentimento* was dedicated to me, as my last novel had been to Lillian, and was doing well critically and in sales, but it was my mother's view that Lilly's politics were and had always been screwy, that she was now bolstering her misplaced faith in Stalin with stories about her early anti-Fascist activities, stories that were apocryphal and insulting to people who had seen Stalin for what he was in the beginning and more quietly turned against him.

Lilly appeared to sense the silent reproach and launched a counterattack meant to shoot down everything from my mother's upper-class background to her chronic emphysema.

But by then Lillian believed that she herself had emphysema and had convinced her doctor of it, largely, I suspect, by having a coughing attack in his waiting room. Anyone hearing her cough would take it on faith that she had a pulmonary problem—anyone at all, let alone a Park Avenue doctor whose practice the cough put in jeopardy since many of his patients, listening to it, had doubtless hit for the hills, or for another waiting room, another doctor. It never seemed to enter anybody's head that a woman who smoked close to four packs of cigarettes a day might have an occasional respiratory spasm during which her lungs rebelled in a frantic but hopeless attempt to push out the last of the smoke. Lillian preferred to think it was emphysema, liking the official sound of the word and having no idea what it meant: once again her body had taken off without her, once again her mind rejected the unruly actions of her physical self. And anyway, Dash had had emphysema too, so it seemed like a loyal thing to come down with.

I'd been trying for years to get Lilly to another doctor, since some of the advice her Park Avenue doctor gave seemed dangerously diversionary. The most recent thing he'd prescribed—a breathing machine—weighed twenty pounds, its voltage adaptor another twenty, making travel of any kind a little unwieldy considering they both had to be hand-carried. Lilly used the breathing machine every six hours with a faith and dedication that would have been touching if she hadn't kept a lit cigarette going in an ashtray next to it. Her friends seemed to share her primitive belief in the machine and one by one they sat waiting reverently like natives with downcast eyes while she used it. Her expression when she did so was that of a high priestess and I used to wonder why each newcomer approached the machine with such awe until I realized she'd brainwashed them. Given a little time, Lilly and anyone were a folie à deux.

Her more recent friends accepted the machine as an essential part of her makeup and toted it around for her when asked. There was for instance Max Palevsky, a new friend, a kind and generous man who was fond of her. Max had made a fortune late enough in life to remember what it was like to dream of having money and one of the things he'd dreamed of was giving a party anywhere in the world he wanted to give it. He wanted to give it in Egypt and he sent plane tickets to twenty friends, some based in Los Angeles, some in New York or Europe, some as far away as Australia. Among them was a pleasantly gruff man named Stanley Sheinbaum.

The day the invitations came Lilly was planning a dinner in New York, as she did about once a week, and I was planning to sell my Los Angeles house, as I did about once a year. (Lilly had phoned that morning to say that Nora Ephron knew of a good property for sale in another part of California.)

April 14

DEAR PROFESSOR FEIBLEMAN:

I will not speak to Nora Ephron tonight for the very good reason that she is getting married and will, evidently, not be available for some days. She is marrying Carl Bernstein who, to make us both feel worse, has just sold his paperback rights for $1,550,000 . . .

Yesterday, Stanley Sheinbaum phoned me and without mentioning your name I asked him once more to read me the list of people who were going on the Egyptian trip. I have omitted most of the names because I could not identify them, nor could he. But here are the ones I know either something or a little about:

Dr. Derek Denton, who is a very famous Australian endocrinologist; Harold Willens, who was well known during the McGovern and, I think, during the Eugene McCarthy campaigns; Jerome Wiesner, president of MIT; Rabbi [Leonard] Beerman, who, according to Sheinbaum, is the most distinguished rabbi in the country, chiefly because he has not been a hard-line Zionist, and has warned Israel against certain of its policies; Terry Malik, who, as you know, directed *Badlands* . . . and, of course, Stanley offered your name and your credits. I said of course I knew who you were.

Sheinbaum himself I think was once head of that Hutchins stuff in Santa Barbara, and I think he is well known for other things but I can't remember what. He is a nice, liberal gent, who married one of the . . . Warner girls, which is more than you have done.

With my warmest regards to you and yours,

Miss Hellman

When you talk to what you call your mother, will you ask her not to mention the [dinner] party [I'm giving] to anybody? I have only been able to ask a few friends, and I already stand the chance of hurting a good many people's feelings. Thank you, my dear friend.

The Egyptian trip was the first time any of Lilly's friends, new or old, were aware of her impending blindness. Till then she had camouflaged the problem by announcing that her eye doctors knew about it and were not at all worried. What she meant was that *she* wasn't worried, which meant that somewhere she was. The glaucoma had advanced beyond the point where surgical intervention could help, she had almost no peripheral vision left and her eyes couldn't adjust at all to sudden extremes. Sometimes with enough light she could still see to walk or read a little and she could sometimes enjoy scenery from a plane window, but flying over the Alps was like looking down at a bright blinding mirror. Other than that we had a good time together on the plane, though the Swissair stewardess who served Lillian's lunch said, after more than an hour of airborne research, that none of the staff on board, including the two pilots and navigator, were familiar with the American term "goy drek."

Egypt from the air is a minuscule ribbon of timeless green in an otherwise endless desert: after a panorama like Los Angeles, so vast in space and tiny in time, it came as culture shock. Lilly had her own reasons for feeling jolted and it was a few days before either of us could think clearly. By then her breathing machine and its adaptor had been installed in her cabin by Max, and Lilly was more or less adjusted to her surroundings.

By the third afternoon she was sitting on the top deck of the boat Max had chartered, trying to figure out why all the temples were on one side of the river, all the tombs on the other. Our guide, the Egyptian curator of the British Museum, had just finished explaining to her that the sun rose on the eastern bank of the Nile and set on the western bank, so that one bank was naturally given over to worship, the other to death, and was himself trying to understand why Lillian, who understood the theory before the words were out of his mouth, couldn't grasp the facts. By the time I tuned in, their conversation had taken on the weight and depth of profound historical surmise, and it seemed foolish to interrupt and tell the curator that Lilly's problem was not a matter of comprehending the mysteries of life-and-afterlife in ancient Egypt as much as it was a question of not knowing east from west. Any discussion of compass points was a tar-baby subject and I turned away from it to a bridge we were about to go under just as another of Max's guests spoke up within Lillian's earshot.

The woman who spoke, Miss Smith, was what Lillian called "formally pretty," a well-known actress with a great amount of tightly curled golden hair, who affected an Oxford-English accent. She was the sort of person who goes to Europe for one summer and crosses her sevens for the rest of her life. It was apparent from the rigidity of her movements, I thought, that someone had once told her she was a statuesque blonde and she never got over it. She had already come to Lilly's attention once by disembarking in one of the first towns we came to with the remains of her lunch in a paper napkin, walking straight through a circle of hungry-looking children to feed a couple of stray dogs; apart from her sincere feeling for dogs she was an ardent supporter of women's lib and she spoke up eagerly now, having noticed something about the bridge our craft was approaching. It was worth observing, Miss Smith announced, that there were several men standing on the bridge, but no women. This, she explained, was a noteworthy and disturbing example of the condition of women in Egypt, and when Lillian started to laugh Miss Smith got up and stalked off to her cabin.

One of the few subjects Lilly had little or nothing to say about was women's lib, not because she didn't believe in it but because she couldn't stand all the jubilee jabber. She believed as I did that it was a matter of economics—equal pay for equal work—and as long as people limited their opinions to the economic view she was supportive. But when the talk got around to who emptied the garbage she was not; concerning that subject she stood on her own record, since her life was proof of what she believed, and she didn't care who emptied the garbage—or who stood on bridges—or who wore a brassiere. The problem, she said, was not whether a woman ought to wear a brassiere, but whether or not she could afford to *buy* one.

Miss Smith was of another opinion and Lilly spent a week riding her about it, suspicious of her dedication, disliking the carefully set gilded curls, the practiced delicacy of her British vowels, and sensing the hostility and hardness beneath. By the eighth day people on the boat were thinking up excuses to keep them apart and when our guide announced one night that we were scheduled to enter Tutankhamen's tomb the next day—and Lilly seemed interested—everyone was relieved.

In the morning the group traipsed ashore and made ready for the long climb down a rickety ladder that was built at a steep angle deep into the earth. After the harsh sunlight outside, the

sudden darkness inside the entrance to the tomb was so intense
that Lillian had no hope of seeing at all, though she wouldn't
admit it. After Miss Smith had disappeared down into the tomb,
traces of her laugh wafting in the air behind her, Lilly made the
difficult descent with two Egyptian guides helping—one holding
her up by the arms and the other supporting her precariously
from the bottom. It took close to half an hour and when she
arrived at her destination she was not in her best mood. The
tomb was black and damp and hot and uncomfortable. "All right,"
Lilly said, "where in hell is Tutankhamen?"

"I'm awfully sorry, madam," a guide wearing a miner's lamp
said, bowing to her politely, "he's in Chicago."

He was. The Tutankhamen exhibit had been in the States
for weeks and Lillian could have seen him at the Metropolitan
Museum in New York within easy walking distance of her
apartment.

Her language during the grueling rung-by-rung ascent back
up the ladder appeared to shake the walls of the ancient tomb as
she covered every subject she could find in the time allotted. The
two Egyptian guides got an earful of information about thought-
lessness, tourism, men's minds, women's lib, women in general,
affected women in particular, stupidity, illiteracy, life, death, corruption, sex, England, Louisiana and Mississippi.

Back on the ship she turned without stopping to fight with
me on the subject of ignorance in language. Having recently posed
in Blackglama mink as part of the series of ads that asked "What
becomes a legend most?" she felt it incumbent upon her now to
say that the advertising company's use of the word "becomes"
was "illiterate past belief" since nobody could become a legend
just by wearing mink. I said they had used the word in its other
sense and Lilly said there was no other sense to it and when I
brought up *Mourning Becomes Electra* she laughed and then swore
at me. We wound up that night in her cabin, eight or ten of us
and two bottles of wine, talking and drinking and carrying on
till Lilly fell asleep, and the day was declared a success.

But the next morning wasn't. Miss Smith began to pontifi-
cate again about women in Egypt and Lillian made a dismissive
and wipe-out remark before anyone could stop her: Miss Smith
ran crying to her cabin—Lillian felt guilty enough to want to
follow and kill her—and Max diverted her attention by going

over plans for the next day. We were, he said, to meet a woman called Omm Sety, a legend in this part of the world where people believed that she was a soul reincarnated from another era, someone who could recall the ancient past. Omm Sety had been born close to the turn of the century in England, had led an average middle-class life there till the day her parents took her to see some Egyptian artifacts in the British Museum; she looked around her, said she recognized everything she saw and went on to claim that she herself had been a part of that ancient world. Nobody paid much attention to her but she believed so firmly in her former incarnation that she went to Egypt, took up residence and lived there for the rest of her life. She called herself Omm Sety, "mother of Seti," because she believed that she had given birth to the child who became Seti II, a pharaoh whose ancient temple and environs in Egypt were as familiar to her as any part of her more recent childhood in England.

The next morning we went as a group to meet her. Omm Sety was a pleasant and mild-mannered English lady—serious and quiet, intent and not without humor. She spoke happily of her life as mother of Seti II, describing those days in detail while Lillian listened in silence and I waited for her to take the woman apart. Half Max's guests expected her to do the same, the other half thought she might be somehow amused by Omm Sety, and we all turned out to be wrong.

Lilly was polite when introduced and for the rest of the day treated Omm Sety very gently, the way a guest would treat a host's decrepit aunt. On the way back to the boat Max asked what she thought of her.

After a moment Lilly shrugged. "Poor old lady," she said quietly. "She's doing the best she can."

It was such a patronizing remark I broke out laughing, then checked myself. Lilly and Omm Sety were not too far from the same age. In terms of general health Omm Sety was probably in better shape than Lilly (she walked with a cane but there was nothing wrong with her eyes) though otherwise Lillian was right: she was doing the best she could. Omm Sety was one of those people who are born old and stay that way. Lillian was to die like a child at seventy-nine.

If there was no friction between them it was because Lillian had no sense of being an age peer: she was more apt to be jealous of a little girl than an old woman.

PETER: *Did you see that child the Simpsons brought over yester-*
day . . . what a beautiful face! She's only two years old—she
told me herself, "I'm two years old."
LILLIAN: *She's three if she's a day.*

The rest of the trip passed quickly. In the evenings our guide
gave slide-show lectures on the things we were to see the next
day and after that there was poker. Lilly had always been a good
poker player and with a bright Tensor light on her cards she
managed, methodically and slowly, to wipe out the rest of us and
walk away nightly with most of the pot.

One evening the captain gave a party for the crew and passengers. There was singing and dancing and after a while the
sailors on the boat took to cavorting with the Nubians who worked
among them—descendants of the Nubian slaves of ancient Egypt—
men who functioned as women or men, as they chose. Toward
midnight one of the Nubians got into makeshift drag and did a
belly dance while the rest of the crew clapped time; most of Max's
guests joined in the fun, but for some reason the idea of finding
herself in a room dominated by loosely defined sexuality irritated
Lilly, who felt left out of things, as she had sometimes felt in
America among groups of gay people. She went to bed swearing
not to have anything to do with the crew.

The next evening we all went ashore in Asyut, a small port
town that hadn't allowed foreigners on its shores for a quarter
of a century. They had broken the rule for us and there was a
long lineup of horses and carriages waiting by the dock: Lilly and
I went ashore and sat waiting in one while the others were filled.
It was the beginning of an evening she was to refer to later as the
night we almost died.

Dusk was settling in the port and clouds of small birds had
begun to screech in the trees; across the town square a small
group of schoolchildren stood watching as the foreigners moved
from ship to shore. In the fading light the faces of the children
were angry and suspicious, the way people appear at the approach of anything they don't understand, and one of them picked
up a stone and threw it at the first carriage. It struck the roof,
the driver swore and the children formed a line and began picking up stones from the street and flinging them one by one, as if
to ward off an enemy.

One of the horses reared, a driver held him down and Lilly

demanded to know what was going on. She couldn't see the children throwing stones and I didn't want to describe them to her since I was beginning to think that getting off the boat at this hour, in this town, had been a serious mistake. A couple of young boys had crossed the square, their faces furrowed with a look of fierce suspicion. It was a curious look, one I was not to see again until a night years later, when an American woman interviewed in Florida spoke out against allowing three young hemophiliacs who had been infected by the AIDS virus to attend the same school as her own children. The look of ignorance and fear—the face of violence—crosses all barriers and is frightening wherever you find it. The first of the schoolboys threw a stone the size of his fist that glanced off a middle carriage and struck the head of the horse in front; the horse bolted, panicked, and one by one the other horses followed suit.

The line of carriages stove fast into the night, the horses running wildly now, carriages following each other much too close, the whole caravan bumping and whipping through the narrow streets of the town in interminable ricochet: wheels screeching from curb to curb, sparks grating into the darkness as the townsfolk looked on with blank round eyes. A few of the passengers had begun to scream and Lilly, who could see nothing, turned pale, and then ahead of us somewhere one of the horses fell in the street and the caravan came to a sudden crashing halt, people yelling, horses neighing, townsfolk laughing in a kind of enraged and awful celebration, a Walpurgisnacht.

I got out and ran ahead to see; I was gone only a few minutes but when I got back a mob had formed around our carriage. The driver was grinning and demanding *baksheesh,* a tip, for getting us out, and Lilly was shouting at him, angered by her own fear, refusing to pay blackmail in whatever harsh and insulting terms she could summon up.

Just then the fallen horse was brought to its feet and the carriages started to clank dizzily back through the town. I gave the driver his *baksheesh* but he still looked grim and when Lilly went on shouting insults at him I took her by the shoulders and pulled her head against me, covering her mouth. The carriage reeled as a hand tore open the door from outside and a man in the crowd reached in for Lillian's purse. When she pulled it free he laughed and grabbed her foot. Lilly was wearing bright gold-mesh sandals and one of them came off in the man's hand: she should have let it go, but she had just that second realized, I think, how blind she was and how helpless. Instead of retreating into the safety of the carriage she opened the door wider, stepped out onto the fender, put her hand out deep into the flowing darkness and grabbed the first man she found in the crowd by his hair.

The man's cap and glasses came off in her hand and Lilly held them up high and shouted into the mob at the top of her lungs like a crazed general: "Tell your friend to sell my goddamn shoe and buy you a new pair of glasses, you son of a bitch . . . and leave my foot alone!"

There was something wild, something majestic about her standing there as the driver roared with laughter and the carriage went careening back through the dark streets and the crowd to the dock. The passengers all scrambled onto the boat, gathered together like frightened mice in the bar for a drink, and the episode was over.

LILLIAN: *Is that a mouse? . . . What is that?*
PETER: *Nothing.*

 PAUSE.

LILLIAN: *Was it a* mouse?
PETER: *It was and it's gone.*
LILLIAN: *Please tell me the truth.*
PETER: *I am.*
LILLIAN: *Where was it?*
PETER: *It started for the kitchen—it went back under the baseboard when I yelled.*
LILLIAN: *Right there? The baseboard of the living room? Oy.*
PETER: *Lilly, it's the same place the mice are every single year. The mice have been there since the house was built.*
LILLIAN: *Oy gevalt. I want to go to my bed now. Will it get up on my bed? . . . Stop laughing at me, Peter.*
PETER: *I'm not laughing. Yes, I am, it's like a bad joke. How can you be scared of a mouse? You weren't scared of a whole goddamn mob.*
LILLIAN: *What mob?*
PETER: *In Egypt, in Asyut, you stood out on the fender and threatened them, don't you remember? You dared them to come*

*get you—a whole fucking mob—how can you be scared of a
mouse?*
LILLIAN: *What's one thing got to do with the other?*
PETER: *I give up.*
LILLIAN: *How big was it?*
PETER: *A two-inch field mouse.*
LILLIAN: *It has no right to do what it did, Peter, it's against na-
ture. We were sitting here having a private conversation—what
right did the mouse have to come out?*
PETER: *I'll have a little talk with it in the morning.*
LILLIAN: *Point to where it was.*
PETER: *Over by the green chair.*
LILLIAN: *Oy.*
PETER: *Will you please calm down?*
LILLIAN: *I'll get Melvin to put a trap there tomorrow.*
PETER: *It won't do any good, Lilly, it never does. Just tell me
this. How can you be scared of a mouse?*
LILLIAN: *What would I be scared of, a man?*

On the way home from Egypt we stopped in London, then
flew down to Paris and rented a car and drove to Lyons.

The café in Lyons was on a corner and we ordered a *pastis*
and a *fine à l'eau* and fed some cracker crumbs to a pair of spar-
rows that skeetered back and forth over the pavement by the
table. It felt like the end of something or other so we made it the
beginning of something else. We had found a way to be easy with
each other for the first time since Sarasota and sitting together
we took to wondering about the time ahead, how to circumvent
the past and second-guess the future enough to include, in a space
of our own, a little pure fun.

For the next few years there are gaping holes in my memory:
some of the time can be filled in with letters, some with pieces of
a journal I kept on scraps of paper or lumped together in a series
of dime-store notebooks from whatever part of the world I happened to be in when I wanted to jot something down. I had a
habit of not dating journals, as Lilly neglected to date her letters,
and the length of time between the entries is not always clear.

For the making of the movie of "Julia" I have very little.

LA. Friday night
L phoned from NY this morning. She sounded down,
said they sent the script for her approval, but it hadn't oc-

curred to her that she herself would be a character in the story.

She made me laugh about the script—there's a phrase in it that puzzles her. It's from a scene in which the two leads—Julia and Lillian—get into a lower berth on a train and hug each other in a "mock lesbian embrace." She called the producer at home to ask what a mock lesbian embrace was, but he didn't know. They're already looking for a lead—he says Jane Fonda's interested.

LA. Sept. '76

L came out here to do some business and meet with Fonda last week. She stayed in my room, I moved into my workroom—I still like sleeping where I work and so does she. Fonda was simple and straight with her; L liked her right away. The script is a literal adaptation turned out by a screenwriter, Alvin Sargent. Lilly says he complained a lot about how hard it was to do, which amused her. "Alvin talks a lot about the agonies of art—it's a fine complaint when you're writing for money."

LA. March

Some kind of change going on in Lilly. Don't know what. Something about the way she walks and turns her head and the rhythm of her speech sometimes. She's aware of it, I think, but I doubt she can define it either. What in hell could it be?

LA. April. Friday

Talked to L yesterday, she's finished a draft of her new book, the one on the HUAC hearings. I still think it's a mistake, I told her so twice when she started. She always said she wouldn't touch that subject in a memoir and she was right: let other people write about that, not Lilly. You can't blow your own trumpet, and you can't be the heroine of your own life. Not in America—not unless you're in politics or some other form of show business.

Something's screwing up her judgment. Feels as if a gear had slipped inside and she was reaching out for help—it's too frantic. What's she so scared of—what is there I still don't know?

This morning I showed her this page from one of the interviews she did for *Pentimento*.*

* Interview by Nora Ephron in *The New York Times Book Review*, September 23, 1973

Q: I wondered why you've never written about the McCarthy period and the blacklist.

A: I tried this time, any number of times. I never can say what I mean. I tried in this book* to say it in the theater piece. I wasn't shocked in the way so many people were. I was more shocked by the people on my side, the intellectuals and liberals and pretend-radicals—and that's very hard to explain. I'm not really saying it right even now. I mean, I wasn't as shocked by McCarthy as by all the people who took no stand at all. Many of them now think of themselves as anti-McCarthy when they weren't. If they say they were anti-McCarthy, what they mean is that they were anti Joe McCarthy himself, not what he represented. I don't remember one large figure coming to anybody's aid. It's funny. Bitter funny. Black funny. And so often something else—in the case of Clifford Odets, for example, heart-breaking funny. I suppose I've come out frightened, thoroughly frightened of liberals. Most radicals of the time were comic but the liberals were frightening.

LA. April 21.

Talked to L again about her book—she's calling it *Scoundrel Time*—I've read it twice and I'll read it again but I still don't know what to say. She's writing against herself, there's a defensive tone when she talks about it and she sounds unsure. She's so damn sure-footed when she's on target—like her voice when she was proofing the collected plays on the Vineyard, she read Regina's lines in *Foxes* better than Bankhead—and went on cutting the plays as she proofed them. Nobody can get in her way when she knows what she's doing. But this is different, this is wrong and she knows it's wrong. So why is she doing it?

LA. May '76

L on the phone this morning:

"They wouldn't allow *The Children's Hour* in London when I first wrote it—the Lord Chamberlain sat me down in his office and said: 'Miss Hellman, we're well aware of the male homosexual problem in this country, which is of course minor. But to our certain knowledge there is not one lesbian in England.' " Says she fell down laughing in his office.

* *Pentimento*

Am leaving for NY next week for a few days, it'll be nice to see her.

NY. May '76

What to do about the jealousy? It crops up in L when you least expect it but it's there all the time.

Yesterday Muriel* came to see me in L's apartment. I've never made any bones about my feeling for Muriel—L likes her too. When she came, L sat down with her and invited her to the Vineyard next summer. Then we sat and talked for an hour or so, then Muriel said goodbye. I went out to the elevator with her and while we were waiting for it, the door to L's apartment burst open suddenly and she stuck her head out grinning and stared at us. It was clumsy of her. She just stood there staring. Wanted to see what we were doing in the hall. Funny to expose her feelings like that in front of Muriel, but she can't help herself.

Funny too that she doesn't mind talking about it—I asked her the other day why schools teach *Othello* as a jealousy theme when it's so clear that it's not: Othello isn't a jealous man, the whole plot is based on that: Iago works hard to make him suspicious. But a jealous person is *already* suspicious—suspicious of everything, of the turn of a head or the flick of an eyelash. Pushkin noted it and so did Dostoevsky. L listened and agreed, said she didn't know why either, and we went on talking about it for half an hour. "I have a jealous nature," she said, but not the way a grown up would say it—she said it like a pugnacious little girl: "I've always had a jealous nature."

I think sometimes jealousy will drive her off the edge. It must feel like having a cloud of gnats around her head all the time. She suffers a lot from it, more than she admits. The only thing that saves her is pride.

LA. May '76

Silly problem: it seems Fonda gave a newspaper interview in which she spoke of L's seductive quality—crossing her legs, showing the lace on her panties or some such nonsense, and L went up in smoke. Says she's going to demand a retraction, can't be insulted that way, etc. etc. Why is a sexual insult always so much more painful than any other

---

* Muriel Rukeyser the poet, a longtime friend of mine.

kind of insult? I told her Fonda didn't mean anything, she was only trying to pay L a compliment and got quoted out of context. L's been quoted out of context a lot, you'd think she'd overlook it, but she can't—she's up in arms over this one. I still can't get over the feeling that there's something happening inside L—nothing large, but cumulative maybe, like a dripping faucet that nobody pays attention to till the sink corrodes or a pipe bursts. She swears her doctor says she's fine except for the eyes. Maybe I can finally get her to go to another doctor, she's brainwashed this one.

> NY. Waiting Room, ICU Unit
> Lenox Hill Hospital

I wonder if I'll spend the rest of my life worrying about the wrong things, the wrong people. Louise* called day before yesterday, to say DSB† tried to kill herself over the weekend. She has cancer, typical of her not to say anything to me. Louise could hardly talk for crying, I couldn't get all the facts straight, but I called the doctor right away—he said Louise came back earlier than expected to DSB's apartment and found her unconscious but still alive. She's in the Intensive Care Unit at Lenox Hill—might pull through, might not. I got on the next plane.

Been sitting in the waiting room for the better part of two days now, they say she'll probably live: I don't know how I feel about that—she wouldn't have tried suicide lightly. DSB wouldn't try anything lightly. I've pieced the story together the best I can, maybe I should put the facts down so I don't forget again—Lilly is already asking too many questions about it. Nobody would believe what goes on in my family. It went like this—

When DSB was five years old her mother caught her playing with herself as children do. She paid a surgeon to come to the house to perform a clitoridectomy, an operation more associated with certain African tribes than it is with Park Avenue. DSB's childhood was a knockout. She married at seventeen, had me at nineteen, divorced at thirty-three. That's when my father told me about her early surgery, giving it as an excuse for the divorce.

The doctor says her reason for wanting to kill herself is

---

* My mother's housekeeper, Louise George, whom I'd known and loved all my life.

† My mother

the cancer—she doesn't want a mastectomy—he doesn't know why, but I do—she's had enough sexual mutilation. She couldn't stop the clitoridectomy, she was only five, but she can stop this. She almost did. On top of everything else both her parents were suicides, thirty years apart in the same apartment—that's the part Lilly remembers so well and she's right. But she doesn't know all the facts and I can't tell her. I would have, I guess, if DSB had died, but she's not going to die and it's not my business to tell while she's alive, but I wish I understood it better. I wish I understood anything better.

I'll go have dinner with L when DSB's out of ICU. Not till then, I can't handle the questions. DSB's story isn't finished yet, I'm sure of that. I don't know how it'll end but I have a feeling I won't be able to help much, whichever way it goes. She's the angriest person I've ever known, but it's quiet anger—my mother never raised her voice in her life. No wonder I'm comfortable with Lilly's temper, at least it's out in the open—I'd rather be in a storm you can see than one you can't. I love my mother a lot, I think she knows that; I'm sorry for her now—more than sorry—I'd take it on for her if I could.

I wish everything in my whole damn world didn't feel so arbitrarily doomed. Dinner with Lilly will help.

LA. June

The dust has settled. [DSB] agreed to a lumpectomy. When she's done with radiation, she promises to come visit me for a while in LA, she wants to be alone till then.

L has taken the whole business calmly. All she knows about is the suicide attempt, so most of her deductions are wrong—but her advice is still good. Anybody with a difficult mother feels comfortable with L, somehow she can steer you right without needing to see.

She talked a lot about her own mother on the phone this morning—said she'd never understood her till it was too late. Her mother wasn't a middle-class lady, she says, though she herself is. She remembers coming home from school one day and asking her mother to have the sofa reupholstered because the stuffing was coming out. The living room looked threadbare, she was embarrassed to ask friends home from school because of it. Her mother turned and looked at her as if she'd never seen her before. "Oh, does that worry you? Of course I'll have it fixed." But she hadn't noticed it till then.

It's one of the clues to Lilly—she cares desperately how the furniture looks and at the same time doesn't care at all— the same ambivalence she has about the rich.

I'll be happy to see her again. I miss the Vineyard house, it's a healing place. I feel as if I'd eaten a handful of razor blades.

In trying to piece together the odd scratchings I call my journal, I find a gap of over two years with only two events to account for them—the publication of *Scoundrel Time* and the opening of the movie of "Julia."

LA. Oct '77

The pub-date of L's new book was cause for a party, but the wrong party, the wrong cause and the wrong book . . . *Scoundrel Time* is well written but it still sounds like boasting. The rest of us can boast, but L can't—not about that, it's asking for trouble—they'll shred her for it, Podhoretz and his right-wing boys are already out to get her, I keep telling her that but she won't listen, and I'm having trouble with my new novel—I'm too self-involved to think of anything intelligent to say. How do you tell somebody who's going blind that she ought to scrap a whole book? She can't *not* work, she doesn't know how.

NY. March '77

Saw *Julia* last night. A good job, but they had too much reverence for the original—Zinneman and Sargent both stuck to the facts closer than L ever did. Gives it a frozen-in-amber quality that's good sometimes, bad others. It's a small story and too lush a decor drowns it. Lilly liked it more than she expected to, the picture as a whole impressed her. "With reservations," she said. "It's up to its ass in good taste."

Vineyard. July 13

Dinner last night at the Hacketts'. I like them more and more. They're much older than L, and Frances is ten years older than Albert—they've got to be in their late seventies or eighties. They're a touching couple, Albert pretends he's older for Frances' sake and this year he's begun to fake deafness because Frances is going deaf.

On the way home L said, "Did you see Albert's face when Frances tripped on the stoop just now? He turned white. He's more in love with her than he ever was. Imagine somebody wanting you that long—just imagine." She opened the back door and went in and stopped again. "Know something?" she said, "there's never been a time in my life I wouldn't have swapped art for real life if I had the choice. Maybe it's a good thing I never had it."

Maybe it's a good thing none of us had it.

Vineyard. July 14

L just bought a second-hand boat with a young fisherman she likes—Jack Koontz. They made an arrangement: Jack will take paying customers out fishing every day, split the proceeds with L, and take her out once a week. He's an interesting man, big and gentle with her, she's already flirting with him. L flirts with trees, cats, lampposts, anything and everything, it's automatic with her by now. Most people respond—Jack certainly does—his face lights up when he sees her. They'll get along fine.

Vineyard. July 16

Ruth [Mrs. Marshall] Field came to stay with L yesterday. Very noblesse oblige, she insisted on carrying her own suitcase down from the car, I doubt she's ever carried one before. Her way of speaking is at least fourth-generation rich, and Lilly teases her mercilessly about it. They have the kind of unspoken code old army buddies have and teasing is allowed up to a well-defined point. When L crosses the point, Ruth freezes, then L backs off and makes manners.

Ruth divides most of her time between a big summer house in Dark Harbor and her plantation in South Carolina. She has an apartment in New York too and a house in Connecticut. According to L, on winter mornings in South Carolina a servant gives Ruth a pair of gloves, a basket and a pair of scissors, and she goes out to the garden and cuts gardenias for the breakfast table. L had the basket and scissors all ready for her this morning, then said, "I'm sorry Ruthie, I don't keep gloves for guests in the country."

"Only in the city?" Ruth said, and sailed out for some roses. She came back and arranged them while L went on teasing.

This afternoon L was washing the lunch dishes and Ruth

went in the kitchen to help her and broke a glass. She insisted on cleaning it up herself, she found a broom in the closet and then stood a minute or two looking at it upside down as if it had descended on her from outer space. You could tell she'd never seen a broom before except in pictures, she had glass shards flying around the kitchen like shrapnel. L finally went over and stopped her. They struggled with the broom for a little but nobody won. Ruth is strong. I went and got the vacuum cleaner and some wet paper towels.

Ruth has no idea that L put a detective on Fiona—just as well. L spent the afternoon telling her she doesn't understand children and never will.

Vineyard, July

We're back to talking about opening a restaurant. Must be a decade since we started planning. So far we've placed it in LA, NY, New Orleans—and the latest choice, the Vineyard—Vineyard Haven if possible, Oak Bluffs if not. We'll have ten or twelve tables and only three entrees on the menu— three that change daily. We'll need a general manager, but L will seat people and I'll oversee the bar. It's beginning to sound more like a permanent dinner party than anything else— still, we'll have a good time. L wants to start making a list of possible menus right away.

We got a little tight after dinner and started talking about new problems and old lovers. I accused her of collecting scalps and she laughed, but it didn't stop her: Herman Shumlin, Jed Harris, John Melby (the one who had a brief fling with her and lost his job in the State Department because of it), the Czech she almost married, the famous university president, the doctor who seduced her in his office when she was a girl, the well-intentioned rich liberal who never went to bed with her (the one Mike used to refer to as Tip-Top Bread)— they're like polyp-events out of the past when she talks about them, as if they'd happened to someone else. It's the same for me, old passions are like remembering a cemetery. But she'll be sexy till she dies and she knows it—she blushed purple when she caught me staring at her. It didn't stop her talking, she just switched rails and jumped to a story about Hammett and Faulkner. She said it was a story she got from Bennett Cerf. Then she pretended she couldn't remember the story and said she'd have to tell it some other time and went up to bed.

Lillian saved the story about Bennett Cerf for years, no matter how often I asked for it, and told it only once, when we were taping.

LILLIAN: *It was when I was teaching at Harvard in sixty-one that Bennett Cerf came round to see me. By then Bennett was head of Random House, he'd bought Knopf, and Knopf wanted to bring out a reissue of one of Hammett's books.*

I said, "Okay, Bennett, I can't stop the reissue of the Omnibus, or anything new you publish at the old terms, but I'm very angry about Hammett's contract. Nobody ever got in touch with Dash when he was in jail—nobody sent him a nickel all through those years, nobody made a telephone call to say how do you feel, nobody came to the funeral as far as I know—including Alfred [Knopf] . . ." And Bennett said, "You're being very severe about Alfred, Lillian, there are two sides to every question— Dash wasn't very pleasant to him through the years." And I said, "No, I agree, he wasn't very pleasant to Alfred. What's that got to do with anything? I've been talking about financial terms, not friendship terms—Knopf made a fortune on Hammett and they can go on making a fortune if they want to, but they'll get a lot of publicity from me for doing it unless the terms get changed." So Bennett said, "Now, Lilly—Alfred can be a very stubborn fellow." And I said, "Okay, Bennett, just go ahead."

It was a standoff, till Bennett said, "Let me tell you something you probably don't know about. A really shameless incident of Hammett's baiting Alfred."

It happened years ago, Bennett said, at the "21" Club— Hammett and Faulkner were having lunch there, Hammett was published by Knopf, but Faulkner was Random House, so Bennett stopped by to say hello on his way out.

He said the two of them, Hammett and Faulkner, were a little tight, and there was a lot of joshing about what wonderful affair was Bennett off to, and Bennett said he was going to Knopf's for dinner that night with Willa Cather and Toscanini. They both jumped at the name Cather—she was the only American writer they wanted to meet—they asked Bennett to phone Alfred and see if they could come along.

Both of them were very excited about it and Bennett wasn't in a position to turn Faulkner down on anything, so he called

Alfred and Alfred said yes, bring them both—he wasn't crazy about having Dash, because Dash drank so heavily, but never mind.

So Bennett told them he'd be back at seven because Alfred ate absolutely on time and never served hard liquor before dinner—just a glass of sherry or something. He promised to come pick them up at "21" . . . Well, clip-clop go several hours, and Bennett comes back at seven as he'd promised, but they hadn't moved. They looked even more unshaven and they were dead drunk—they'd been drinking all day long.

Bennett got them out to a taxi but he did it reluctantly—he knew there'd be trouble. They were filthy-looking, and he had a terrible time getting them into the cab. They all got out at Alfred's and Bennett got them upstairs.

They sat down on a couch and Alfred said to Faulkner, "It's a great honor to have you here, Mr. Faulkner—I have a number of your books . . . I wonder if, before the other guests come, I could bring them out and you'd autograph them." And Faulkner said, "Yes, indeed, sir, it'd be a great honor for me to do that for you." So Alfred brought out all his books and Faulkner began to autograph them, and Dash fell off the couch and passed out on the rug.

SOUND OF LAUGHTER.

SOUND OF COUGHING.

LILLIAN: *Bennett asked me if that was an unusual thing for Dash to do, and I said no it wasn't at all, when he did it he was out for a couple of days. Anyway, Knopf was very upset. "Isn't that a disgrace? A once talented man—look what's happened to him, look at that . . ." And Faulkner got up from the couch with great dignity, put his books aside and said, "Where I come from, sir, people don't talk that way about their guests. That man's done nobody any harm—no harm at all, just sleeping away as nice as he can be," he said, "didn't steal a horse and ain't let a pig out. That man's my friend, and I can't stay in a house where my friend is talked about that way—we don't allow that where I was born."*

So Faulkner started out of the room to the elevator, still with great dignity, and Bennett followed and tried to persuade him to

come back. But Faulkner said that would be against his princi-
ples and as he said it he fell down drunk and hit his head on the
radiator and passed out and had to be taken to the hospital.

SOUND OF LAUGHTER, COUGHING AND SNEEZING, ALL AT ONCE.

LILLIAN: *Isn't that a wonderful picture of two writers? They never*
did meet Willa Cather.

Vineyard. Monday Oct 11th
We had a nice time today, the kind we used to, a beach
picnic at Gay Head. L made meatloaf sandwiches, I made
chicken salad, we took hard boiled eggs and a bottle of wine.
The air was crystal, Indian Summer—October always was the
best month on this island. We got a couple of beat-up beach
chairs out of L's shack and then didn't use them. She still
sticks to her ritual of undressing under a towel, then standing
up naked—I still laugh but she doesn't mind.
We were both in a good mood and lying in the sand L
said the only large-sounding thing of its kind she's said since
I've known her. It didn't come out of a conversation, she said
it in space, "You're the first since Hammett."

LILLIAN: *Did I say that?*
PETER: *Yes.*
LILLIAN: *I think I must have meant that you were the first person*
I'd . . .

PAUSE.

LILLIAN: *Oy.*
PETER: *What's the matter?*
LILLIAN: *I was about to say you were the first person I'd slugged*
it out with.
PETER: *Uh-huh.*
LILLIAN: *Terrible word. Terrible idea.*

PAUSE.

LILLIAN: *Or maybe it's not, maybe it's all right. If it comes out*
right in the end, it is. I meant that you and Hammett were the
only two people I've loved, for a totally different set of reasons.

PAUSE.

LILLIAN: *You're also the only two people I've never forgiven.*

Vineyard. October 23

Preparations all day today. L is revving up for a dinner party. She got another anonymous call this morning, told me about it at breakfast. Whoever it is, you'd think they'd get tired—the purpose is still to warn her about me and my phi-landerings, I gather—precious little to report these days. L didn't dwell on it, she brushed past the subject and went back to her guest list.

The party sounds like one of the dinners she gives when she's feeling rattled, like a general amassing his forces and putting them through a dress review. She senses trouble, I think, but it's not coming at her from outside: she's wrong about that—the trouble is inside.

Too many unexplained goings-on in my world. I hope I'm not having a crack-up and don't know it.

Vineyard. October 28

Went to NY on Monday, lunch with magazine types, dinner with DSB. I wonder sometimes if my attachment to L came out of some idiot rebellion. Not that it matters. Once somebody owns real estate in your gut, why you sold it to them is unimportant. The point is, you sold it.

But why do I always feel like such a stumblebum with my own mother?

That was the winter Lillian and I had a disagreement that we sometimes referred to in later years as "the ashtray fight." It was the end of an annual discussion we'd been having about a couple of ceramic plates I kept in my house, given me by my mother.

LA. January, '78

L is staying for a couple of months, in the big bedroom as usual, and last Friday we decided to cook dinner for some friends. An hour before they came we both started to straighten up the living room at the same time. L took the two ceramic platters, the ones I use as ashtrays, off the coffee table and put them out in the kitchen. I found them in the sink, rinsed them off and put them back in the living room. A minute later they were back in the sink. I carried them in again and stood in front of her with them. "These go on the table," I said.

"I don't think so," she said.

"It's not a question of what you think," I said, "that's where they go."

"Forgive me, but you're wrong," Lilly said. "It's foolishness to put them in the center of everything, they're hideously ugly and there's no room—I need the space for the steak tartare."

"Tartar steak," I said, "not *steak tartare*. Saying it in French is affected, you learned that from some headwaiter. And they're not ugly."

"Yes they are, darling," Lillian said.

"I happen not to think so."

"Really? I'm surprised at you," she said, "you usually have such quiet taste."

"I do compared to you."

"That's an unnecessary remark."

"This whole discussion is unnecessary," I said, "they're my fucking ashtrays and it's my fucking table and I'm putting them back."

"Well, of course put them back if they're that important to you," Lillian said, smiling, "I had no idea you cared so much about them. You can see why I was confused—to me they're just cheap-looking Mexican junk from Tijuana."

"They're not Mexican," I said, "they're not junk, and they're not from Tijuana. You know perfectly well where they're from, we go through this every single winter. They're fine ceramics, they're from Istanbul, and they're a present from my mother."

"Why don't you put them on the wall?"

"I don't want them on the wall—I want them where they are," I said. "I'll put you on the wall."

"That would be foolish," Lilly said, "I'm not a present from your mother."

"I'm not so sure."

"That's a disgusting thing to say," she said, "I'm going to my room now . . . I'll pack my things and leave right after dinner—I can't stay in the house of a man who thinks so little of me, I'm very pained by that remark. Your mother and I live in different worlds. It's a tribute to my feeling for you that I tell you the truth about those ashtrays, and in return, you insult me."

"Let's not get so high-minded," I said, "you've been gunning for those ashtrays for years. Maybe it's time you remembered they're just ashtrays."

"It's time one of us remembered," Lillian said.

She stalked upstairs to pack her things and I went out and smashed both ashtrays on the terrace. We managed to get through dinner without killing each other by being extra polite to other people and L didn't leave, but she stopped speaking to me for three days.

LA. Thursday

Nora Kaye called this morning to talk about a screen-play, something to do with ballet dancers, said she'd been thinking about it a long time and Herb* will direct. I told her I couldn't work on anything till I finish my novel and this afternoon I got another call from [a studio executive] who wants me to do a polish on the script I wrote for them. I said the same thing, he told me to shelve my novel, and I told him to shove his script. Lilly overheard both conversations.

"Can't you talk to people without sounding so raw?" she said. "It's time you learned."

"Learned what?"

"The nobility racket," Lillian said.

The nobility racket was the subject of many lectures and sto-ries through the years and was intended in a helpful way, though I couldn't seem to put it into practice successfully no matter how hard I tried.

LILLIAN: *You never did get it right, I've been telling you forever.*
PETER: *Tell me again.*
LILLIAN: *You have got to be willing to go through with it—you never do. The nobility racket works fine if you're willing to go through with it.*
PETER: *Tell me.*
LILLIAN: *All right, but this is the last time. First you figure out the noblest possible reason for what you want to do—then you reduce it to the most modest terms. You never use the word sac-rifice or anything like that. And you count on the fact that your hand may be called by certain nasty bastards (laughing) and you get yourself ready for it.*
PETER: *Give me an example.*

---

* Herbert Ross, film director and Nora Kaye's husband

LILLIAN: *Well, let's say you've been writing a script and you want to get out of it, okay?*

PETER: *Okay.*

LILLIAN: *Okay. You say, "Look, you paid me x amount plus expenses for research, and I've done a great deal of investigating about the subject—I've researched it thoroughly, and I know now that I can't do the story as fiction. It must be done as a documentary, because its power lies in its total truth. But the mistake is mine. I thought it could be done the other way, and I was wrong, so I must pay for my mistake." Then you walk away from it.*

PETER: *And then return the money, right?*

LILLIAN: *Wrong, dopey. You simply say, "I have no money but as soon as I get another job, I'll return to you half my expenses. That's as fair as I can be. But you'll have to wait until I get another job . . . thank you very much, I'm sorry, and I'm grateful to you." Of course nobody's going to take you up on the offer, but you have to be willing to go through with it if they do. That's the secret.*

PETER: *That's the secret?*

LILLIAN: *That is absolutely the secret. Once your shot is called, you have to make good your word, because the news will get around, and you want it to get around, that you're a fine upstanding character.*

PETER: *I see.*

LILLIAN: *A person of honor.*

PETER: *Uh-huh.*

LILLIAN: *I lived on that for a long, long time in Hollywood.*

PETER: *You did?*

LILLIAN: *Certainly I did. I've a reputation as a result of it. That's what Diana Trilling's remark comes from.*

PETER: *What remark?*

LILLIAN: *She said whatever happens to Lillian Hellman she's going to come out looking like a rosy nun.*

PETER: *She did?*

LILLIAN: *Said it very angrily, I'm told.*

PETER: *I hope to God you can keep it up.*

LILLIAN: *Why shouldn't I keep it up?*

PETER: *Scoundrel Time, I keep telling you.*

LILLIAN: *You sure took a dislike to that book, didn't you?*

PETER: *I don't dislike it, I think it's a mistake.*

LILLIAN: *Maybe. I've made mistakes before. I didn't use the no-bility racket on Sam Goldwyn soon enough—even if I did make up for it later. That was a very long time ago, of course.*

PETER: *What happened?*

LILLIAN: *Oh, I once wrote a picture called* North Star. *It was a very good script, I think, a documentary—or a semidocumentary. Willy Wyler was going to shoot it, but he was called into the army. I won't bore you with that part.*

PETER: *Go on.*

LILLIAN: *It turned into a fictional picture with Lewis Milestone directing. You remember Lewis Milestone?*

PETER: *Sure.*

LILLIAN: *Well, I got him Aaron Copland to do the music, and Ira Gershwin to write the lyrics and then I went home to New York. But after a while Goldwyn began to fight with Milestone, and one day I got a panic call from Goldwyn. "The picture is won-derful," he said, "but it would be best if you came to look. Cer-tain cutting must be done."*

I very reluctantly flew out to the Coast and sat in the projec-tion room with him, and after about half the picture, I started to bawl. And Goldwyn got very angry. He said: "I want you to stop that immediately—what are you crying for? What's the matter with you—this'll be one of the greatest pictures I've made in my life! My name is Samuel Goldwyn and I do not turn out junk!" Then he stood up and said: "How dare you cry over my pic-ture?" And I said: "Go fuck yourself. It's a piece of shit, you've allowed this fool to do anything he wanted—it's a piece of whole comedy shit, that's what it is."

That was a Friday, and I went back to the Beverly Wilshire and cried for about two days—Sam called and called, but I wouldn't answer the phone, I didn't want to see anybody. But he called so much on Sunday that I finally gave up and went over to his house.

This is how he greeted me when I walked in . . . He said, "You go around Hollywood telling people you found Teresa Wright. You did not find her, I found her." I walked past him into the living room and he repeated it. "You tell everybody you found Teresa Wright . . ."

I said: "I have no interest in who found Teresa Wright or who didn't, and I've certainly told nobody I found her." (*Of course I had found Teresa Wright, I found her for* Little Foxes.) *I said: "I haven't talked to anybody and I haven't seen anybody—I've been crying about your goddamn picture. My work's gone, that's all I care about." Sam lost his temper immediately and said: "I want you to get out of this house!" I said: "I'll get out of this house when you get out of this room and not before."—I don't know what made me say that idiot sentence—and Sam said: "I'll put you out by force, I'll carry you out!" I said: "If you come near me, you bastard, I'll kick you in the balls, and if I do you'll never walk again. Remember I'm a good twenty-five years younger than you are."*

PETER: *How old were you?*

LILLIAN: *Oh, about thirty-eight.*

PETER: *Uh-huh.*

LILLIAN: *No, wait, it was before I went to Moscow—I was younger than that, about thirty-six, I guess.*

PETER: *Go on.*

LILLIAN: *Well, at this point, Frances flew across the room. You know Frances Goldwyn, don't you?*

PETER: *Uh-huh.*

LILLIAN: *Well, she came flying over, but not at me—at Sam. She said: "I'm taking you out of the room, Sam, please don't talk this way. I'm ashamed of you—Lillian's your friend . . ." And I was saying, "Don't worry, Frances, it doesn't matter—the picture's a piece of junk, that's all that matters . . ." And Sam let Frances quiet him down. But he took it out on me later . . .*

PETER: *How?*

LILLIAN: *Well, I had a very special contract with him . . . Sam had to submit three pictures a year and I could turn them all down if I wanted to . . . but if I turned them all down, I had to add another picture. You see what I'm saying?*

PETER: *Sure.*

LILLIAN: *He said, "You have a submission coming up, you'll be back here in two months to do it." And I said: "I'm never going to work for you again as long as I live. Never." He said: "Then you will never work in Hollywood again." I said: "Okay. We'll see. You go to your lawyer, I'll go to mine."*

Of course I didn't go to any lawyer, but Sam did—I got a letter saying, "This is to notify you that you are to accept no work other than from Mr. Goldwyn." And about a month after that, North Star *opened in New York. They had a very fancy preview and I went. And right in the middle of it, to help things along, the print broke . . . I flew out of my seat on one side of the theater to the projectionist's booth, only to see Goldwyn running from the other side. . . . I heard myself say, "You bastard. You can't even get a good projectionist. And Sam said: "Don't you talk to me! I'll kill that goddamned projectionist! Get out of my way!" He was a man with a terrible temper, but he never got to the projectionist's booth, somebody came and held his arms down.*

    Anyway, to come back to the nobility part . . .

PETER: Yes.

LILLIAN: *There was no money to be returned, because I hadn't taken any—not for future work, I mean—but I refused to accept any more checks from MGM, and word got around that I wasn't for sale at any price—that I was standing on principle. When Darryl Zanuck offered me a picture, I explained what had happened and he said he'd buy my contract from Sam. But he called me the next day and said: "I've never been so yelled at in my entire life—everybody's seen Sam in rages but I've never seen him like this . . . anybody touches you is going to get killed . . . he told me he was going to break me—have me demoted." You know Zanuck was the president of Fox.*

PETER: Yes.

LILLIAN: *No studio runs that way anymore, on one man's say-so, but in those days Zanuck was as powerful as Goldwyn. Anyway, he couldn't budge him.*

PETER: Could anybody?

LILLIAN: *Hal Wallis, finally. Meantime Sam offered me a better contract, at twice the money, and I refused, and word got around again. Hal bought my contract for three times what Sam had paid me . . . it was the talk of the town—my price went up forever. It was unheard of to buy a writer's contract, movie stars got bought, not writers. Who cared about a writer, you know?*

PETER: Of course.

LILLIAN: *Anyway, that was that. The problem was over.* North Star *was a dismal failure, but I was still a success.*

PETER: You never saw Goldwyn again?

LILLIAN: *Oh, sure, Frances arranged it about ten years later. In*

*the name of deep feeling and decency and friendship, she said.
Frances was pretty good at the nobility racket herself.*

SOUND OF COUGHING.

LILLIAN: *That's a bad example of it, the Goldwyn business, but
you know what I mean . . . it's the only way to survive in that
kind of snake pit . . . it's called standing up for a principle, see?*
PETER: *Yes.*
LILLIAN: *A noble principle.*
PETER: *Right.*
LILLIAN: *As noble a principle as you can come up with.*
PETER: *Uh-huh.*
LILLIAN: *And while they're looking at the principle, you get the
money.*

⊱⊱⊱⊱⊱V

I WAS STILL WORKING on my new novel in the autumn of '79, when Lilly went to Barbados for a vacation and I couldn't break stride long enough to go with her. I had a habit of writing letters and forgetting to mail them and I called Barbados to tell her I would be going to the post office soon.

> Heron Bay
> St. James
> Barbados, W.I.

DEAR PETER,

I write again, although I do not really think it is dignified, to tell you that there are many people of sound mind in this country who do not believe you have ever written me a letter to Barbados. But this is to tell you that I am not one of them: you wrote it and you ate it under some ketchup and some kumquats; you sold it to a rare bookdealer; you sent it to Jack Klein.* Much could have happened and, obviously, much did. I really only want to reassure you about my own deep belief.

Mrs. Kitty Hart is visiting my neighbors. Last night she admired the caftan you gave me from Bergdorf—everybody admires it—and when I told her you had given it to me she did not seem to cry, but she asked kindly for you . . .

I continue to work but I dare not reread . . . I

---

* Lillian's accountant at the time, and mine

have a nice doctor visiting me, funny, Viennese . . .
Hannah has, of course, long departed. . . .

I will call you. This letter is only to confirm my
deep belief in your devotion and in mine.

I guess I am fairly o.k. I sleep most of the time;
life is less tough that way. I have lost the wedding ring
you never gave me.

Anyway, I am grateful.

> With the greatest respect to you and
> your lady mother, I am, sir,
> Miss Hellman

When she came back I flew to New York and spent Christmas and New Year's there, but as soon as the holidays were over
I went home to work and in January I had to tell her again that
I couldn't travel with her, this time to London, where she was
scheduled to give a couple of lectures.

I called her again as soon as she got there.

> Claridge's. Wed.

DEAREST MR. PETER,

It cheered me to hear you last night—cheered me
so much that I gave the taxi the wrong Russell address
for dinner and was 40 minutes late. And it wasn't a
good night for him—his Pa had just conked off, leaving
him Lord [BLANK], but his half brother had gone back
fifty years to contest the legality of his birth. (Do you
remember I told you that he had been known as the
bath-tub baby?) The papers are full of it and it's pretty
silly stuff; poor soul, pretending he doesn't care. I've
just talked to Marti* and if I can get back from Robert
Lowell's in Kent, we'll have supper together on
Sunday.

It's been nice here, anonymous, without care, suspended. I don't think it's self-pity, but my life has always been so full of earning a living, or the
responsibilities that came and that I asked for, I guess.
It isn't that I regret them—I don't think I'd be much
without them—it's that it's nice to have them gone for

---

* Marti Stevens, a friend to whom I had introduced her

a few weeks. And it's a beautiful city, very changed from when I first saw it young, but handsome in that 18th Century way that I think begins to be the period I understand.

I think about you very much. I love you very much.

Lillian

Claridge's. Sat.

DEAR MR. PETER:

This is now the third time I have written this week with no written word from you. Twenty years ago, I would have been a suicide; now it simply seems life's text-book, the way of the world. But it certainly keeps me from giving you Maclean's* compliment about your last book.

Today I am going to Macleans in Kent and then to Lowell's—a few miles from there—for lunch tomorrow. *That* makes me nervous. You were living in Spain and so did not see me through the years with Lowell, nor his bouts of insanity, nor his former wife's famous attack. And this wife, Lady Caroline Guiness, I knew very slightly years ago, silent and I believe, empty. But no emptier, I think, than the talky ladies I've had for the last few days. I may make a new rule: never to listen to anybody who summarizes themselves. "I never care about money." "I always—" "I sometimes."

It's wonderful weather. For the first time in years I've slept my head off, smarty—it's a dead world and very attractive—I bought you an English 1st edition of Dostoevski and then found out it cost $2300. I canceled it. But money hasn't to do with love and love won't have to do with much either unless you find time to write to me instead of standing over a charcoal grill.

Most sincerely,
Miss L. H.

Claridge's. Monday.

DEAR SIR,

Last Wednesday when you were kind enough to call me, you told me you had already written. I be-

* Her British publisher

lieved you for reasons not worth this paper, and when your letters did not arrive on Saturday, I caused such a fuss downstairs that they sent, at great cost to me, a messenger to the Central Post. Your letters arrived this morning bearing a postmark of last Friday! I guess there is sense in writing and not mailing, perhaps if you mean to use the documents in a journal for your later years, but then please say so and do not tamper with the human heart as you certainly would not deceive the heart of a dog.

I had dinner last night with Marti . . . it turned out most pleasant. She is deeply devoted to you and she is a nice lady . . . she insisted upon buying me dinner—it had been arranged the other way—and now I must limp four blocks to find a florist.

I had a nice weekend. The Macleans' for Saturday, a pleasant house, and two funny, nice children. Then they took me ten miles away to Cal Lowell's and his newish bride, Lady Caroline Guiness, in a magnificent house, very run down, but very grand, and I stayed for lunch which was long enough but didn't see their new . . . son because at the age of 5 months he was out swimming in the English Channel. . . .

My London agent just paid a visit full of gloom about the possibilities of the book* but so, at this minute, am I, except I don't think about anything much, except sleep. And you.

I hope you will see fit to write me again and to find somebody to mail it.

I miss you very much and wish you would stop talking about work and tell me what work. I am not a tattle tale.

Much love,
L.

DEAR MR. F.

This is my second note today, perhaps because I miss you so much.

_____

* *Scoundrel Time*

For the same reason I called your ma. I cannot repeat the conversation because I do not understand much of it. Except she says the doctor speaks of "remissions" but not a cure. Cure! Two months ago she had a week to live. You are the craziest lot I have ever known and may even be the most dangerous.

> Admiringly,
> LH

DEAREST PETER.

I left two weeks ago today and this is my third note this week and it is enough to make me cry because of course, you have not written to me [since Friday] and have, in fact, denied knowing me to three royal ladies and two fags. I am crying.

I write under great handicap as you well know. There is only one remedy for the terrible rejections that *Women's Wear* has already printed about me—sell your Hollywood house and give me all the money.

> Miss Heartbroken

For a week or so after she got back to New York Lilly went on writing letters. I had sent a section of my new novel to her apartment so that it would be waiting for her when she got back. After reading it she called, then followed the call with a note.

DEAR MASTER.

This is a good day. Please always think you've written another fine book and a long, good serious life is ahead of you. Maybe—and I have thought a great deal about it—the so-called lost years were not lost at all: they were, obviously, preparation.

> Yours in admiration, respect, love
> Miss L. Hellman
> Prophet, Seer

DEAREST PETER,

It is now four hours after my last letter. I have felt the need, as I felt it last night in my second call, to separate what I sense from what I know. I do not, however, know enough to write in detail about the hows or whys, but, for a long time, except for work, I have thought you are marking time. There is nothing wrong with that, maybe even good, but there are signs of self injury along the way . . . and maybe you and I come under them, although that is not my worry in this letter. The new book is going to be wonderful and already speaks for itself. But you are getting sick more than you realize; you have a kind of lassitude that maybe you need from time to time, but that neither you nor any of us should accept for very long. And all kinds of other, more mysterious lockings-away. I do not mean to lecture or to take the place of a doctor. I mean only my deep concern for you and the work, now as close to me, maybe closer, than my own.

Much love
Lillian

I said a foolish thing last night: I blamed what I sensed on Los Angeles. Foolish because I don't know that.

DEAR LILLY:

Glad you're back in civilization. No use gadding about the Midlands, you know how you are.

I do not know how you are, but I hope to soon, and I hope it will be from observation, not just hearsay. Get your ass out here, Lilly, it's March and I love you.

P.

DEAR MR. FEIBLEMAN.

It is not easy for me to write, but it is necessary now to tell you that not only do I love you very much, but I believe you have come, will continue to come into a fine, sensible, almost responsible place in this world and that will lead to many fine things including splendid work . . .

My warm regards and good wishes to your family.

Lillian Hellman

DEAR MISS H:

I never was much of a correspondent, but I liked your phone call last night. Am I to wait now until I know which plane madam will be taking?

It is my view that you should know that you are missed.

Regards,
Mr. F.

P.S. I've been working long hours and am lonesome and extremely sorry for myself. Any time you have the need to write a letter telling me how much you miss me, I want you to feel free.

DEAREST P.

This is my small, sad, crippled writing. But it will tell you I love you and miss you and need you . . .

Love,
L.

DEAR LILLY:

More.

Love,
P.

DEAR MR. F.

I cannot write a love letter because I cannot write anything [because] I have such trouble following lines. But I do love you, almost, or on some days to the point of reverence. Not every day, but many days, and that is not usual for my nature. I also think you are a very good writer, handsome beyond belief, courteous, generous, very educated for a Jew, witty, healthy when you want to be, and more charming than Don Juan ever could have been. I think a few other things, too, such as maybe you are crazy, but you can't help that when we consider the loins from which you sprang. I miss you deeply and wish you were buying me dinner at Lipps and I could see well enough to cut it. Life slapped me hard the last few years and in these last weeks it seems to me all stuffing has come out. But maybe a little will come back although now it is not a question of hope: I am beyond that, I think. I live on typed words and nothing means much.

But you do and this is my love letter and has taken me a half hour to write. I love you.

Miss H.

When she had caught her breath from the London trip Lilly came to see me in Los Angeles and I put her in what we had both come to think of as her room. I knew from her tone that she needed to be fed and tucked in for a while, like a small child who has been away too long at camp. But after a week or so she began wandering downstairs around seven in the morning in a busy way, only to sit, looking lost, at the dining table, where the sunlight was too bright for her to see unless she had her back to it, and then there was nothing to look at.

It was time for her to go to work but work was getting harder because of her eyes and we began in the evening to talk of writing something together. For a long time she'd been keeping an idea for a movie tucked away in that badly lit, amorphous root cellar of the mind—the place writers use to germinate stories. She told it to me in a sentence or two, a good film idea, the kind you know is good the instant you hear it, and we began to talk about it, making notes on odd scraps of paper.

The idea was that many people live on the brink of something most of their lives without being aware of it, so that a chance circumstance can tilt them over into danger. It was to be dramatized like this:

There is a gathering place in a given city—a restaurant, say, where people meet before a concert or an opera. Eight or ten of the tables are always reserved for the same clients, most of whom are known to each other at least by sight. At one table is a distinguished lawyer who is up for political office; at another a couple of music students; at a third a pair of elderly women who have been best friends all their lives; at a fourth a successful young businessman with his fiancée, etc.

Into the restaurant walks a mystery woman—a visitor to the town—who asks for a table alone. For the next few minutes, a couple of people at each table think they recognize the woman as someone out of the past . . . and in each case her appearance precipitates a dangerous situation. The lawyer thinks she was once witness to an unsolved murder that would ruin him if it were made public; another man thinks she's a woman he was once in love with, and so forth. Maybe a couple of tables agree upon who she is—maybe not. The rest of the movie is devoted to each person's story. By the end, fear has taken over the town and someone will try to kill the woman, still identified only as "Madame A" since no one can be absolutely sure who she is—and so she is a threat to all.

Lillian's idea grew as more detail was added and by the end of a week we had most of the characters. The notion of a miniseries was still relatively new in television, only a couple of them had been made, and no one yet knew whether the form would catch on. But we talked to one of the networks about the idea, sold them an option and went to work.

We worked at opposite sides of my round dining table overlooking the city and Lilly's typewriter had to be moved with the daylight so that the sun could be kept behind her, the light on the page. She worked hard, typing in upper case, chain-smoking all the time, condensing her story to the fewest possible scenes, the least dialogue. The segment she'd chosen to do was about the lawyer's family and the long-ago murder and she flattened the tone of it every step of the way, taking out any hint of unnecessary drama and providing no help to the reader in the form of descriptive narrative. The distillation she was left with was dry as a bone. It was odd, I thought, that a playwright accused of melodrama should diminish the rumble of her own story to such a degree that it would take a director—or an imaginative reader— to know the dramatic possibilities it contained.

I made up my own characters and story to fit the general plan and when we were done we put the two together and submitted the whole script-synopsis to the network, which kept it a month, paid us, and said they couldn't use it. A few weeks later another network made an offer for my section alone and we turned it down, but no executive at any network seemed able to read Lillian's work in this form—maybe in any form—and know what it was about: her name was said to suggest something called "serious writing," a term considered lethal to any television project, and no amount of doctoring or talking fixed that. (Today, in the light of recent world events, the script of *Madame A* has a curiously modern quality, the strength and sharpness of the drama come across better than ever and the story is strong and clear.)

LILLIAN: *You never learned how to talk to those television people, did you?*
PETER: *Sure I did.*
LILLIAN: *Forgive me, but I don't think so—I heard you at that meeting we had about* Madame A. *Either you go hats-over-the-windmill and blurt it all out, or you try to sound shrewd. You can talk any way you like, honey, but for God's sake don't get shrewd. You're not, and those kiddies are—it's all they are, they have nothing else, but they're shrewd past belief. Take a high moral stand. It's the only thing that buckles them.*
PETER: *How can you take a moral stand about nonsense?*
LILLIAN: *You've heard me do it often enough, you ought to know how by now. You have to use words like "dignity" and "truth" and say things like "I don't believe decent writers should be treated this way." It's not hard—it's tone mostly. The trick is to sound high-minded. Haven't you ever heard me sound high-minded?*
PETER: *I always think you sound high-minded.*

> SOUND OF LILLIAN LAUGHING.

> SOUND OF LILLIAN COUGHING.

LILLIAN: *Go fuck yourself.*
PETER: *You're not high-minded?*

> SOUND OF LILLIAN LAUGHING.

LILLIAN *(laughing): Go fuck yourself, honey—just go fuck your-self—go fuck yourself and stay fucked . . .*

After the script was turned down by the network, Lilly began to fear blindness more than ever and she went to talk to a friend, Milton Wexler, the man she'd come to depend on when she needed a certain kind of advice. Milton was the only person I had ever known who could be counted on to speak the truth however unpleasant and no matter what the circumstances, a quality Lillian trusted more than any other; she felt better for seeing him and in April went back to New York more cheerful than she had been in a long time.

In June of that year we met on the Vineyard and went on

with our plans for a restaurant, though Lilly couldn't see well enough to play hostess and I was working too hard to do much else. But thinking it probably wouldn't happen didn't stop us from trying out dishes for the menu and we spent the early part of the summer cooking. We were both controlling-people, and controlling-people are angry people, so we made it a rule for the sous chef never to contradict the chef; but by the second week even that didn't help. When it was my turn to be chef Lilly stood behind me and said things like, "Forgive me, but I wonder if you *mean* to be doing that."

I put the wooden spoon down and turned to face her.

"Do it yourself," I said.

"Have I offended you in some way?"

I said nothing.

"Forgive me, but you don't take criticism well about cooking," Lilly said. "Personally, I like criticism, I think of it as a compliment. It's how I learned to make puddings and sauces . . . I listened to criticism."

"That must be why you curdled the hollandaise yesterday."

"I did not curdle the hollandaise yesterday, and it's highly offensive of you to accuse me of it. Rose came over to ask my advice about something and I left the flame on by accident."

"Okay," I said, "it curdled itself."

"At least I don't burn things."

"Are you saying I burn things?"

"Somebody burns things," Lilly said. "There's a cloud of smoke behind you."

"Will you please get out of the kitchen?"

"Certainly."

"Thank you."

"You're welcome," she said, "and I'm not coming back."

"Good."

"You have a very childish nature, if I may say so."

"You may not."

"I'm going out for my dinner."

"So am I."

But neither of us did and when we sat down to eat we were always polite about what had been cooked—each secretly convinced that the other was a cripple in the kitchen and therefore to be treated with pity and respect.

In July my mother came to visit for a weekend, an event that made all three of us edgy. Her cancer was still under treatment and Lillian felt upstaged by the disease. By then there had been extensive chemotherapy and more surgery for malignant lymph nodes—terms Lillian was familiar with only in the haziest of ways—and on top of that my mother had emphysema. Emphysema was a disease Lilly considered her private turf. In the last years, rather than sit home alone, my mother had gone on trips to places like Siberia and East Africa and the Galapagos Islands, expeditions related to subjects that interested her in science or anthropology.

The morning of her arrival Lilly passed me in the hall and stopped. "I've been meaning to tell you—your view of your mother is distorted," she said, "nobody sees their parents very clearly . . . I had contempt for my mother, I always saw her as careless. And you see your mother as courageous. Too courageous. You ought to begin to see through that."

I said I didn't think I should begin to see through it an hour before her plane landed.

"You have to start sometime," Lilly said.

She marched off down the hall and left me thinking about it. I decided she was wrong but when I picked my mother up at the airport an hour later I thought she was older-looking than I'd ever seen her and I wished she had on a brighter-colored dress.

A little while after that the three of us were sitting out on the deck waiting for the Herseys to come over for a drink. A silence had settled over the table that did not bode well.

For some reason I've never understood, one of the laws of nature has it that any two people you love enough to bring together in the hope that they'll like each other are going to make fools of themselves and hate each other on sight. I hadn't exactly brought Lillian and my mother together, they had known each other for decades and the visit was their idea—they were doing it, they said, to please me—but I hadn't altogether discouraged it either.

Sitting on the terrace, Lilly lit a cigarette and eyed my mother as if taking her measure for the first time. "What's the name of those islands you just visited?"

"The Galapagos," my mother said.

"The Galapagos, yes," Lillian said in a voice meant to sound interested, "how were they?"

"Interesting," my mother said.

There was a silence.

"I saw a postcard you sent Peter from there," Lillian said, "something about stepping around in guano."

My mother didn't answer for a moment and I knew what was coming. Lilly's knowledge of geography was only an extension of her knowledge of anatomy and you could tell from the overcareful way she had pronounced the word that she wasn't sure what *guano* meant. (It turned out later that she thought it was a small country somewhere east of Nairobi.)

"Guano *was* a problem," my mother said slowly, watching her, "but there were thousands of birds—that was fun—and you can see what hooked Darwin. It was worth the trip."

"What did she mean about Darwin?" Lilly said later when my mother had gone up to rest. "She certainly thinks of herself as well read, doesn't she? I wonder what she was *really* doing in guano."

"Guano isn't a place, Lilly," I said, feeling more and more hopeless, "it's birdshit."

"I think it is too," Lillian said in a satisfied way. "I'm glad you're beginning to see through her."

The rest of the weekend didn't go any better. The two women seemed intent on appearing stupid to each other and nothing I could do or say made any difference.

> Vineyard. Sunday afternoon
> L gave a dinner for DSB last night and they both had too much wine. DSB drank out of nervousness, she knows better than to drink with the chemotherapy, and she began to look sleepy right away. Her eyes were closing and by the end of dinner she sounded fuzzy when she spoke. I had expected her to impress my friends and when she didn't I wanted to kill her and put her out of my misery. While she was looking drowsy, L had some more wine and got argumentative over nothing. All in all, the evening was a disaster, but it was only a disaster to me—they were in fine shape this morning. I'm a basket-case.
>
> Why in hell has my gut been in turmoil all weekend? Why can't I relax with it and let people be who they are?

As soon as the weekend was over I resolved to streamline my life, wanting it simple and easy now, hoping to clear the air of leftover smoke from old battles. I had a sense I was going to be needed and I was beginning to know that friends could help each other as long as they base the need on pure affection. The best of friends are empty-handed. Lovers carry loaded guns.

Lilly spent the rest of the summer trying to work and make winter plans. It seemed more important to her than ever to know what she would be doing next January, next March and in early spring as well. She'd always felt lost without plans but there was another incentive now, an unspoken reason for wanting to lock in far-off dates, as though by ensuring a fixed time and place to do something, anything, she might somehow control the future. And so when Max Palevsky offered to charter a yacht for next year and take some friends around the Caribbean for a week, Lillian agreed at once. Next year would come before you knew it, she said. Meantime she went on churning in place, like someone treading water while the tide goes out.

⊱⊱⊱⊱⊱VI

ON THE FIRST of August the summer before the Caribbean trip I found a package in my room, a birthday present from Lilly. It was a portrait of her painted by Luis Quintanilla—a painting Hammett had liked so much he kept it with him wherever he went. It wasn't a flattering portrait, her face seemed too hard and full of makeup, the brow too worldly-wise. I thought it made her look too old and Lillian thought it made her look like a three-times divorced editor of *Vogue*. But you could tell she approved of something about it and it was accompanied by a note.

> For you, for me, and for your mother for a winter's tale.
> Miss Hellman, The Glory of the Continent

Dinner parties were fast and furious that summer, as were house guests: Hannah Weinstein came to visit; Mike and Annabel Nichols came; Dick Poirier, who hated the Vineyard, came as well. People seemed to sense something in the invitation and rallied without knowing why.

By September Lilly's face had begun to take on a determined expression—a hard look that could turn into a radiance when something amused her enough to pull all the lines up into a laugh. Whatever was shaky about Lillian, you could still trust her laugh, but by then a lot of people, many of them strangers, had begun to tell her that she had a beautiful face—a compliment that made her nervous.

"I know exactly what they mean," she said, "it breaks my

223

heart, I was never pretty. When I was young, women used to say 'Lillian has lovely hair.' It meant they couldn't think of anything nice to say about my face—it's what that remark always means— and now that I look old and tough and haggard, they say I'm beautiful. Women ought to shut up—they talk too much."

Early in October she went back to New York and I went home. After that she called twice a day, sometimes three times, and when she didn't have a reason she made one up, though it was seldom necessary, since her life never seemed to want for incident.

LA. Oct. 2nd

L phoned this morning to report on something that happened in her neighborhood liquor store. The owner of the
store called to tell her a strange man had been hanging around
asking questions about her. Somehow my name came into it,
she said, and she was worried: "It's the same man who's
making the anonymous calls, it's got to be, who else would
bother to spy on me? I'm beginning to be afraid, I don't like
his coming so close to where I live . . ."

Something about her tone embarrassed me more than it
scared me and I felt like blushing for her, I don't know why.
Lilly fussed and fumed a little, then hung up. She called back
an hour later to talk about something else.

Why do I keep expecting disaster?

Scoundrel Time triggered some bad press but Lilly's fame was still on the increase and there were a lot of interviews that year in print and on television. In December she called to tell me that a young journalist had come to interview her, a woman who was in such awe of Lillian she was tongue-tied. "She was a very intense young lady—early Radcliffe, I think, the kind that lean on their pearls."

I asked how you could lean on pearls.

"Oh, you know," Lilly said, "she wore a single strand of them with a plain white blouse and a tweed skirt, and while she was asking questions she put a finger inside the strand and leaned forward. I think it was meant to look simple and sensitive. Anyway, she said she worshiped me, that's the kind of lady to look out for, and this morning she mailed me the interview she'd writ-
ten. Here's her description of me . . . are you listening?"

I was.

"Okay," Lilly said. "Quote: 'When Lillian Hellman smiled, I sat admiring her face. That wonderful stone face that looks as if it had fallen off Mount Rushmore.' "

She coughed for a few seconds while I chuckled. "It's all right for *you* to laugh—nobody said *you* fell off Mount Rushmore. The bitch. It's getting so I can't let strangers in the apartment, I'm a sitting duck here."

She went on for a few minutes about it and swore she wouldn't give interviews to strangers in the future, then about a week later called to say that a French movie director was coming to see her and she was going to do some detective work.

The object of his visit was of great interest, she said, not to her but to me. It had to do with a novella of mine called *Fever* that had been published long ago and been picked at by people ever since; Lilly went back over its history to make sure she remembered it accurately and could refer to it, if she had to, with the French director. The novella was about a friendship between the dying madam of a New Orleans whorehouse and a little boy, and had been lifted whole by another novelist, Romain Gary, who had, according to Simone Signoret, gone off the deep end toward the end of his life and begun to plagiarize other people's work: along with a couple of stories he had lifted from other writers, he took *Fever* and transplanted it in Paris, a fact that had caused a minor twinge in the French press because Gary's version won a prize before anybody recognized it, and because the original, *Fever*, had already appeared in Paris years before, published by Gallimard and translated into French by Simone, who wanted to play the madam.

At the time Lillian had vacillated between telling me to sue for plagiarism and encouraging me to forget about it. "If I had a penny for every writer who lifted Regina out of *Foxes* I'd be a rich woman," she said. "You can waste your life on that kind of thing—better use the energy to write something else."

It was good advice and I had followed it, by which time Katharine Hepburn had taken *Fever* to Warner Brothers, saying she wanted Simone to play the part and that she, Kate, would direct it; Warners bought it, paid me to write a script, then decided that Simone wasn't a big enough star in America to carry a movie alone. Things came to a standstill until Simone, out of pique, did a French film of Gary's plagiarized version; the movie she did was called *Madame Rosa* and was shown in the States to enormous critical approval. Simone began to feel guilty and called from Paris saying she was willing to testify for me if I wanted to go to court; Lilly reversed herself and thought I should sue. She had her own reasons for anger at Simone, who'd done *Foxes* on the stage in Paris several years earlier, and, Lilly said, tried to make Regina appealing and "vulnerable." "Goddamn that word," she said, "it's the most misused word in the business—it's all actors think about these days, they don't give a damn what they play, just so they look vulnerable. I wonder what Simone would do with Hedda Gabler. Go all cow-eyed, I suppose. There ought to be a law—actors shouldn't be allowed to think. . . ."

By then she wanted me to sue the French movie company along with the French publisher and by then I didn't want to sue anybody: Romain Gary was dead and so was the issue. Lilly's original advice seemed better than ever and her reversal of it made me suspect once more that something had begun to affect her judgment.

But then quite suddenly there was a new wave of interest in *Fever*. This time it started with Hannah Weinstein, who decided to move the whole thing back in time to the days of Storyville, the New Orleans red-light district that had been torn down in 1917. Hannah spoke to a French director, Louis Malle, and Malle considered it for a while, then decided to drop it and do something of his own in Storyville, using only a couple of elements from the original. The movie he was planning, called *Pretty Baby*, was to be about a young girl rather than a young boy and would star a new and unknown teenaged actress named Brooke Shields.

Then all at once, with no warning, Lillian got a letter from Malle asking if he could come and talk to her about it.

"I'm sure Malle wants me to work on the script," she said excitedly on the phone, "he must know I'm from New Orleans. But I doubt he knows how close you and I are, so he'll probably bring *Fever* into the discussion. I'm a pretty good detective—Hammett taught me. I'll see what I can find out and call you when he leaves, maybe he owes you a nice fat chunk of money."

She called me the second the meeting with Louis Malle was over and I knew from her voice that she had something special to report—I settled down with a cup of coffee to listen.

"Malle didn't want me to work on the script," she said, "I

was wrong about that, he brought his own screenwriter with him. It's some woman named Platt—I think they must be going together, she did most of the talking. She jabbered a lot about the story—it seems one of their characters is the aging madam of a whorehouse—you sure started something, kid, that madam's going to appear in an ice show next. Anyway, they began to discuss what movie actress should play the dying old madam and Miss Platt began to nudge Louis and say things like, 'Oh, please, Louis, let *me* tell it.' And Louis said okay.

" 'See, Miss Hellman,' Miss Platt said, 'we were getting ready to cast, but we still didn't know the *character* of the madam— what she was truly like and all—so we couldn't make up our minds what actress should play her . . . then one day I started leafing through a magazine, and I saw this remarkable picture. It was an ad, a black-and-white photograph of you wearing Blackglama mink, and you looked so elegant, Miss Hellman, I couldn't believe my eyes—I've never seen a woman look that elegant—so I turned to Louis, and I pointed to the photograph, and I said, "Louis—*there's your old whore!*" ' "

Lilly's voice had risen before it stopped and I laughed so hard I dropped the phone and broke the connection and had to call her back.

"Just go on laughing," she said. "First Mount Rushmore and now this."

I asked what she had done with Miss Platt.

"Offered her another cup of tea," Lilly said. "What else?"

I asked why she hadn't thrown her out.

"You don't understand anything about life," Lilly said. "If a strange woman came to my apartment and made a semi-nasty remark about one of my plays I *might* throw her out. But if somebody calls you an old whore, you just hand them a cup of tea—and pretend you didn't hear it."

I said it must have been a hard thing not to hear.

"Not really," she said, "Miss Platt wasn't trying to be unpleasant, she was trying to talk me into playing the part. Peter, please stop laughing."

"I can't," I said, "are you going to play it?"

"That's not a nice question," Lilly said.

The next spring was the cruise Max had planned in the Caribbean and I picked Lilly up in New York and flew to Martinique where the boat was anchored. There were nine of us in all, including the Herseys; a publicist named David Garth, known as the kingmaker for his talent in helping elect politicians; a friend of Garth's; Milton Wexler; Max himself and Max's wife, Lynda.

The trip began smoothly.

> Max's boat. 2nd day out.
>
> The boat is a knockout, the weather has held, the crew is good with Lilly. She chews them out every so often, trying to find where things are in her cabin, but they know she can't see much belowdecks and they're gentle with her. She's got Therese* with her, that helps some, but the placement of the breathing machine was a major production and so is everything else in her cabin. No danger of her falling, not on a boat, it's the one place she can't lose her balance, but she's always crashing into things—she's black-and-blue from it. A footstool carved out of teak, an ivory-base lamp, a remote panel that works the lights in her cabin, they all get in her way. When she talks, she sounds as if she were being per-secuted by furniture. "I'm going to have all the fancy junk taken out of my room," she said this morning. "What's goy for amenities?"
>
> I said goys didn't have a word.
>
> "They must have," L said, "I can't very well tell the steward to get rid of the amenities, he won't know what I'm talking about."
>
> But he did know and it didn't help.

On the third day I found Lilly sitting by herself outside on the main deck staring up at a white noon sky. She had her head back and her dark glasses on and I thought she was asleep but when I started to move away she said: "Always leaving me, aren't you?"

I said I wasn't.

"I'm not asleep," she said, "I was thinking."

"What about?"

"The plays," she said, "the 'well-made' plays."

It was a term people had been using in criticism and inter-views lately and it was on her mind more than usual because she

---

* Lillian's housekeeper

wasn't working on anything. The most recent interview had been very specific.*

> Q: There's another common criticism that your plays are too well made . . .
>
> A: . . . The charge of too well made, I suppose, means too neat, too well put together . . . it's basically, I think, a rather foolish charge against anybody, because what is too well made?—why should something be badly made? . . . I think what people do mean by it is that perhaps sometimes the sewing shows, and there I think sometimes it does in my plays. I don't think too often. I hope not, but I think sometimes it does . . .

Sitting on the main deck with no land in view Lilly was silent for a time and then said: "I know what they mean by 'well made' and by 'melodrama' too . . . and the other things I'm accused of now. It's overplotting, that's all. Just overplotting."

She was quiet again and I took it to mean she was getting her thoughts in order to talk about it. The year before, when the subject first came up, I had looked up *melodrama* in the dictionary and found that its original meaning was a drama with a happy ending. Lillian's definition was drama without purpose, but her plays all had purpose—sometimes too obvious a purpose—so it wasn't that.

It wasn't till much later that she said it plainly and when she did she went into detail.

LILLIAN: *The trouble is, it now seems clear to me that the criticisms of me may have been wrong in essence, but they were right in certain facts. I didn't know how to plot, you see . . . I was always struggling with it . . . and by* Autumn Garden *I began to understand that I mustn't plot as much as I had been—began to understand it instinctively—and in* Toys in the Attic *I proved it. Almost. But I'd gone through too many years of plot troubles . . . I wasn't able to carry all the plot twists and turns that Hammett did. It took me years to figure out that he had trained me to the plot idea without at all meaning to—because he didn't like plotting himself. He did it but he didn't like it.*

SOUND OF COUGHING.

* Interview with Fred Gardner on audiocassette, Jeffrey Norton Publishers

LILLIAN: *It was the worst mistake I ever made. . . .*

There was something impressive about Lillian's courage whenever she confronted anything wrong in her work and sitting on the boat deck that day I waited for her to go on but she didn't. When I looked at her eyes under the dark glasses, she was asleep.

By the fourth day of the trip her knees and arms were cut from bumping into things and then something else began to happen, something more ominous.

It started with Lilly going to sleep wherever she happened to be on the ship, in public or not, a piece of behavior that was totally out of character for her. We all ate at the same table in the ship's dining room and several times during lunch or dinner her eyes would close. Then she'd wake up a minute later, startled, and doze again.

It was an old joke between us, the subject of sleep, I'd been kidding her for years about refusing to admit she slept. The denial was always the same—"I wasn't asleep, I was thinking"—and down through the decades she had said it in trains, planes, sofas, chairs, movie houses and theaters, on kitchen stools, rocky ledges and once standing up in a bus. On land, sea and air she had declared her inability to sleep in a voice that brooked no argument and I had always gone along with it, as a Southern gentleman is taught to do. The lie was her birthright, part of her heritage and tradition. Only insensitive ladies slept during the heat of summer in the antebellum South, and what shattered the tradition was not the Civil War, but air conditioning. It was gone with a cold wind. After that, ladies of a certain class didn't sleep not because they couldn't but because sleep was considered vulgar, a more personal act than certain bathroom functions. To sleep in private was possible; to sleep in public was out of the question. But to doze off at meals, in the middle of the dining room—at the same table as the other guests and in full view—was not even plausible. The only explanation was that she didn't know she was doing it.

> Max's boat. 6th day out.
> She does it every breakfast, lunch and dinner, like narcolepsy. I don't get it. Too many sleeping pills? She's been taking one every night for years, maybe she's doubled the

dose. But she doesn't sound like it, her speech isn't thick and her mind is clear. The little spasms of sleep never last more than a couple of minutes.

I lectured her again this morning about changing doctors. She ducked it by saying she'll take care of it as soon as "this situation ends" and she has time to think. But this situation won't end because there'll be another situation by then and she won't have time to think because she doesn't want to—not about that. It must feel like thinking about death, but so what? The ends people will go to in order not to think about death are always surprising but if you're going to knock down their defenses you'd better have an alternative and I can't think of one.

Max's boat. 9th day out.

It's still happening. Worse, if anything. What's chilling is that nobody on board takes any notice of it. When L dozes off they avert their eyes as they would from a street accident—there's polite conversation right across her snoring.

By the start of the second week of the cruise I began to have the feeling Lilly could have dropped dead on deck without attracting too much attention and there was nothing I could do to alter that or help. The sense of impotence was frightening, as it is in dreams. When she was awake she dominated all conversation, but no one seemed to object to her abrupt and rude interruptions. With a few exceptions, the other guests took it all in their stride and treated her a little like a geriatric appendage. I minded that more than anything and by the end of the cruise I was furious, not at them, but at Lilly.

It's true that children are sometimes angry at their parents for looking old and frail, as it's true that a certain kind of woman can't tolerate weakness in her husband—and a certain kind of husband will never forgive his wife for failing to look her best at a public event. We are validated by the plumage of those who love us and their feathers matter more than our own. Strength is a better credential for a lover than love is, but Lillian fell between parent and lover for me, so I wound up confused and irritable. She could pull herself together if she wanted to, I thought, Lilly can always do what she wants to. . . .

The last week of the cruise was the same and when it was over the ship dropped us all back at Martinique. The other guests flew home but we had decided we wanted to spend a week in a beach hotel on the island. After everybody had taken off for the airport we stood on the pier watching the yacht move with a slow dismissive air out of the harbor. The sun was high and the dock smelled of shellfish and iodine and there was a breeze off the hills in the trees behind us.

"Pretty, isn't it?" Lillian said. It was but she couldn't see it. "Postcard-pretty," she said, "the entire Caribbean is a pig in a poke if you ask me. It'll blow up in people's faces one day. Where's the hotel?"

We caught a taxi and drove for twenty minutes. Martinique is one of those islands that doesn't seem to have recovered from the last eruption of its volcano: the town was peaceful and there were children on the streets and bright birds in the eaves of little bright houses and I didn't believe any of it and neither did Lilly. The hotel looked comfortable and we checked in and walked along an interminable corridor that barreled down one side of the building and up the other to a pair of rooms at the end overlooking the sea.

Lilly walked slowly, grumpily, complaining about every turn and asking whether we were there yet every thirty seconds like a spoiled brat. She asked the bellboy how the weather had been for the last week and what it would be doing by tomorrow and the day after. She went on asking questions until after I had tipped the bellboy and he had departed and the door was closed and locked.

Then she fainted.

LILLIAN: *Goddamn old age. Everything that's wrong with you crystallizes. Goddamn my eyes and my pacemaker and goddamn my arteries.*
PETER: *I wish you'd stop talking about your body as if it were out to get you, Lilly.*
LILLIAN: *It is.*

I lifted her onto the bed and took her pulse; it was fast and fluttery and her face was like chalk. But her breathing was deep and regular and I picked up the phone to call a doctor and then thought better of it and told the main desk to send the bellboy back with a wheelchair if they had one, two carts if they didn't.

When I hung up, her eyes were open and she was staring at me curiously from the bed. "Why can't I stay awake?" she said.

At the airport I sat her on a sofa in the waiting room and went to the desk of Air France. I said it was an emergency, that we had reservations back to New York next Sunday, seven days away, but couldn't wait. It was imperative, I said, that we get there at once, on the very next plane. The man behind the desk listened boredly and said he was sorry but they were booked until the weekend—next weekend—when we already had seats. But he would put Monsieur and Madame on the waiting list, he said, there were so many emergencies these days, it was formidable about the emergencies, but he promised to put us on the first available flight.

The thirteen hours we spent in the airport in Martinique passed with a kind of sedentary slowness, like time in a hospital. There was a tedium that nothing could crack. Troops of French tourists traipsed in and out every so often, filling the room with chatter and cigarette smoke, departing in a flurry, vacating space for the next group. I made Lillian stretch out on the sofa and covered her legs with one of my jackets. She slept most of the time, drifting in and out of it easily. Now and then a tourist would push her legs off the sofa to make room and toward evening I had a fight with a Parisian who didn't know she was ill, and when he did, didn't care. We argued for a little and I hit him backward across a table and held his suitcase over him until he agreed to leave Lillian's legs alone.

After that things were quiet again and I don't remember much else that happened until a voice said: *"Vous pouvez monter, monsieur, il y a deux places, porte numéro trois."*

I got Lilly to her feet and half-led, half-carried her through the crowd to the plane. Once we were seated things seemed better and once things seemed better I got mad at her again. "You're to do as you're told," I said.

"Yes, darling."

"I'm sick of you, you understand me?"

"Yes."

"You'll see a new doctor when we get to New York or I'm through."

"Of course," Lillian said happily. She was feeling safe and her color was better.

"You'll do as I say from now on."

"Yes."

"Will you swear?"

"Yes."

"You're lying, aren't you?"

"Yes, darling," Lillian said.

⇥⇥⇥⇥VII

FROM A NOTEBOOK kept by Lillian's secretary, Rita Wade:

> January, 1979. I went to Miss Hellman's apartment thinking she was in the Caribbean. (It was agreed that I would be off that week.) When I opened the door I saw valises in the foyer. Miss Hellman called out to me to come into the bedroom and said, "I didn't expect you. I'm glad you came." I said I had come in because I had a lunch date and wanted to check the mail. She said I could keep my lunch date but would I stay with her until Peter Feibleman came back. (He had gone to his hotel to change clothes.) She told me how she'd gotten sick and had been sleeping off and on for days. She said, "If I fall asleep be sure and wake me." No sooner had she spoken than she fell asleep. It took a while to wake her and I said I thought she should call the doctor. She said, "Oh, he will only tell me the same thing . . . that I had too much to drink, or too many sleeping pills." I began to open and read the mail and she fell asleep again. She seemed to me to be near death. This time I woke her and said she really should call the doctor. Reluctantly, she asked me to get him on the phone. I forget his exact words, but they didn't amount to anything. Peter Feibleman came back shortly after and made some more calls and got her an appointment with a different doctor—Jay Meltzer. He took her to Dr. Meltzer's office. I canceled my lunch date and waited for a call. (I was sure she was near death.)

Jay Meltzer was a cheerful doctor with a hail-fellow-well-met manner who had been recommended by someone I trusted and I led Lillian into his office and handed her over to him. Along with Lilly I gave him a sheet of paper I'd asked Rita to type, listing all the medications Lilly was currently taking. I left the two of them alone and went out to the waiting room but before I had time to sit down, Meltzer was behind me. He was staring at the list.

"She can't be on this much stuff," he said, "I wouldn't even have to examine her. Some of them are contradictory, I don't think it's possible. She'd be toxic."

He read the list again and I didn't say anything.

"All right," he said, "all right. I'll call the hospital."

From Rita Wade's notebook:

> Dr. Meltzer said she was overmedicated and he was putting her into Columbia Presbyterian Hospital for detoxification. Meltzer told her when she recovered that she didn't have emphysema, but a bronchial condition from smoking. She didn't need the breathing machine at all, he said. (But [her previous doctor] had said she had emphysema, and wherever she traveled in the US, she had to carry an AC breathing machine and a DC breathing machine in European countries and the Caribbean, along with the medicine and tubes that went with them.) It was a relief to get rid of that equipment.

The sixth day of the month she spent in Columbia Presbyterian, I went to visit her. Till then I had stayed away at the suggestion of Meltzer, who had taken her off all medication and said she needed as much sleep as she could get. I knew she would be weak and and depressed and lonesome: mad at me for staying away.

I stopped at the nurses' station on her floor and asked if she could have visitors.

The head nurse looked up from her desk in a weary way. "If the visitor's a man, she'll manage," she said.

"How is she?"

"Feeling better today."

"That's nice."

"For you, maybe," the head nurse said.

I had brought a box of chocolate truffles for Lillian but something about the head nurse's expression made me change my mind. "These chocolates are for you," I said, "they're a present from Miss Hellman, she asked me to leave them at the nurses' station."

"What's in them," the head nurse said, "cyanide?"

"I gather she's a little difficult."

"You might say that."

"How's she eating?"

"She's not," the head nurse said, "the doctor put her on a no-sodium diet. She threw her lunch tray on the floor. We had to take her phone out of the room this morning."

I asked why.

"To keep her from ordering pastrami and corned-beef sandwiches from the corner deli," the head nurse said. "With extra pickles. And saltcellars. At least I think that's where she gets them— she's got four saltcellars hidden under the mattress."

"Didn't you take them away from her?"

"The night nurse tried. Miss Hellman hit her with a lamp and called her an asshole. She uses that word a lot."

"She doesn't mean it," I said quickly, "it's just the worst word she can think of."

"Oh, no, it's not," the head nurse said.

"She'll eat if somebody feeds her."

"The day nurse tried—Miss Hellman called her a silly bitch and said the food was kike drek."

"She doesn't mean any of it," I said—"she probably doesn't even know the day nurse is Jewish."

"The day nurse," the head nurse said heavily, "is black."

I went down the hall to Lillian's room. I knew she'd be in tears from feeling abandoned and upset at my not showing up, and I had my explanation all ready. Halfway down the hall the sound of guitar music wafted past me and grew louder as I came closer to her room. Two other patients were standing in the corridor staring at Lillian's door. She would have to turn the volume down on her radio whether she wanted to or not, I decided, and I knocked on her door and opened it.

The room was cheerful and bright. Lilly was lying back on her pillows with a lazy expression. Seated next to her on the bed was a tall, good-looking intern who was singing softly and pluck-

ing the strings of a guitar. Lillian had a cigarette in one hand and
the other hand on the intern's leg.

"Hello, darling," she said as I came in, "this is Jonathan.
Jonathan's been taking good care of me. He's very musical—
aren't you, Jonathan? Aren't you musical?"

"That's right, Lilly," the intern said.

⤛⤛⤛⤛⤛VIII

BY THE THIRD WEEK Lillian had a makeshift bar on a shelf in a corner of the hospital room for the use, she said, of any visitor who might be thirsty. It wasn't a complete bar, she explained—apologizing to each person who came to see her—just the basics: vodka, dry vermouth, Scotch, bourbon, gin and some mixers. The white wine was being chilled in the refrigerator off the main hospital hall, below the plasma. The head nurse complained for a while and then gave up.

One Sunday afternoon I went for a visit and found Lilly presiding over what she called "a little informal gathering" in her hospital room. Mike and Annabel Nichols, Claudette Colbert, Maureen Stapleton, Richard Avedon and Leonard Bernstein among others were lounging around or standing with drinks in their hands while Lilly held court from her hospital bed. The head nurse followed me into the room.

"I'm sorry, Miss Hellman," she said in a hollow voice, "you can't keep your smoked salmon in the hospital refrigerator, it's out of the question. It smells."

"It won't if you don't open it," Lillian said. "Just leave it inside the waxed paper."

"I'm afraid not. We need the space."

"How much space can a little packet like that take up? It's only a pound. Put it on top of the white wine."

"You've got two tins of caviar on top of the white wine," the head nurse said. "Miss Hellman, people are dying in this hospital."

"I don't blame them," Lillian said, "if I had to eat the rat-fuck you serve up here I'd be dead too. Fortunately Mrs. Nichols brought me some smoked salmon."

"She'll have to take it back with her," the head nurse said, "I'm not going to permit it. I'm not. I don't care what you say."

She went out before Lillian could answer.

"Let her alone," Lillian said to no one in particular, "she'll simmer down."

I said I didn't think so.

"She will if she wants Mr. Davis to stay sober tonight," Lillian said.

"Who's Mr. Davis?"

Lillian pointed to a short bald man sitting in a chair in the corner. He was wearing a hospital robe and slippers and pouring some Scotch into a glass with a trembling hand.

"Mr. Davis is here for something-cardio-something," Lillian said, "they've scared him half to death with their talk. Haven't they, Mr. Davis? The poor man was shaking like a leaf this morning. I found him out in the corridor looking white as the walls. Have a nice cheese sandwich, Mr. Davis, there's a platter of them just behind Mr. Bernstein. It's terrible the way they treat people in hospitals these days—just terrible. . . ."

After a month, Dr. Meltzer declared that Lillian had been detoxified and she left the hospital with the last remnants of her bar bottles, three unopened bottles of chilled white Bordeaux, two tins of cocktail sausages, a jar of Dijon mustard, a jar of Savora mustard, five lemons, three limes, a jar of capers, a pound and a half of pastrami, the tall musical intern whose name was Jonathan LaPook, and Mr. Davis. She had arranged for Mr. Davis to be released at the same time because she had told him so many horror stories about the hospital he was scared to stay without her. Lilly dropped him at La Guardia Airport—Mr. Davis lived in Detroit—and stopped on the way home at Schaller and Weber to pick up a dozen weisswurst.

Jonathan LaPook turned out over the next couple of years to be a good friend to Lilly, taking what time he could from the lethal schedule of interns to explain to her whatever medical fact she was currently unable to get down. He was able somehow, a day here, a day there, to ease her anxiety about her old enemy, her physical self. For a few weeks following her time at Columbia Presbyterian Lilly felt stronger and the spasms of sleep disappeared, but the memory of the episode stayed, and the thing that had been dripping inside her was louder. It was in her eyes now and she was aware of it without knowing why or how.

That summer we went back to the Vineyard and Lilly had fun, as her kind of nature always had, but with a difference. Sometimes she would sit quietly by herself with a curious expression, bewildered and a little suspicious—listening for something. One day I found her out on the deck with a glass of beer, smoking a cigarette and looking at the sea as if she were expecting a visitor who was inexcusably late. I sat down beside her and kept still. After a minute or two Lilly turned her face to me and smiled.

"What were you listening to?"

After a little she said: "I don't know."

"Where's it coming from?"

"I don't know," she said again and changed the subject.

It was a strange time for both of us that summer. I had my own problems—my new novel was in its third or fourth draft depending how you counted and I had rewritten long sections of it time after time, but I couldn't get it right. It was the only time in my life I had ever known how a story would end before I began it and the knowledge had wrecked things: I was stuck with the ending now and so were my characters, but they refused to be manipulated into it. I tried several ways of enticing them but they wouldn't go and I knew better than to force them but I couldn't shepherd them either. I couldn't do anything with them.

Then Lilly asked me to read it out loud. She couldn't see enough to read the typewritten page and careful listening wore her out: it took three weeks because she had to keep stopping to think.

When I was done Lillian gave me her opinion. She said it very straight and simply in the clear deep cool-water way of speaking she sometimes used about writing, the tone Hammett had used with her. "It's nearly there, it's closer to finished than you think. Just throw out the plot."

After a moment I said: "Just what?"

"The plot," she said, "it's in your way. The people are fine. It's time to go ahead with them, but they have to do what they want now. Not what you want. Let them go, Peter."

I hadn't liked hearing it but I started over that same day and now I was going fine. I had to watch myself every second not to allow the old plot back in and I didn't have the kind of heroic restraint Lilly thought I had—that was the problem now.

The other problem was my mother, who had been sick again, seriously sick, though she hadn't told me about it till she was getting better; she was still the angriest person I'd ever known, the quietest, and the most tender. I had by then spent half my life pacifying angry women, and by then I knew why.

Lillian said, on the beach: "What's got into you?"

"Nothing," I said.

"Okay," she said. "If that's the way you want it."

We were lying in a place we often used, an imaginary rectangle of sand about six feet by ten, directly below the house. There were two beach towels, a beach umbrella, a hamper of thinly sliced chicken sandwiches with watercress and homemade mayonnaise, fruit and cheese and a bottle of chilled Valdepeñas in a wine cooler. We had around us the glassy heat off the water and the sound of insects and echoes of other summers. Save for an occasional slap at a sand fly, nobody had to move. A stillness had settled over us while we watched the sailboats and the fat ferryboats as they waddled off to Woods Hole. The view from Lillian's beach was always pleasant to look at.

"Split an apple with me, will you?" she said.

I said I would if there was a knife.

"In the basket—I don't know how sharp it is."

"I can sharpen it in the sand," I said, "If I can manage to . . ." I shrugged.

"Go on."

"With what?"

"There's a sentence you come close to finishing, but you veer off," Lillian said. "You've been doing it for years. Say it or forget it. You nurse it too much."

I said maybe I was getting forgetful.

"I don't think so," Lilly said, "I think you're scared of knives. Of what you might do if you picked one up on the wrong day. It's got something to do with your growing up, I think. Something to do with New Orleans."

She fell into silence and sat there. It was such a good guess I couldn't think of an answer to it and she had made no sign, till that day, that she had any clue. She was often given to guesses about people, many of them way off the mark, but once in a while she'd reach through everything and put her hand on some fragile truth nobody knew about, not even the person of whom it was true.

"What's the thing you were most scared of in the whole world when you were growing up?" she asked.

"Being a sissy."

"Me too," she said.

"A girl can't be a sissy."

"Forgive me but you're wrong," she said, "all men think that. Boys think they have a corner on the sissy market, but it's not true—girls can be the worst sissies of all."

I turned on one elbow and watched her. It didn't make sense to me, but it wasn't the sort of thing Lillian would lie about. I said: "You're not a sissy."

"No," she said. "Not now. I have to face blindness. Neither are you."

"I'm not so sure about me."

"I'm sure," she said.

I got up and brushed the sand off my legs. The heat was getting uncomfortable and so was the conversation.

"What the hell," she said, "you're not responsible for what you feel, nobody is. Only for what you do about it, and you've done all right. In the main I mean, you've done stupid things like the rest of us, but you've mostly done all right. You ought to take pleasure in that, and a little pride maybe. A little pride wouldn't hurt you."

She broke off and I kept quiet. I'd had the feeling while she was talking that something unspoken had passed between the words. It was like a thought that rode in on other thoughts, a kind of piggyback fact that came in that way because it couldn't stand on its own, like the time at the Cape Poge lighthouse when I saw the broken swan and buried it. Only this time there was nothing to bury.

"Listen here. About my horseradish," Lilly said suddenly, changing the subject, "I got a call this morning from a woman I hardly know—she heard about it and wants some, my horseradish is getting famous. This is the sixth time this summer somebody's asked me, isn't that amazing? If you'll pull up a couple of roots from the place below the garden where it grows, I'll grate them and give her a small jar of it."

I didn't answer and she headed up the path toward the house by herself. Halfway up she called back: "Kay wants some horseradish too . . . so does Rose. Hurry up, will you—I'm famous for my horseradish."

Her hair glittered and while she was cleaning the sand off her feet I picked up the picnic basket and towels and the beach umbrella and went after her. When she went inside I could see her outline through the kitchen window but I knew she couldn't see much herself once she was out of the light. It was getting late, the sun was already behind the house.

Walking up the path, I watched her: she was waiting for me by the sink. The light was crumpling over the grass and getting ready to shatter on the water. It was one of those days you know you're going to remember all your life and never know why.

Kidding on the Square

$$\succ\succ\succ\succ\succ I$$

> OSPREY . . . "bone breaker," in Pliny the name of
> a bird of prey . . . see OSSIFRAGE.
> OSSIFRAGE . . .
> The ossifraga of Pliny is identified by modern nat-
> uralists with the Lammergeyer, which swallows and di-
> gests bones, and is said to let them fall from a great
> height upon rocks and stones so as to break them . . .

From a notebook of mine dated November 6, 1985:

> But where is it now? Where do ospreys go for winter?
> Where do people go when they die?

> *L: I saw the most appalling thing at the hairdresser's
> today. Remember how you used to make jokes about my
> coming home with my hair still up in curlers? I can't stand
> sitting under a drier at all now, I can't read a thing in that
> light. Paul David's a good hairdresser, he does a fine job,
> but my God the people who go to him. There was a rich
> lady sitting next to me—one of those conservative blue-haired
> bigots from West Chop, she was about my age. When her
> hair was done she opened her purse and took out a little
> gold whistle—you have my solemn word of honor—a little
> tiny gold whistle in a Tiffany felt bag. She put it in her mouth
> and blew it.*
> *I watched her in the mirror and I thought, What kind
> of life must you lead that you blow whistles for things? Then*

*I remembered that I'd seen a black woman sitting in the front
seat of a car outside when I came in. Just sitting quietly, not
complaining. Not the type that can. If you grew up in the
South you always know those eyes.*

*And when the blue-haired lady blew her whistle I heard
a car door slam and the colored woman came in to fetch
her. The rich lady was sitting there with her hair all finished
and sprayed and set for the evening and I thought, How dare
you? Just how dare you? How can you whistle for her—who
in hell do you think you are?*

*But I only thought it. I didn't say it. It would have been
pointless to say anything. So I did the only thing I could
think of.*

*I emptied my coffee cup over her head. It wasn't very
hot, but it was hot enough to startle her. She sat there staring into the mirror with the coffee dripping down her nose
and her hairdo melting all over her face. That's for you, lady,
I thought, blue-haired lady, for all you ladies who blow
whistles for people and dirty the world for the rest of us.
That's for you, I thought, but I didn't say it—I just smiled
at her in the mirror and walked out.*

Lilly walked all the way home from the hairdresser that
afternoon rather than call anyone to come get her in the car. She
walked down the street and down the driveway and into the house,
moving in the same slow unflagging interminable and determined
way she had been accustomed to moving when she could still
trust her eyes, and when she came into the living room and
stopped, she still looked as though she were going forward.

By then it was late in the season and we left the Vineyard a
week earlier than usual because we both had lectures in New
Orleans; we'd arranged them so that we could be together in the
city at the same time.

A few friends came along with us for company—the Palev-
skys from Los Angeles and Claudette Colbert with Lilly from
New York. Lillian had often visited Claudette at her Barbados
home and liked her company. My lecture was first and the next
day we all trooped down together to hear Lilly speak at Tulane.

When we walked into the auditorium at Tulane people were
sitting on the floor, in the aisles, wherever they could. There was
a high tension in the house, the kind of held-breath hush that

happens before a big religious event. When the lights dimmed there was absolute silence and Lilly walked out very slowly from the wings; she did it like a dream figure, somber and erect and somnambulant, it was a great entrance. They went on applauding long after she'd sat down. There was a table on stage with the Tensor light she'd asked for in front of her and she sat quietly while somebody introduced her and then she began to read "Julia" from beginning to end.

I remembered then Lillian warning me when my first play was produced about something in the theater that can wreck a performance. It happens when fifty women reach into their handbags for a Life Saver and fifty men clear their throats or blow their noses. Onstage it's heard as a faint rustle, a breeze moving through a small forest, but it's the moment playwrights dread because it signals a slump in interest no actor can cover unless the actor cavorts outside the limits of the play. The fault is on the page, not on the stage, and if it goes on for too long the play may never recover.

It happened early in Lillian's reading and when it did I saw her jump a few paragraphs, turn two pages and go on without a break. I knew she wasn't following the text but she'd told me two days before the lecture that she tried cutting "Julia" and couldn't do it.

The second time it happened I saw Claudette, who was beside me, sit forward in her seat staring at the stage.

What was remarkable was that Lilly was cutting as she went along, without any marks to help her, using the pulse of her audience as her only guide, but managing it so seamlessly that nobody could tell. When she heard the rustle, she jumped forward in the text, making up a bridge-sentence, something to retain the thread of story. When the silence was complete—so complete you could hear the car horns outside—she slowed down.

About three quarters of the way through, she reached forward to put a cigarette out in what she thought was an ashtray and turned out to be a wad of white tissue she had dropped on the reading table when she first sat down. Presently a long plume of smoke rose out of the wad and meandered up in front of her like a feeler in the air; Lilly didn't see it but within seconds it thickened into a column, the beginnings of a smoke screen, and still the audience was silent. The man who'd introduced her was sitting in a chair near the proscenium frozen in horror: he did nothing. Claudette made a sound and nudged me and I climbed up and grabbed the tissue and sat down with it crumpled in my hand till it was out. Then the reading was over and we all went outside and you could still hear the applause.

Not long after New Orleans there were some other lectures and Lilly flew out to Los Angeles and made her base with me while she did them; the first was Cleveland and I went along for company, though I wasn't scheduled to speak at the same time till the following week in Marin County.

I took some work along and shored up in my hotel room while she got ready. An hour or so before the lecture she wandered in and sat down for a while, smoking.

"I've done it this time, haven't I?" she said. I asked what. "Overshot the field. I'm too big a name. There'll be a wave of attack against me soon, I hope I live past it—I made it through the last one all right but I was younger in the McCarthy days. Will you come with me today and stand in the wings?"

It wasn't the kind of thing she was given to asking in space so I quit work and went with her.

Lillian was used to working in a small theater, but this was an amphitheater: she couldn't see the hands go up for questions, so she got somebody to do it for her, a young man from the staff who volunteered to sit with her on the stage.

Halfway through, a woman stood up wearing jeans, an old army jacket and thick boots, her hair cropped close to her head. Her question was, "Have you ever endorsed gay lib?"

The young man who had volunteered to field questions for Lilly nodded approvingly and repeated, "Have you ever endorsed gay lib?"

"No," Lillian said.

"Why not?" the woman asked.

"Why not?" the young man repeated.

"The forms of fucking," Lillian said, "do not need my endorsement."

Later, back at the hotel, she ordered a drink and sipped it curiously. "I've never heard an audience cheer a remark like that," she said, "were they standing up?"

The entire amphitheater had risen to its feet like a football field after a winning touchdown and the cheering had lasted several minutes.

"Funny how it affects people when you tell them the truth," Lilly said. "It's considered refreshing."

When we went back to Los Angeles I found a package in the mail. Inside was a long piece of antique lace—the Spanish altarpiece Hammett had bought for her, the one Lilly had thrown in his face and tried to return to the shop. With it was a note that said: "With my kindest regards, L. Hellman."

I hung the lace on a wall in my house but Lilly would have nothing to do with it. "I hate the thing," she said. "It's still painful and I'm still mad at him—dead or not, I'd like to kill him for it—I'm only giving it to you because I can't see it now," she added and turned her head away whenever she passed the wall where it was hanging.

But one day when she thought I was upstairs I caught her standing in front of it staring at the lace with a faint smile—almost a look of pride. I tiptoed upstairs and made a loud noise and when I came down again she was sitting on the sofa with her back to it.

It was somewhere around that time that a dinner was arranged with Barbra Streisand, who lived near Paradise Cove just outside of Los Angeles. Sue Mengers, Streisand's then agent, drove us up the Pacific Coast Highway and on the way chatted about the incident that was still making waves in Hollywood, the one involving an executive named Begelman who had forged an endorsing signature on a check made out to Cliff Robertson from Columbia Pictures and been caught red-handed. The scandal had both embarrassed and shaken the film community because the check involved, ten thousand dollars, was a sum Begelman could have demanded from any of his friends, who would have happily given it to him to keep him in line: the attention caused by what he'd done was a major threat to those around him who were embezzling far greater sums every day and getting away with it.

"He's a friend and I'm saddened by it," Sue said. "Whenever I stand up for him I know how you felt in the McCarthy era when you stood up for all *your* friends."

Lillian, who was in the backseat, bristled. "How can you compare them?" she said. "My friends were decent people—Begelman's just a cheap crook, he's one of the sleaziest characters in America."

"Pick, pick, pick," Sue said softly, and Lillian, who liked

her, laughed on and off for the rest of the way to Paradise Cove.

The dinner was pleasant and friendly, not the kind of meal she had expected, and the food was good, which surprised her. When Streisand showed her around the estate afterward, Lilly was impressed despite herself.

"I wish I could afford to live that way for a little," she said on the way home. "That's what's dangerous about Hollywood— it makes you envious . . . no wonder I always got out just in time. . . ."

Her next lecture was with me at the College of Marin and we flew to San Francisco together and took rooms in the Huntington hotel; Lilly had hired a college student named Heather as a traveling companion to help her dress and she'd brought extra clothes so we could have a night on the town. But the night we checked in she complained of pains in her chest and the hotel doctor, who came at two in the morning, told her she'd have to go to a hospital. It wasn't the sort of thing to tell Lillian the night before a lecture—her lifelong fear of making any kind of commitment was based on her inability to break one once it was made—and when I picked up the phone to call Marin and cancel her appearance, she stopped me. "I'll feel better in the morning," she said, "you'll see."

In the morning she felt worse but no medical threat made any difference and she refused to cancel the lecture no matter what. I started to lay down the law and changed my mind. What kept Lillian going was work, and the idea that her health might prevent work could knock the rest of the stuffing out of her. For someone of that much raw force, too much concern was pity, and pity was the subtlest form of contempt. I arranged for an ambulance to pick her up in the hotel room with a stretcher, take us all to the College of Marin, wait there and take Lilly to the hospital when it was over.

There's a raucous tilt to crossing the Golden Gate Bridge in an ambulance that gets to you sooner or later, especially on the way to a lecture at a university, but she didn't seem to notice it, and by the time we were past the halfway mark she was chain-smoking despite the driver's orders and a couple of signs around the oxygen tank. Then she complained of the bouncing and asked to sit up but there was no room: Heather was in one corner of the ambulance, I was in the free corner studying what I was to read aloud. But she kept at it like a child and I fought with her a few minutes then gave up and swapped places with her. For the rest of the trip she blew smoke at the ambulance driver, leaning over the back of the front seat to see what Sausalito looked like through the windshield, while I lay flat on my back on the stretcher trying to read.

The ambulance pulled up at the rear entrance to the lecture hall and somebody maneuvered Lilly into a wheelchair and pushed her into the wings. But when the houselights went down she stood up and walked onto the stage by herself. Since the stroke in Avallon, her left leg wouldn't always support her and she used a crutch to propel her out of the wings to a chair onstage. I introduced her and she made it through the lecture fine and when it was done, rose by herself into the applause and stepped forward and took my arm in maybe the most graceful and certainly the best-timed gesture I ever saw.

She refused to take the ambulance back because, she said, it was too bumpy, but got into a limousine instead and said: "That idiot woman almost pushed the wheelchair onstage, did you see her?" I hadn't. "Why can't people learn a little stage presence," she said.

A large group of students surrounded the driveway clapping and yelling encouragement. "Somebody hold me up to the window," Lilly said. Heather did and she waved until the limousine had turned a corner and the students had disappeared. Then she asked for a cigarette and lay down in back and shut her eyes.

They kept her in the hospital over two weeks that time and diagnosed the episode as an angina attack brought on, the cardiologist thought, by excessive smoking. Lillian chain-smoked her way through the entire time and drove the staff crazy, the nurses crazy, the nearest deli crazy and Heather crazy. She picked a minor fight with me the first day and I let her have it—it was becoming one of her few remaining ways of making love—and after that she cheered up and asked me to lock the door when I came so we could fight in private. The attending physician frowned on the ritual shouting till he saw the improvement in Lilly and then he gave the staff orders to leave us alone.

From that time on the erosion of Lillian's health took place with relentless regularity; her mind held watch while her body betrayed her as she'd always suspected it would and it happened in a programmed way according to which every few weeks some mysterious payment was made, as though she were dying on the installment plan. The usual people wanted to help her—Hannah, Mike and Annabel Nichols, Max, Dick Poirier and always the Herseys—but there was little to help with, nothing to be done unless one of them could think of a way to stop her from smoking, and nobody could. Lillian's random falls began to take on another meaning now, a sense of purpose, though the purpose remained hidden; as the blindness increased, camouflage became her main concern. In a sunset world shadows are longer than the objects that cast them and brightness is all.

During the time in Los Angeles I'd managed to set up enough electric lights for her to see by and I'd rented a typewriter with extra-thick boldface type. Lilly had begun work on what was to be the fourth book of memoirs, the shortest of all, a book written under the harshest kind of circumstances since an hour a day was the most she could use her eyes. Even a minute or two longer caused a severe headache and until the trip to the College of Marin I had done whatever I could think of to make things easier for her; but the doctor had been explicit about what would happen if she went on smoking and from then on I told her I wouldn't travel with her, visit her, see her at all unless she quit. But instead of the declaration of war I meant, Lilly took it as a piece of unreasonable nonsense and while I stuck to my guns she wrote me notes and letters.

> The Cosmopolitan Club
> New York
>
> This is my new club. I wait on the bed until the Charity organization tour of my apartment ends. There are 800 people here. This club is full of well bred liberal ladies. I am a fool. It is raining. I met a Bishop.* The Bishop has a beautiful cross hanging from him. He is Episcopal. He says he will come and sit on a rock with me. He says I can be Episcopal. I do not lie. He is handsome. He is rich. You are also handsome. You

---

* Paul Moore, Episcopal bishop of New York

are not rich. In ten minutes I leave to have my brain examined . . .

Most sincerely, your friend
Lillian

The Cosmopolitan Club
New York

I have returned from the brain department. I have had eighteen needles put in my head. They said to relax. I said they should find other word . . . How you think, Mr. Feible?

Best regards
A headache

DEAR MISS HELLMAN:

I'm sorry you had your brain examined and even sorrier for the doctors who examined it. I don't know what they can possibly find in there short of a wheel with a dead squirrel in it, unless they can spot acute stubbornness on a CAT scan.

Knock off the brain stuff, Lilly, it's nonsense, you get headaches because you have eye trouble and you're working long hours. Cut down on the hours and the headaches will stop. Then you can pay attention to the thing you're ignoring, the smoking, which will kill you if you continue to bypass it. The last time I counted you were up to four packs a day.

You asked on the phone if I don't feel heartless for staying away till you give up cigarettes. No. It goes like this, Lilly: you have a perfect right to kill yourself any way you choose. And I have a right not to watch. Those are the rules . . .

If you *do* stop smoking I will not only come see you but will pay you, and handsomely. All you ever wanted was my money anyway. I am enclosing a dollar on account.

I do miss you,
love,
Peter

P.S. My ex-publisher's partner is a louse.

P.P.S. The LA County exterminator just came to the house. There are rats in my cellar and attic. I suppose you'll have an opinion about that. He killed one of them half a foot long. (No one we know.)

Why does everything, including you, happen to me?

Love,

P.

I can't find a dollar, so I'm writing a check. Please don't jimmy it up with extra zeros or I won't send you any more money. P.

Vineyard Haven. Monday.

DEAR MR. FEIBLE, SCION OF SCHOLARS AND RABBIS,

I am on my way to having your check framed. In my opinion, you, of course, may have another, it should go next to the Toulouse Lautrec [poster hanging in my apartment] in N.Y., where we can hang it together or hang ourselves perhaps.

I have worked hard this weekend and went nude bathing only once, and then in Gay Head . . .

My date of return may have to be pushed up; nobody [here] does decent research work and I may sooner than I thought need a library. I tried to talk Thornhill* into some free research but got no place. I don't think he knows what the word means.

I now do want us to meet. I am still worried about the ground rules or even if there can be any. My worries stem from a place about which you have never known: what pained me and what didn't. I think you know a great deal about people—or, at least, it is there when you write—but I am not sure that you weigh each person for their own eccentricities or kinks or just plain, simple take-what-you-can-take. Maybe the answer is to go back and read your own books. Or to pay me highly for an hour's lecture on individualism.

I am sorry about the rats. Are you sure they are all in the attic? Too cheap to talk about the belfry. . . .

---

*Lillian's publisher, Arthur Thornhill, president of Little, Brown

Dashiell Hammett appearing in Washington in 1953 before the Senate sub-committee headed by Senator Joseph McCarthy

Lillian in her New York apartment

Halsman

Lillian in her thirties

VanDamm Studio

Dorothy S. Broido, Peter's mother,
in her thirties

Lillian with Marshal Tito

Roy Stevens

Peter with Carson McCullers at Columbia University lecture attended by Lillian, 1958
(See page 52)

Lillian and Peter at dinner in Egypt

Lillian, with failing eyesight, pretending to examine the interior wall of a tomb in Egypt with Lynda Palevsky

Lillian and Peter having breakfast on the boat in Egypt

Max Palevsky dressed as an Arab on his chartered boat

Lillian, blinded by sunlight and glaucoma, showing Egypt to Peter

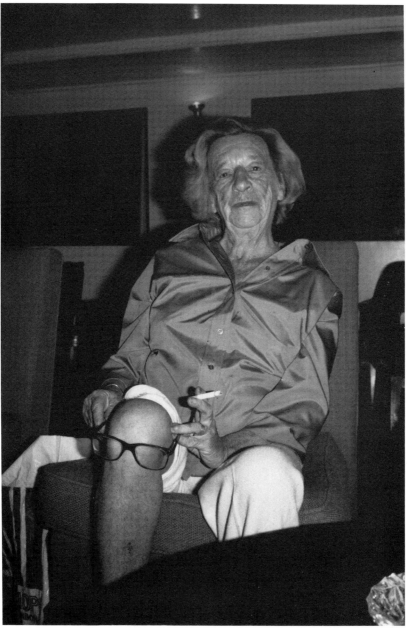

Lillian doing an imitation of Irving Lazar

© *Jean Pigozzi*

Talli and William Wyler

John Hersey, Carly Simon, and Robert Brustein

Betsy and Walter Cronkite

Lillian with Warren Beatty

Maureen Stapleton and Elizabeth Taylor in *The Little Foxes*

President and Mrs. Reagan congratulating Elizabeth Taylor backstage after the opening of *The Little Foxes* at the Kennedy Center in Washington, D.C. (Unseen in this photograph, Lillian and Maureen Stapleton stand arguing behind President Reagan.)

Lillian with Hannah Weinstein

Rita Wade

Claudette Colbert

Lillian playing Scrabble on the Vineyard

Dr. Jonathan LaPook

Alice Wexler, Lillian, Dr. Milton Wexler, and Jack Koontz on Lillian's boat, *Julia*, at Martha's Vineyard

Lillian on the deck of Vineyard house

Israel Shenker

Lillian in living room of Vineyard house

Courtesy of Cornell Capa

Annette Lein

Lillian, taken four years before her death

Yes, I know about your ex-publisher. People go around saying they would like to know the true story. But what true story is there ever in this life, my dear boy, and that's the way my book is written and you must start feeling sorry for me. Get on with your own [book] and forget those horrid little twists you consider plotting. You didn't start that way, it's my influence on you. Mine and maybe Hammett's on me. Go back to what you were. I have an instinct this is going to be a very good book for you.

Much love,
Mme. L

Hotel Villa Magna
Madrid. Thursday

DEAR L:

Decided to chance it here, and I was right—things in Spain are much looser now and there's no danger to me as long as I don't start a revolution. Stop worrying, Lilly, after *The Columbus Tree* was published I was warned to keep away till Franco cooled but there's amnesty for everybody now, even the likes of me.

Yesterday I was having a drink in the Ritz bar when a scruffy kid in his teens tried to break in and was stopped by the doorman and led off by the police. I felt sorry for him till I found out that all he wanted to do was distribute leaflets for the Falangist party. I never thought I'd live to see that one—what the hell is going on? I thought Spanish-flavored Fascism was buried with Franco.

Other than that, a nice silence: old sights, pieces of myself and somebody else I was, an unchanging city despite the high-rises. It all helps in some way. Strange, though—some of it nice, some not.

I miss and think of you and love you. That part's nice but it would be still nicer if you weren't such an ass about the cigarettes and we could travel together.

I'm off to Rome on Thursday, then Venice as planned, unless Italy is on strike. Will keep in touch.

My love,
P.

Vineyard Haven
Thursday

DEAREST PETER,

It's dusk and thus a bad time for me, but I finished the book today and I have no feelings about it except surprise. I must have really wanted to be a writer although I never believed that.

I write in space to tell you that I can't believe I can't phone you tonight. My dependence on you is evidently greater than even I thought. Ah well. My love to you and spit for Zizi.*

Miss H

Rome. Tuesday

DEAR L:

Just spoke to you and got the news about your finishing. Goddamn you, Lilly, you're stubborn, touching and a royal pain in the ass. This letter is merely to inform you that I care about you a great deal, a fact you will by now have taken into consideration and one you have doubtless counted on, having decided in the smugness of what you call your unconscious that I'll come back to you whether you're smoking or not— dying or just having lunch. I might. But why press me? Why not go that one extra step and make me believe in heaven? You've already convinced me of hell, what can it cost you?

I do love you and you are
enough to defrock the Pope.
P.

P.S. You mentioned on the phone that you have a new eye disease—"something called Drusen of the Macula," you said. There is no such thing as Drusen of the Macula, Lilly, it sounds like an unfinished novel by Thomas Hardy. What you have is macular degeneration of the retina, and what the doctors are scared to tell you is what I've already told you: glaucoma destroys periph-

---

* Zizi: like Miss Gigglewitz, a generic name Lillian used for any strange woman

eral vision, leaving you with tunnel vision, and macular degeneration destroys the tunnel. It's a bitch of a prognosis but it's not life-threatening. Smoking is.

Love sometimes is too.

P.

DEAREST PETER,

I have had three small communications from you, but I must not complain because it is two more than I expected. You sound fine in spite of the complaints, although a little more news would not put me to sleep.

My ms is finished, Mr. Poirier will read it today, it is in the mail to Billy. Our Mr. Thornhill is at the Frankfurt Book Fair and I am not going to mail his until he returns. I do not want it bouncing around among that silly group. I think I like the title, but I am not sure: "The Camerons, Maybe." What do you think? Not that I would pay any attention to you on titles . . .

I guess this is all stalling to tell you that by the time this can reach you the eye operation will be over. I go in on the 7th and they operate, supposedly only on the cataract, on the 8th. There would have been no sense to your canceling your trip, although, if it turns out a disaster, I will want you to come to be with me for a little. I am hoping I will at least have an address for you to which Rita can cable. I am told there is a fair chance of success. I have also been warned by [the opthalmologist] of the chances of failure. I am, of course, scared to death but Milton [Wexler] will be here with me the last few days and that has to be of some help. I tell myself now that for the first time in my life I cannot believe in a future, and having said it, I feel in some way consoled. It seems to me it has happened to a stranger—I had expected, if I ever thought much, [trouble that might come from] lungs. But *eyes*! Very odd is life, my friend.

Mr. Poirier reported an hour ago that my ms was, he thought, wonderful, although he would have a number of changes to suggest. Anyway, it is over and I think its title will be either "Perhaps" or "The Camerons, Maybe," neither of which you could possibly like because they have to do with the subject.

I know that it is impossible for as removed a man as you are from the human condition to understand how much I miss you and need you. *You* need Zizi or a stupider form of you-know-who for peanut butter.

Say a large prayer for me. The next weeks will be hell. Then maybe if things go well and although I have a hard time thinking they will, maybe I can come and meet you and you can sneak me past Zizi who won't care much anyway because she just finished with Peter Viertel in Irwin's show.

> Much, much love
> L.

I did go back to her as soon as I got home, despite the smoking, because her doctor now believed that a total and abrupt loss of cigarettes might precipitate a heart attack. He suggested a less drastic cutback, from four packs to half a pack a day, and I knew that if he tried to enforce that, Lilly would give *him* a heart attack. So I negotiated with her and we settled on three quarters of a pack, my final offer.

The eye operation didn't improve her vision and I found her in New York looking through her checkbook in a state of high anxiety. What worried her now was not blindness or disability or even death but the thing that had been the preoccupation of much of her life and work: money.

> LA. Wed. night.
> Saw L week before last in NY. She's beginning to have daily waking nightmares of going broke, she poor-mouths all the time now, she used to hate people who did that. Her biggest worry is the possibility that she may need nurses. "I can't afford nurses all the time, maybe I can't afford to die."
> I told her she was right—you have to be really rich to die—she might as well live, it's cheaper.

What was confusing about her concern was the timing: Lillian had had money troubles before but she didn't have any right to them now. Recently, her aunt Florence Newhouse had died, leaving her enough to live on no matter what happened, and she had money of her own as well. The obsession with it was like a way of not thinking about death—filling an emptiness that had become too scary. But she went on telling everybody that she was close to broke and one morning Max Palevsky called and asked me the name of her accountant so he could send her a monthly check without her knowledge. "To keep the wolf away from the door," he said, and I didn't have the heart to tell him that the wolf wasn't even in the neighborhood. Max's affection for her was genuine and he went ahead and set up the payments without any bother or fuss.

A week later Lilly called to say she thought Max might make an effort to help her soon and please to go along with it and not interfere. "I'm going to need all the help I can get—I'm sick of worrying about the rent."

I said there wasn't any rent, since she owned her apartment and the Vineyard house, both without a mortgage.

"The symbolic rent, dopey," she said. "Just shut up when Max calls."

I didn't tell her he already had called, any more than I'd told Max she didn't need the money, and I began to feel like a dim-witted Robin Hood in some psychotic glade of Sherwood Forest where you're not supposed to rob the rich to give to the poor, you're just supposed to stand there.

But Lilly couldn't sustain the financial worries believably for long because, in the year that followed, she had a sudden and totally unexpected windfall of money. It started with a phone call from the Coast.

For a long time she'd kept her best-known play, *The Little Foxes,* off the market in big cities in order to prevent its popularity being sapped by bad productions, or by one of the many actresses who always wanted to play Regina, some of whom weren't suited to the part. "When I wrote it, I was amused by Regina—I never thought of her as a villainous character—all I meant was a big sexy woman." Tallulah Bankhead had been sexy, and on the stage she had looked tall. She was Lillian's favorite Regina and from time to time Lilly liked to recall the deep thrilling offstage laugh before her first entrance, a laugh that had affected the audience like an electric current; Bankhead's energy had carried her like a firebrand through the Broadway run but halfway through the road-company tour Lillian had closed the show to put an end to her increasingly wild, cocaine-induced cavortings. "Tallulah had the whole cast running around like circus animals . . . it wasn't their fault—you can't *not* respond to an actress like that if you're in a play with her." I asked if Bankhead had ever successfully kicked the cocaine habit. "She wouldn't even admit it was a problem," Lilly said, "when I confronted her with it, she said: 'Darling, I *know* it isn't habit-forming, I've been taking it every day for twenty-five years.' "

Bankhead's Regina was an act nobody had been able to follow, except for Bette Davis in the movie version; what Davis lacked in sexuality she made up for in theatricality, but all that had been long ago, and Lillian no longer expected to see a star of such magnitude play Regina in her lifetime, so it came as something of a shock when she got a call from a producer saying Elizabeth Taylor wanted to do the play.

The casting of Elizabeth Taylor crossed a frontier that had not often been crossed with any success. Few good screen actors make good stage actors, just as few good stage actors know what to do in front of a camera—the techniques are so opposite as to seem almost unrelated. Elizabeth Taylor was a bred-in-the-bone movie star. She had never been on the stage in her life.

Yet her appearance in *Foxes* guaranteed the run of the play: Hollywood, the town so often accused of operating on the "star system," was nothing now compared to Broadway, where a movie personality meant more to the box office than a stage star—and a television star meant more than both. The cost of mounting a Broadway play, once modest enough, was up so high it required some sort of guarantee and there was no more bankable guarantee on both coasts than Elizabeth Taylor.

For a playwright like Lillian facing the end of her life, the main source of work income came from stage productions, since the movie versions of her plays, once sold, were gone forever. *Foxes* had long since been bought by Samuel Goldwyn, who made the Bette Davis movie in 1940, and when Goldwyn died his rights passed to his son. Lillian had begged Goldwyn Jr.'s permission to tape Mike Nichols' 1968 Broadway production of *Foxes* for television but Goldwyn Jr. had refused. He owned it—she did not—that was that. He could do as many versions of *Foxes* as he liked, on film or tape, theatrical release or television, without paying her any royalties, and when he died his heirs could go on doing them—all Lillian owned was the play. One day in the future some claim should be made that no early playwright or novelist like Eugene O'Neill, say, or Ernest Hemingway or even Lillian Hellman ever intended to sell rights for a given work *in perpetuity,* with no hope of getting it back no matter how many versions were made, but such a case would have to be decided in the Supreme Court; too much money is at stake for a precedent to be established easily, since every studio in the country would buck it.

And the problem didn't end with movie rights or even television rights. With the advent of cable and cassette, the world's greediest industry became conscious of the cash value of *all* subsidiary rights, and the vast haggle of lawyers retained by every studio in Hollywood perked up its ears and took out its pencils. Soon the fine print in studio contracts became finer—and funnier. Three months before Taylor's bid to do *Foxes,* I'd shown Lillian a contract for the sale of one of my novels that announced a studio was purchasing "all rights to said property forever . . . in the universe and elsewhere." Together we sat down and wrote a serious letter in response saying the author wished to reserve the cable rights in Elsewhere. We mailed the letter to the studio with a certain reverence, checked the mailbox every morning and at the end of two weeks a letter came back saying the request had been reviewed by the legal department and denied. The answer was no: the studio wanted *all* rights in Elsewhere. We answered that with another letter and kept the correspondence going back and forth for months, until my agent called and told us to quit horsing around or we'd kill the sale. After I'd been paid, Lilly wanted to write them and ask what would happen if somebody invented a pill you could swallow that would enable you to see a movie in your brain, but it didn't seem worth it.

It did seem worth it to let Elizabeth Taylor do *Foxes* and Lilly bargained a very short while over terms and signed the contract fast; she had always been a good deal maker and a stubborn one. "Negotiating is like gambling—you have to be willing to lose. If you need the money, you're dead. But if you can take the money or leave it you're in good shape, and if you're in good shape you can double it."

She didn't double the terms for *Foxes* but she didn't need

to—by the end of the Elizabeth Taylor production Lillian's royalties alone came to almost a million and a half. Considering the
fact that the combined annual royalties for all her plays the year
before had come to $100,000, that was a vast jump. She had
backed away from contractual discussions with Taylor's producer, Zev Bufman, the moment she realized she wasn't dealing
from strength: her star play was not the star now—the star was.
That notion combined with Taylor's legendary beauty didn't put
Lilly in the best of moods and when she went to see the first dress
rehearsal, she was honed up and ready for a fight. If she didn't
get one it was due to Taylor herself, who turned out to be as nice
a woman as everybody said she was.

Elizabeth Taylor's gentleness with Lillian was remarkable
considering everything else about her. It was known that she didn't
show up on time for rehearsals and when she traveled through
New York traffic to the theater it was in a caravan made up of
three limousines, one in front and one in back. If you didn't know
a famous lady was making an entrance when Taylor walked into
a room you did by the time she sat down—she had been a star
since she was a child and knew no other life.

"Elizabeth's never been in a supermarket," Lillian said one
day in shock, "in any kind of market. She's never in her life stood
in line to use a public phone—a public anything. It's like depri-
vation. Elizabeth's an innocent—a true innocent. Every time she
gets laid she gets married. Nobody ever told her you can do it
and stay single. I wonder if she gets lonely—I wonder if she misses
a family. . . ."

If she did, it didn't prevent a fierce sense of loyalty to her
friends that included a respectful attitude to Lillian, who was hell-
bent on being as ornery as possible. When it came time to cast
the rest of *Foxes,* Lilly insisted on Maureen Stapleton for Birdie
and Taylor agreed with, she said later, a qualm or two. It's no
secret that distinguished stage actors are not always fond of movie
stars, and nobody knew how well they would hit it off. For the
first few days of rehearsal Lillian plied Maureen with phone calls,
hoping to wedge a rift between the two women and then get the
credit for repairing it, a piece of mischief she'd sometimes played
on married couples, a tried-and-true trick that usually worked.
But it didn't work this time. Maureen and Elizabeth liked each
other on sight and within a few days were having their meals

together like sisters; after a week they were so close that Lillian, whose fear of rejection was always dressed and waiting in the wings, felt left out, and irritability set in. "What's the matter with Maureen, she spends more time with *that woman* than she does with her own children." The answer was that Maureen's children were grown up and she liked Elizabeth Taylor. "I doubt it's that simple," Lillian said mysteriously, "there's something unpleasant at the bottom of it."

But it was that simple and there wasn't. After another few days of talking about Taylor as "that woman," Lillian gave up and took a closer look.

"I watched a dress rehearsal the other day," she said to Hannah on the phone, "I can't see much, but Elizabeth made her first-act entrance in a dress Flo Ziegfeld would have picked. It must have cost a cool fifty thousand dollars—it was more of a ball gown than a dress—it sure wasn't anything Regina would wear at home during the day, let alone for breakfast. And besides that she was wearing the headlight diamond Richard Burton gave her—she looked like something off the prow of a carnival float. I had to put a stop to it, so I went backstage and sat down in her dressing room. 'Look, Elizabeth,' I said, *'The Little Foxes* is a play about how the middle class in America got to be the upper class. If you wear that dress on your first entrance my whole play goes out the window.' I sat there waiting for a fight—I'd told her the truth so I'd be on record when things got nasty—but Elizabeth only stared at the floor for a few moments, thinking about it . . . and the next dress rehearsal I went to, she had on a different dress, a much simpler one, and the diamond was gone. Maybe Maureen's right—maybe there *is* something special about her. . . ."

There was, and Lilly was impressed despite herself, but her awe was short-lived. Taylor managed to get through the play like a trouper every night but she wasn't at home on the stage and it showed. That by itself wouldn't have thrown Lillian, who expected it, but who didn't expect what happened the first time there was an audience. In the end the play went out the window anyway, not because it was badly performed but because no one in the theater had come to see it: they had all come to see Elizabeth Taylor and they let her know it from the time the curtain went up until long after it went down. Every gesture, every turn, every sound she made caused an echo in the audience ranging from a soft murmur to a muted cheer. They laughed at whatever she said or did, funny or not. It would have taken monumental restraint not to acknowledge that kind of response and Elizabeth did her best—she never once turned and winked at the audience, though the tenor of her performance had a kind of hidden wink in it, the kind Ronald Reagan has when he talks about telling the truth. You couldn't call her shot on it because her fans loved it and presently Lilly got angry at her all over again.

Instead of complaining, she called rehearsals whenever she got the chance, called them weeks after the play had opened, called them in New York, Washington, D.C., and Los Angeles. Elizabeth always went along with it, only once or twice asking why it was necessary to have a three-hour rehearsal that ended two hours before the performance, when the theater was sold out for the entire run, and the people who bought tickets applauded the same no matter what she did or didn't do. Lillian ignored the question and called another rehearsal the next day. The play, she said, demanded a certain style, and this production, which was badly directed, had no style at all. Maureen, of course, knew what she was doing—Maureen could act off the back of a truck—but nobody else did, and Lillian went on calling rehearsals until Elizabeth's good humor started to crack.

"Why doesn't she let the lady alone," Maureen asked me one night at dinner, "would you mind telling her that Gary Cooper *can't* play Regina?"

But Lillian's hammerings at the company only increased, until Elizabeth snapped, though only a few days later she relented and asked Lillian to tea at her rented house in Beverly Hills.

I picked Lilly up and took her there late one blustery afternoon. After the requisite electronic security gate, the maid and the producer, Elizabeth appeared wearing what Southerners still call a shift and looking very pretty without any makeup. For the next hour you had the sense that a couple of three-year-old girls were determined to have a tea party just like grown-ups. They talked like grown-ups, they passed scones like grown-ups, they said please and thank you and remarked on the weather just like grown-ups. But what they really wanted to do was get behind the furniture and throw mud at each other and after an hour and a half Elizabeth said: "May I ask you something?"

"Do, Lizzie," Lillian said.

Elizabeth leaned forward politely and said: "Please don't call me Lizzie."

"All right, honey, I won't," Lillian said, "what was it you wanted to ask me?"

"That's it," Elizabeth said, "that's all—I don't like being called Lizzie. I'd rather you called me Elizabeth."

"I'd be happy to," Lillian said. "Have I ever called you Lizzie?"

"It's all you call me," Elizabeth said.

"If it is, I humbly apologize," Lillian said, "I know the feeling—I hate it when people call me Lil. I much prefer Lilly or Lillian."

"I like Elizabeth, Lillian," Elizabeth said carefully. "What I don't like is Lizzie, if you don't mind." She smiled.

"Why would I mind? God knows I have no wish to offend you—I'll call you anything you like, Lizzie," Lillian said.

Elizabeth fell silent and stared at her a moment, then suddenly burst out laughing and came over and kissed Lillian several times and sat down beside her, her own face flushed and excited. She seemed to realize for the first time that beneath all Lillian's anger and willfulness was a great clumsy glob of innocence you couldn't help but trust, and she sat holding Lilly's hand for the rest of the visit.

On the way home Lillian sat smoking a cigarette with a disgruntled look and I asked what was wrong. "I like her," she said. "It makes it hard. I don't like liking people, it's a waste of time." We drove in silence for a while.

"And she's wrong," Lillian said, "I've never in my life said Lizzie."

From Rita Wade's notebook (this entry written several years later to recall the facts):

March, 1981—I went to Washington D.C. with Miss Hellman for the opening of *The Little Foxes*. We stayed at the Watergate. March 17th we ate dinner at the Kennedy Center, went to the opening, and the party afterwards. She was fine. Next night, March 18th, we dressed and were ready to go out. (She didn't have anything to drink.) As I turned to reach for her purse, she fell. I didn't think she was hurt because she had fallen on a rug and was wearing a long fur coat. I went to help her up, but she said her head had hit the wooden arm of the chair and she wanted me to let her rest for a minute. She was in a sitting position with her back against the arm of the chair. After a while I checked the back of her head and found it was cut and bleeding. I washed the cut and helped her up. She put on a hat to hide the blood that had matted her hair and we went downstairs to the dining room in the Watergate for dinner. At the theater she told the company manager she had fallen and hit her head. He said he would have a doctor look at her during intermission. When the doctor saw her he told us to go immediately to the George Washington Hospital where it took five or six stitches to close the wound. They did not, however, take any X-rays, although she had complained that her back hurt. The next morning, March 19th, I put a hot water bottle to her lower back and that gave her some relief. She stayed in bed all day but we went to dinner that night at the Kennedy Center, then to the theater and the party afterwards at the Pisces Club and stayed until midnight. When we came back to the hotel there was a message for me to call home. I did and was told that my husband had had a heart attack and died at 8:30 PM. I left on the first shuttle in the morning after calling Cinda Thompson to come to Washington. (Miss Hellman didn't at all mind staying alone for the two hours.)

Her fall in the Watergate Hotel was Lillian's second noticeable stroke, the first having been the episode at Avallon. But by now I'd begun to have the feeling that the danger wasn't so much in strokes that were obvious as in the ones that weren't. It was as if all the capillaries in her body had taken to popping in an aimless and indiscriminate way, whenever they felt like it, sometimes inside the brain sometimes not, so that she had probably been undergoing innumerable tiny strokes for years without knowing it, like a constant small leakage of the system. If she was conscious of what was happening it was not in a sudden or dreadful or even very clear way, but rather in a growing awareness of the unexpected, of trouble in the wings, and it gave her a kind of gloomy satisfaction at seeing her old enemy, her body, show its true colors and go sour on her as she had always known it would.

She continued to ignore it and went about her business. The run of *Foxes* in Washington was followed by a special performance for the Reagans, who planned to come backstage afterward and congratulate the actors and author. This was tantamount to a royal command performance, American style, and the company looked forward to the event with some trepidation: given Lilly's blunt and often articulate opinion of Reagan and everything he stood for, an attitude that was not exactly new in her, the prospect of a one-on-one confrontation was a matter of concern to everybody in the neighborhood.

The Watergate hotel-room fall had produced among other things a splintered bone, so that Lillian was back on crutches, a precursor of what life was to be like in the not-too-distant future and one that made her grumpy. Maureen took it upon herself to stand beside her during the event, a decision based more on affection than sense. They had known each other ever since Maureen's marriage to Max Allentuck, and for years afterward—years that included the birth of Maureen's two children by Max, her divorce from Max, her sustained friendship with Max long after the divorce and her continuing career: Maureen and Lilly had always supported each other as old friends do with an occasional phone call, a note when a note was appropriate, lunch at home, dinner in a restaurant. Through times that were trying and times that were not they had stayed close and it seemed natural now for Maureen to be with her during this most trying time of all.

Before the president and the first lady came backstage, several of Lillian's friends sat her down and lectured her about it, everybody saying more or less the same thing, that it would be better to skip the meeting entirely than to make a mess of it and disgrace herself in front of the Reagans. It was not a political event and must not be construed as one. Lilly had given her solemn word of honor to behave herself and Maureen had promised never to leave her side.

On the night of the command performance, the actors lined up dutifully backstage. At one end of the line was Maureen—then Lillian—then Elizabeth; a place between them seemed to guarantee Lillian's safety from anything, including herself, though the unexpected can happen from time to time no matter what you do.

On the way down the line of actors, President and Mrs. Reagan came to a halt in front of Maureen. Mrs. Reagan said: "Hello, Maureen," and Maureen said: "Hello, Nancy." After that, the president spoke briefly to Maureen and they passed on to Lillian.

While everyone in line held their breath, the president and the first lady told Lillian how much they had enjoyed her play and Lillian accepted the compliment politely. Their meeting was brief, it went according to protocol and the presidential couple moved on to Elizabeth.

While the Reagans were speaking to Elizabeth, Lillian turned to Maureen slowly with a shocked expression and said, in a voice full of reproach: "You *know* her?"

Maureen shook her head in silence. She only wanted to postpone the conversation, she explained later, since Lillian's voice even at whisper level could be heard across the theater.

"You *know* her," Lillian repeated in disbelief. "You *know* her. *She* said: 'Hello, Maureen,' and *you* said: 'Hello, Nancy.' "

"She used to be an actress," Maureen whispered, "I'm an actress. Actresses call each other by their first names."

"That doesn't explain it, and you know it doesn't. Oh, my God . . . You know them," Lillian said accusingly, her voice growing louder, "you know them both. If you know her, you must know him too. *You know her . . . you know her . . . you . . .*"

The next day, when it was all over, Lillian told the rest of it this way: "Maureen would never have answered if I hadn't backed her against the wall . . . it's not the sort of thing a woman likes to admit about her husband, even an ex-husband, but I wouldn't let her alone no matter what she said—I just went on shouting, '*You know her . . . you know her*' till Maureen told me the truth. She said: 'I don't know her. Max fucked her.' "

Lillian paused and sighed. "Well, that was that—I laughed so hard my crutches went flying out from under me and Elizabeth and Maureen had to carry me into the Green Room and lay me out on the sofa. Even then I couldn't stop guffawing and wheezing and gasping for breath and coughing all at the same time. They almost called the doctor."

I asked why they hadn't.

"I sat up and stopped, of course," Lillian said. "I didn't want to disgrace myself in front of the Reagans."

II

A JUG OF WINE AND THOU

LILLIAN: Why am I eating this pickle?
PETER: Maybe you like it.
LILLIAN: I don't. My stomach is making noises, can't you hear it?

PAUSE.

LILLIAN: My stomach was cutting up badly last night—it kept me awake. I never heard such goings-on in my life.

PAUSE.

LILLIAN: You know what I was thinking when I couldn't sleep? I was thinking how many people spend their lives with their inferiors . . . there's a terrible price to be paid for that.

PAUSE.

LILLIAN: Seems to me one has to do almost the opposite. The only people who can keep you in check are the people you have some respect for . . .

SOUND OF COUGHING.

LILLIAN: People who are superior to you, I mean, or your equal in something. The writers who have nothing but bootlickers around them always seem to suffer for it in their work . . . like [BLANK BLANK], for instance—I thought his last book was awful. Didn't you?
PETER: Yes.
LILLIAN: Worse than awful . . . cheap. All of it, including the fine writing department. I found the sex all whomped up in it

*too. There was something quite phony about the whole book—
phony-large.*

SOUND OF COUGHING.

LILLIAN: *I was at Christopher Lehmann-Haupt's house one night
last winter when John Cheever was there . . . Cheever and Norman Mailer, both—I don't know Cheever very well, but I've always thought of him as a rather kindly man—well, not kindly,
he can be very sharp—but a not ungenerous man . . . and I
suddenly heard him say, across the room, "I think it's one of the
most contemptible books I've ever read in my life. I've nothing
but contempt for the book and the writer." And I said, "Who,
John?" And he said, "[BLANK BLANK] and his new novel." He
said it in a voice that was hair-raising. Just hair-raising . . . I
said, "Why the writer along with the book?" He said, "Why not?
The man wrote the book, didn't he?"*
PETER: *What did Norman say?*
LILLIAN: *Nothing. He was grinning.*

PAUSE.

LILLIAN: *Are you getting drunk, honey?*
PETER: *Pleasantly so. Nothing to write home about.*
LILLIAN: *Me too. Pour me some more wine, will you?*

PAUSE.

LILLIAN: *I had a nice chat with Mike Nichols this morning, did I
tell you, he's doing a new play, it sounds wonderful. We talked
about that and about . . . well, I don't know how Los Angeles
came into the conversation but it did . . . Mike began to joke
about all the trips I've taken—not joke, exactly, when I was young
it was called kidding on the square. Mike's good at that, so
are you.*
PETER: *What's kidding on the square?*
LILLIAN: *It just popped into my head after all this time—after
forty years, I suppose . . . I really don't think I've heard that
expression in forty, fifty years. Kidding on the square . . . I'm
not sure I can tell you what it means, it's been too long. Wish
Sid Perelman was alive. He could tell you.*
PETER: *Sending somebody up with a straight face?*
LILLIAN: *Partly, only I'm not so sure it had to do with another*

person . . . it had more to do with a sort of attitude, a talk . . . know what I'm trying to say?
PETER: *Sort of.*
LILLIAN: *You kidded on the square about . . . oh, the hell with it, I should shut up. I've had too much to drink and it's been too long.*

PAUSE.

LILLIAN: *I guess I'll go to bed now.*
PETER: *You can't.*
LILLIAN: *Why not?*
PETER: *You owe me a story.*
LILLIAN: *I do?*
PETER: *Uh-huh.*
LILLIAN: *Are you sure it's my turn?*
PETER: *Yes.*
LILLIAN: *Okay.*

PAUSE.

LILLIAN: *Well, there was a girl.*

PAUSE.

LILLIAN: *That's the story.*
PETER: *That's not a story.*
LILLIAN: *It is.*
PETER: *It is not.*
LILLIAN: *She died.*

PAUSE.

PETER: *Of what?*
LILLIAN: *I don't know.*
PETER: *Come on, Lilly.*
LILLIAN: *Nobody ever knew.*
PETER: *The storyteller's got to know.*
LILLIAN: *Snakebite.*
PETER: *Snakebite?*
LILLIAN: *Uh-huh.*
PETER: *Where was she?*
LILLIAN: *In bed.*
PETER: *With a snake?*

LILLIAN: *Uh-huh.*
PETER: *Just like the rest of us.*
LILLIAN: *Just like the rest.*

SOUND OF COUGHING.

PETER: *Go on.*
LILLIAN: *She didn't know it was a snake. She thought it was a prince.*
PETER: *At least we knew.*

SOUND OF DRUNKEN LAUGHTER.

PETER: *Was she happy with the snake?*
LILLIAN: *No.*
PETER: *Why not?*
LILLIAN: *It wasn't affectionate enough—it only came to see her when she fed it.*
PETER: *She wanted a snake that loved her for herself?*
LILLIAN: *Yes.*
PETER: *Go on. What was the snake's name?*
LILLIAN: *Karl.*
PETER: *German snake?*

PAUSE.

PETER: *Irish? . . . Jewish? . . .*
LILLIAN: *German-Jewish.*
PETER: *German-Jewish snake?*
LILLIAN: *Uh huh.*
PETER: *Was she Jewish?*
LILLIAN: *She was Scotch-Irish.*
PETER: *Scotch-Irish, was she suicidal?*
LILLIAN: *No.*
PETER: *Honey, if a Scotch-Irish lady gets in bed with a German-Jewish snake, either she needs therapy or he's very rich.*
LILLIAN: *He was rich.*
PETER: *And he bit her?*
LILLIAN: *Uh-huh. What the rich always do.*
PETER: *And what happened?*
LILLIAN: *She died.*
PETER: *What did people think she died of?*
LILLIAN: *No one knew.*

PETER: *How old was she?*
LILLIAN: *Eighty-one, eighty-two.*
PETER: *How old was he?*
LILLIAN: *Forty-one, forty-two.*
PETER: *He fell in love with a woman twice his age and then killed her?*
LILLIAN: *Sure.*
PETER: *Why sure?*
LILLIAN: *It's what he did for a living.*
PETER: *I thought you said he was rich.*
LILLIAN: *That's how he got rich.*
PETER: *So she was rich too.*
LILLIAN: *Uh-huh.*

PAUSE.

LILLIAN: *Can I have a cigarette now?*
PETER: *No.*
LILLIAN: *Why not?*
PETER: *You've already had your quota for the day. The only reason you want to go to bed is because you've got a fresh pack hid under the mattress. Don't get off the subject, you were telling me a story.*
LILLIAN: *I did tell you a story.*
PETER: *That's not a story. I know a story when I hear one. A Scotch-Irish lady who gets bit by her lover is not a story.*
LILLIAN: *A* snake.
PETER: *It's still not a story. It's an event.*
LILLIAN: *I say it's a story—you say it's an event.*

PAUSE.

LILLIAN: *I must be right, I'm older than you are.*

SOUND OF DRUNKEN LAUGHTER.

PETER: *How old are you these days?*
LILLIAN: *Who knows? I've lied so much about my age I don't know hold old I am myself anymore.*
PETER: *You ought to be proud of your age.*
LILLIAN: *You think so?*
PETER: *Sure.*
LILLIAN: *Well,* you *be proud of it, honey.*

PAUSE.

PETER: Wasn't it Bernhardt or somebody who lied the other way—made herself older than she was?

LILLIAN: Shaw did it too.

PETER: He did?

LILLIAN: The one time I met him he did. He added a whole year to his age.

PETER: When?

LILLIAN: I only met him once—in forty-four I think it was. Willy Wyler arranged it with Gabby Pascal.

PETER: Gabby?

LILLIAN: Gabriel Pascal. Shaw's movie producer.

PETER: Oh, him. Wasn't he the producer who had that correspondence with Shaw—the one who wrote and said he wanted to do a very artistic film of one of the plays—that he deeply believed in its artistic truth?

LILLIAN: That's right. And Shaw wrote back and said, "The difference between you and me is that you're interested in art, and I'm interested in money."

PETER: So they wound up friends.

LILLIAN: Great friends. Pascal took me along when he went down to see him. And Mr. Shaw was very nice to me—very, very nice . . . I don't think he knew who I was, but he was nice. Charming.

PAUSE.

LILLIAN: We spent a long afternoon there. It was touching to see this old man's affection for Pascal—he was the only producer he'd allow to do his work. . . . I remember Shaw came out on the lawn to see us off. He had a pleasant modest house. Very modest. He stood on the lawn by the car, talking, for a long time . . . and later on Pascal said, "He likes you," and I said, "How do you know?" And he said, "He never does that except with people he likes."

PAUSE.

LILLIAN: He probably made it up.

PETER: Why would he make it up?

LILLIAN: I don't know, maybe he didn't . . . I'd just come out of Russia and it's true Shaw was interested . . . I told him I'd raised

*a fuss about getting royalties out—I had raised a fuss, a big one—
I said, "I hope it does you some good too, because they perform
you all the time." And he said, "Oh, my dear child, perhaps it
would be best if we both left our royalties there . . . we may
need to go there one day . . ."*

SOUND OF COUGHING.

LILLIAN: *He said, "We may all need to get out of the Western
world."*
PETER: *Did he?*
LILLIAN: *Uh-huh. I thought he was very handsome.*
PETER: *Figures.*
LILLIAN: *Remarkable face. Except for the skin. Very blotched, you
know—whatever that disease is that people get—the one Red Lewis
had—Sinclair Lewis—I don't know what it's called. . . .*
PETER: *How old was Shaw?*
LILLIAN: *When I met him? I'm not sure anymore. I think he said
he was eighty-nine, and when I looked it up he was only
eighty-eight.*

PAUSE.

LILLIAN: *How old do you think I am?*
PETER: *Oh, about seven.*
LILLIAN: *Pour some more wine for me. I think you're charming
too. What makes you so charming?*
PETER: *I have a beautiful nature.*
LILLIAN: *How beautiful?*
PETER: *Too beautiful. I try to think one ugly thought every day.*

SOUND OF DRUNKEN LAUGHTER.

LILLIAN: *I love you. Whatever that word means. I've come to
know less and less what it means . . . all I know is what one is
willing to do about it. Who you're willing to take an action for,
who you're not, that's all I know—that's all there is to know
about love. Do you really love me?*
PETER: *Yes.*
LILLIAN: *I wonder.*
PETER: *Take that back.*
LILLIAN: *I take it back. I can't afford to wonder.*

SOUND OF DRUNKEN LAUGHTER.

LILLIAN: I want to come sit on your lap.
PETER: Okay.

PAUSE.

LILLIAN: I'm about to kill myself on this light cord.
PETER: Step over it, honey.
LILLIAN: I can't see to step over anything.
PETER: I'm right here. No there . . . this way . . . there
we are . . .

PAUSE.

LILLIAN: You've got a new bone.
PETER: That's my collarbone. It's always been there.
LILLIAN: Since when?
PETER: Since I was born.
LILLIAN: I never felt it before.
PETER: Sure you have.
LILLIAN: It's gotten bigger.
PETER: Collarbones don't get bigger.

PAUSE.

LILLIAN: I'm going to kiss you now.
PETER: Thank you.
LILLIAN: You're welcome.

PAUSE.

LILLIAN: You don't want to be loved.
PETER: Oh, shut up, Lilly. Everybody wants to be loved.
*LILLIAN: Everybody but you. Promise me something. When I die,
don't let Rose turn my funeral into one of her social events.*
PETER: I can't promise that, it's too hard. Ask me something else.
LILLIAN: Please don't do our things with other girls.
PETER: Okay.

PAUSE.

LILLIAN: This collarbone is certainly new stuff.
PETER: It is not new stuff.
LILLIAN: It's never been this sharp.
PETER: My collarbone has always been where it is and what it is.

PAUSE.

PETER: *I sure hope nobody ever hears us talk, they'd lock us up.*
LILLIAN: *Nobody would lock you up . . . you're much too darling to lock up.*
PETER: *They lock up darling people.*
LILLIAN: *Not you, I wouldn't let them take you. Not unless you had a lot of money. I'd fight like a tiger.*
PETER: *How do tigers fight?*
LILLIAN: *Mean.*

   PAUSE.

LILLIAN: *Know what? I think you're a very funny man.*
PETER: *Thank you.*
LILLIAN: *You're welcome. I never have loved anybody in my life that I didn't think was funny.*
PETER: *Nice to know I fit on the list.*

   PAUSE.

LILLIAN: *Peter-pie.*
PETER: *Yes.*
LILLIAN: *You know what I think? We've had a lot of problems, but we've come out fine, in the end . . . haven't we?*

   PAUSE.

LILLIAN: *Haven't we, Peter?*
PETER: *It's not the end yet.*

$$\leftarrowtail\leftarrowtail\leftarrowtail\leftarrowtail\leftarrowtail \text{ III}$$

ITEMS SELECTED FROM Rita Wade's notebook:

1981—Summer: Linda Lightner hired for the Vineyard and drove rented car to the Vineyard. Met Miss Hellman and Peter Feibleman there.

1981—Sunday November 22: Around 1:30 p.m. Miss Hellman and Linda were shopping on Lexington Avenue for a micro cassette recorder. Miss Hellman began to complain of pressure in the chest area. She also said she had a headache, although she said she had no pain in the chest. She appeared to have difficulty breathing.

Around 3:00 Dr. McCormack came to the house and examined Miss Hellman. He said he thought she was having a heart attack and advised her to go to the hospital immediately. Miss Hellman was fully conscious throughout this time, although she appeared to be in great discomfort.

Miss Hellman was taken by ambulance at around 4:00 to Columbia Presbyterian Hospital and was first examined in the emergency room, where she remained for about 30 minutes. She was then taken to the intensive care unit.

1981—Monday November 23: Dr. Allan Schwartz, the cardiologist, reported that during the night Miss Hellman's heart had stopped beating for a period of four seconds. She remained in intensive care for more tests. A temporary pacemaker was installed.

1981—Tuesday November 24: Enzyme tests revealed that Miss Hellman had not suffered a heart attack. Her condition was described as a "sick sinus," in which the nerves which control the heartbeat malfunction. In Miss Hellman's case the heart was beating too slowly. Tuesday night a pacemaker was installed (permanent).

1981—Wednesday, November 25: Miss Hellman was moved from intensive care to Harkness Pavilion, Room 1136, where she remained until 4:00 p.m. Tuesday, December 1st.

1981—December: Miss Hellman was sitting on the toilet and suddenly found herself falling over the bar (fitted over the side of the bathtub) and into the tub, cutting her left shoulder and hand very badly. Because it was Sunday I wasn't there and it took the elevator man and the doorman to get her out of the tub and over onto the bed. Dr. Meltzer was away and Dr. McCormack came and gave her a prescription for a salve for the cuts. For the next couple of weeks she had trouble with her left side and arm. At first we thought the arm was sore because of the fall, but as time went on the arm grew weak and painful. It was obvious she had had a small stroke.

1981—December 31: New Year's Eve: I was in her bedroom when she got up out of bed. When she attempted to stand up (I was helping her) her left leg became powerless. Her left foot was turned to the right and she could not control it. I would turn her foot straight out, and it moved easily, but she could not move it. We called Dr. Meltzer and he immediately made an appointment with Dr. Linda Lewis, the neurologist, and we spent most of that New Year's Eve in Columbia Presbyterian for a brain scan. (Dr. Lewis said her brain cells were those of a woman twenty years younger.)

1982—Winter: The Beverly Wilshire Hotel—In hotel room she toppled over and cut her head and hand against the edge of a television set. Saw Dr. Grode, the neurologist recommended by Dr. Lewis. He thought the fall was due to very low blood pressure.

Lillian's troubles went on like an extended punishment that year and I spent the winter flying back and forth between Los Angeles and New York. My mother was in the hospital and Lilly was still competing with her about who had the most serious illness: the morning after the episode that preceded the implant of her pacemaker, when her doctor told her that her heart had stopped beating for four seconds, she phoned me.

"Darling, I was pronounced dead last night. I didn't call you because I didn't want to worry you. You have enough to worry about with your mother," she said happily. "Save yourself."

Because of her eyes she couldn't read and because of the paralysis in her left side she couldn't move by herself. When she couldn't sleep she began to watch television at night—a new experience for a woman who had in common with my mother that she thought the entire function of television was a way to get the news if you couldn't find a newspaper.

When she had first tried the tube as a soporific, she went straight to the talk shows, and had just turned on the *Dick Cavett Show* when Cavett asked Mary McCarthy what she thought of Lillian Hellman's work—and McCarthy said: "Every word she writes is a lie, including 'and' and 'the.' " Lilly laughed out loud when she heard it but the next morning called her lawyer and told him to sue. "Watching television is all that's left," she said later on the phone. "I only turned the set on out of desperation and look what happens . . . somebody comes through it and insults me in my own bedroom. I can't let Mary's poisonous nonsense go without taking a stand, can I?"

She expected me to agree and I didn't. Miss McCarthy's attack seemed regrettable but not, I thought, without precedent: taking potshots at a celebrity, and so garnering some of the limelight, is hardly a new game, it's the oldest game in town, and the public spats of writers often make the front page if at least one of them is famous, witness Lillian and Diana Trilling or Norman Mailer and Gore Vidal. Now and then it was not unheard of for someone to be jealous of Lillian's talent, her fame, her sex life or her chutzpah. And Miss McCarthy's attack was to be expected on other grounds: she had been a Trotskyite and, with the exception of Vanessa Redgrave, anybody who had been one hated Lillian.

Apart from that, sixteen years earlier, in 1964, the *Paris Review* had printed the following:

INTERVIEWER: Can you comment on your contemporaries . . . Arthur Miller?

HELLMAN: I like *Death of a Salesman*. I have reservations about it, but I thought it was an effective play. I like best *View from the Bridge* . . .

INTERVIEWER: And Tennessee Williams?

HELLMAN: I think he is a natural playwright. He writes by sanded fingertips . . .

INTERVIEWER: Mary McCarthy wrote in a review that she gets the feeling that no matter what happens, Mr. Williams will be rich and famous.

HELLMAN: I have the same feeling about Miss Mc-
Carthy.

INTERVIEWER: She has accused you, among other
things, of a certain "lubricity," of an over facility in answering complex questions. Being too facile, relying on
contrivance.

HELLMAN: I don't like to defend myself against Miss
McCarthy's opinions, or anybody else's. I think Miss
McCarthy is often brilliant and sometimes even sound.
But, in fiction, she is a lady writer, a lady magazine writer.
Of course, that doesn't mean she isn't right about me. But
if I thought she was, I'd quit. I would like critics to like
my plays because that is what makes plays successful. But
a few people I respect are the only ones whose opinions
I've worried about in the end.

An interview in the *Paris Review* calling Miss McCarthy a
lady magazine writer would not have escaped the attention of
Miss McCarthy, who lived in Paris, and her response on the Cavett show sixteen years later when Lillian's name came up was
hardly astonishing. I thought Lillian ought to overlook it and I
told her what she would have told me: forget it and get on with
your life.

"What life?" she said. We argued about it for an hour or so
and I gave up.

Despite her siege of trouble that year Lilly flew to Los Angeles and made plans to see people, since she never permitted the
deterioration of her health to affect her social life if she could
help it. By then she needed a part-time nurse and a live-in housekeeper, a bigger staff than I had room for in my house, so she
rented a place in Beverly Hills.

One morning after a dinner with some friends in an Italian
restaurant in West Hollywood, I got a call from the Guatemalan
maid who worked in the rented house. "Miss Hellman, she need
see you," she said.

I drove over and found Lilly in the living room listening to
Brahms. "Hello, darling, I left my teeth in the restaurant," she
said. "This is going to be one of those days, I can tell. Would
you mind calling the owner and asking him for them?"

I called the restaurant owner, who had made a great deal of
Italian fuss the night before over the honor of having Lillian Hell-

man in his establishment, and told him the problem. About twenty minutes later a taxi pulled up in front of the house and the driver knocked on the door with a hand-written note, a bunch of dark red roses, a container of freshly made pasta and Lillian's teeth.

"That's the second time I've lost them," she said. "I'd better quit taking them out of my mouth. You know what happened the last time."

I couldn't remember.

"I left them in the pocket of my mink coat at Lally Weymouth's black-tie dinner last November," she said, "and when that awful banker came up to kiss me good-night, I put my hand in my pocket and bit myself. I've got to think of a better solution . . . this won't do."

That morning I stayed and read to her for a while, as I had been doing two or three times a week. It was the morning we started *Absalom, Absalom!* and we went on with it all that month. Lilly had always loved being read to, but now blindness made it necessary, and when a ringing phone broke through the reading she got mad, then tactful, in that order.

The phone calls that came during the week of *Absalom, Absalom!* required more tact than usual: Lillian had managed to involve herself in the personal lives of a wealthy Beverly Hills couple, John and Mary Smith, each of whom had taken to using her as a kind of confidante and personal adviser. It was Lilly who had told them to get a divorce in the first place and we were in the final chapter of the book when the phone started ringing.

"It's Mary Smith," the voice said, "John is offering me five million dollars in alimony, plus five hundred thousand a year in child support—and the Beverly Hills house. What do you think?"

"I think you have to turn it down," Lillian said, "it's an insulting offer—John is a very, very rich man, and you've given him thirteen years of your life. Have a little pride now. Say no."

She hung up and I went on reading to her and twenty minutes later the phone rang again. Lillian sighed. This time it was John.

"I offered her five million dollars, plus five hundred thousand a year in child support, and the house," he said, "she just turned it down. What do you think?"

"I think she's an ungrateful cunt," Lillian said and hung up again. "I wish I had the willpower to turn the phone off the way you do," she said wistfully, "it must be so restful. Go on reading, honey . . . I think they'll let me alone for a while now."

Reading often led to writing for Lillian as it does for most writers. She tried using a tape recorder, often letting it run for hours, but it wasn't any good, since dictating is not a viable option for a writer who has lived by the look of words on a page: a playwright can time the length of a play by the look of it. Having given up the theater, Lillian no longer thought in dialogue, but for prose she was more than ever dependent on her eyes. The only thing I could think of that might bridge the gap was a maverick form, like screenwriting. But for Lillian's kind of writer the word was a contradiction in terms, since the truth is you can't write on the screen. You can only write a story structure and some dialogue with a little description and hope the director sees things as you see them.

In looking around for something that might interest her and be possible for her to dictate, I took to fiddling with the notion of a sequel to *Foxes* written for film or television. Lillian thought it over for a few days and one night began to dictate the outline of a plot into a small tape recorder she kept by her bed for sending messages to Rita Wade.

The story she started had to do with Regina's daughter, Alexandra, a long and intricately planned story of revenge. After a week's worth of fighting with the machine she asked me to take it away, have the outline typed up and finish it myself in rough draft. I did, and she began to fiddle with it again until the outline took off and began to have a life of its own.

But the sequel to *Foxes* was never made, because the day the outline was finished Robby Lantz, Lillian's agent and friend, called to say that he had researched it and found that she did not own the sequel rights. Goldwyn Jr. owned them and Lillian had no legal recourse. After the phone call she was too exhausted and dispirited to do anything for weeks and no sequel seemed worth it. By that time Lillian was tired of Regina, tired of Alexandra, tired of trying to stay alive—and ready as a writer to go on to something new.

The last thing I remember about that winter is a concert Lilly went to at some theater downtown. The couple who invited us were heavy-going do-gooders and I copped out and told Lilly I'd meet her for a drink afterward. The concert had had a lot of attention in the press because the visiting musician, a talented

Italian violinist, was the newest star that year in the world of classical music, the disciple of a famous conductor. It was rumored that the violinist had been the conductor's lover.

When the concert was over I waited for her in the bar of the Beverly Wilshire. Lilly's host and hostess drove her back and she walked in alone on crutches looking wobbly and tired, a glint in her eye. While she was waiting for her drink she talked about the concert.

"That violinist is great," she said. "But I didn't have a very good time. Blindness is an inconvenience apart from everything else . . . the drive back here from the auditorium took forty-five minutes and I couldn't see a thing. There was nothing to talk about with those people—they're the worst kind of liberals—they were going on about an orphanage and all the other fine causes they'd contributed money to this year, and I suddenly thought I can't stand any more of this self-serving crap, I just can't. So I started cutting up. I began by asking whether it was true about the Italian violinist and the conductor being lovers, and I used all the words I could think of—the ones high-minded people like that hate. 'I wonder how it worked,' I said, 'did the conductor screw the wop or did the wop screw the conductor?' The words were barely out of my mouth when a voice out of the backseat said: 'I'm in the car, Miss Hellman.' "

There was a pause while Lillian sighed and sipped her drink and I asked what she'd said then.

"I didn't say anything," she said. "I thought silence was better at that point. More tasteful. When we got out, I said, 'I can't take back what I've said, sir, because I've said it. But I'm very sorry if I hurt your feelings.' He turned out to be a very nice man. He put an arm around me and said: 'You didn't hurt my feelings, Miss Hellman, I don't know why you didn't, but you didn't.' So we got to talking about that, and now I'm having dinner with him tomorrow night. Just the two of us," she added. "I hope you're jealous. All that gossip is nonsense, he's not the conductor's lover at all. He's a very tall heterosexual Italian man with a lovely voice. Good-looking too."

I asked her how she knew he was good-looking if she couldn't see anything.

Lillian smiled. "Oh, well," she said softly, "I can see *that* much."

The week after the concert we were having dinner at a restaurant when some people at a table across the room began to wave: Herb Ross and his wife, Nora Kaye, old friends of Lillian's and of mine. Lilly asked who it was and when I told her, she turned away sharply to prevent them from coming over. "I can't be nice to Nora Kaye," she said, "it would be disloyal to Hannah. They had a fight over the same man and Hannah's never forgiven her."

After dinner we got up and went to the door but while Lilly was putting her coat on she changed her mind. "What's the matter with me?" she said. "It was a spat between two women and it's been over for twenty years—I like Nora—I'm going to tell her so."

She felt her way back blindly to the Ross table and by the time she got there everyone was standing. "Hello, Nora," she said, throwing her arms around the first person she came to. When she came back to the door she said: "Nora's *much* shorter than I remembered, and she's wearing the wrong perfume. She smells like an old tangerine."

"You weren't kissing Nora Kaye," the captain of the restaurant said reverently in hushed tones, "you were kissing Ray Stark— Mr. Stark is the most powerful producer at Columbia."

Lillian laughed but when we were outside and the parking attendant had gone for the car, she stopped. "Dottie was right about hating the blind. I bet I'm the only woman in history who kissed that big a movie executive and didn't get paid for it."

The week after, she went back to New York and the following month we met on the Vineyard. It was a jittery summer because Lillian had an important decision to make at the end of it, a decision she'd been chewing herself up about for months: a cardiologist she'd been consulting had suggested that she have an endarterectomy, a surgical procedure in which the carotid arteries, the two arteries in the neck, are opened and reamed in order to clean them of plaque that has built up around the arterial walls. The plaque, he said, was responsible for her series of strokes and might be preventing the flow of blood to the brain. Lillian didn't understand any of it and asked me to explain it to her about once a day, but she couldn't get the facts straight and didn't want to: she put off making the decision from week to week. Twice in early August she fell, fracturing a rib the first time and cutting her hand so badly the second that she was taken to the emergency room at Martha's Vineyard Hospital to have it sewn up.

The summer wore on, we spoke of other things, and toward the end of August the tension was palpable. I didn't like the way Lilly looked or the wandering sudden way she spoke, as if her mind were going off in a direction she didn't want but couldn't avoid. Once I knocked on her door and went in to find her staring at the ceiling—or at something beyond the ceiling—beyond the house maybe or even the island.

"It was a very bad dream," she began as if I'd asked, "the kind that makes you think you've dreamed the same thing before. Familiar nightmares are the worst—I'd rather be scared by something new than something like that. He was lying on his back in the earth. It was soggy, like that place we went to in a skiff, the swamp outside New Orleans, and he was sinking back into it— he held out his hand and he was staring at me. I didn't like the way he was staring and he kept smiling and beckoning to me with his hand . . . isn't that an awful dream?"

"Hammett's buried in Arlington Cemetery," I said, "Arlington's nowhere near New Orleans, it's not soggy earth and he couldn't get you to join him there if he wanted to, it's for veterans."

"Don't tell me," Lillian said. "Tell Dash." She rolled over and stared at the wall.

The dream about Hammett haunted her for a week though she never had it again, and on the last day of August I called Elaine May and asked if she'd come to the Vineyard for a few days to visit Lillian and cheer her up. It was one of those 2 A.M. ideas that seem brilliant when you have them and turn into disaster by daylight, but I didn't know what else to do and I knew Elaine's visit would come as a total surprise. Lillian had been angry at her for over twenty years, nurturing a grudge that started because Elaine was Mike Nichols' friend and continued because she was my friend, which was like purposely poaching on Lilly's private territory.

Not everybody is good in times of trouble but Elaine is and if anyone could distract Lillian she could—that much I knew. So I lied and told Elaine that Lillian very much wanted her to come. What I wasn't sure of was how to tell Lilly she was coming, so I made it as casual as I could and reminded her of an open invitation she'd once made to any close friend I wanted to see.

"You picked a fine friend to start with after all these years. That woman hates me," Lillian said.

I had a hunch she knew it wasn't true and I didn't argue with her. But driving Elaine from the Vineyard airport back to the house I began to have doubts and by the time I got her into the living room with Lilly I was sure I'd made a mistake, having told Elaine one story and Lillian another. I beat a retreat into the kitchen with a book and stayed there for upwards of an hour.

When I went back they were sitting on the sofa together laughing and holding hands; Elaine had a volume of *Autumn Garden* open in her lap and was asking Lillian questions about it. Lilly, I noticed, had put on fresh lipstick and was trying to comb her hair with her good hand. I tiptoed back into the kitchen and had a couple of stiff drinks.

The weekend went better than anyone could have predicted: Elaine was a postgraduate in the school of survival for people with difficult mothers and anyone with those credentials was apt to find a familiar challenge in Lilly, though almost nobody handled it as instinctively as Elaine. She knew without asking that humor was the key, she knew when and how to argue with Lilly and for how long. While Elaine was working her half of the street, Lilly was working the other half: what she knew was how to play a character that was a kind of cross between a world-famous courtesan and a grumpy little old lady in a way that would touch Elaine, and her performance was dazzling. She was much the better flirt. Together they waltzed through the weekend like a well-oiled dance team. Not since Dorothy Parker had Lilly sat down with a woman who could partner her in all the games she liked, silly and serious games and games not yet invented—someone she could count on to play fancy champion badminton with words and never drop the bird.

Apart from game playing, the two shared a sense of pure fun, the rarest of all pleasures at a certain level and the hardest to come by in a pinch when it's the only thing that helps. If you're in trouble, and you suspect it's bad trouble, serious thinking is advisable. But when you know you're dying, laughter is the best medicine of all.

Elaine left on Monday promising to come see Lilly again and I stayed on the Vineyard another three weeks and then went back to a script-fixing job I'd taken in Los Angeles. I hadn't been in my house long enough to unpack when Rita called to say there was a problem. The wires of Lillian's pacemaker had broken out and were dangling loose; she'd been flown to Massachusetts General Hospital in Boston, where the pacemaker was to be removed and reimplanted. Mass General was the hospital where the endarterectomy was tentatively scheduled for September, pending Lillian's decision, but now there was no telling what might or might not happen. No one was in charge and Lilly was too frightened to cooperate: she wouldn't eat, Rita said, didn't want to listen to doctors and was refusing to consent to a surgical procedure of any kind until I got there: she had put my name down on her chart as next of kin.

I swapped soiled shirts for clean shirts, went back to the airport and got to Boston so late I spent that night in a chair by her bed. She was scared the way a baby is scared, and the next morning, after arrangements had been made for private nurses, I checked into the Sonesta Hotel across the river from the hospital where my room could be seen from hers and she would know I was within walking distance. I didn't know it then but she would need private nursing around the clock for the rest of her life; it was the beginning of a never-ending search through one registry after another as Lillian unleashed her spleen at nurse after nurse, chewing them up and spitting them out like so many paper dolls, until no self-respecting uniformed woman or man would come within fifty feet of her. She seemed to know by instinct, upon meeting a nurse, which button to push, what to say that would have the effect of shredding the newcomer and rendering her harmless, and the nurse would be left standing at Lillian's bedside spluttering and shaking with anger. When cornered, Lilly could always resort to her old trick of reproducing her own rage in the person she was talking to, and she was still good at it.

Her stay at Mass General was to last for three long months as she was shuffled from floor to floor, test to test, operating room to operating room, while I waited in the hotel across the river. By the end of that time I had come to think of modern medicine as a clumsy and rather primitive form of torture practiced by a series of skilled, abysmally innocent and faintly sadistic selectmen who mistook a gland for a human being and a college degree for an education. Attending Lillian were seven eminent specialists, each at the top of his field. Among them at one time or another were a cardiologist, a neurologist, two vascular surgeons, an anesthesiologist and a urologist: every part of her body was picked at by a specialist and each specialist consulted with all the other specialists. There was a constant stream of them bobbing in and out of her room, bowing gravely to each other as they passed like dolls with keys in their backs, wind-up replicas of ancient Mandarin wisemen. They were smarter than ordinary mortals—more learned than everyday physicians: they were distinguished scientists, and she had them all at her disposal.

The only thing she didn't have was a doctor who treated her like a person. She was approached only as the legal possessor of various parts and organs whose permission it was necessary to obtain before you could experiment with them, the way an architect must go to the head of the zoning board for permission to knock down an existing wall or put up a new one. Most of the specialists who paraded in and out of her room wore exasperated expressions, as though it demeaned them to seek approval from anyone for such high-minded work, let alone from a woman who didn't know her ass from a teakettle. They were paternal, they were patronizing, they were condescending—and certainly they were knowledgeable. What they weren't, I thought, was human.

It was as if each of them was out to prove on his chart that he had extended Lillian Hellman's life by a certain number of months and weeks and days. What the quality of that life might or might not be didn't seem to concern them—quantity was all. First and foremost they were provers and like all provers they appeared more concerned with themselves than with their patient, as the world's most famous prover, Don Juan, was more concerned with his own masculinity than he was with women. It was not Don Juan but Casanova who really loved, and he would have made a lousy surgeon.

What Lillian desperately needed was an old-fashioned doctor—an internist, a layer-on of hands—someone gentle enough to alleviate her fears and come between her and everybody else. But she had only specialists. There was apparently no one at the helm to collate the information provided by the tests, no one to view the organism as a whole, let alone as a woman. It was beyond the comprehension of the seven eminent men that a writer as famous as Lillian was ignorant of the workings of her own body, yet it was they who were ignorant of the workings of her mind. The imaginary split between mind and body came into play when they tried to explain things to her and Lilly panicked and couldn't understand what they were saying. Each time there was another surgical procedure to face they sat down with her and went over it: an angiogram; a digital subtraction test; an endarterectomy on the left carotid; the removal of the pacemaker from the right side; the implantation of a new pacemaker on the left side; a second endarterectomy on the right carotid—a jumble of words like a mouthful of dead leaves. She spat them out and asked for a Scotch and soda.

In the beginning, when there was nothing but talk and a few noninvasive tests, I asked if I could take her out to dinner in the evenings. The hospital agreed as long as I had her back by nine o'clock; that made it like a date and a date was what she needed. When I asked her, I said I wouldn't take her anywhere unless she got dressed up, and she swore at me like a sailor; but she had one of the nurses help with her makeup and Robin Hogan, the best of her college-student companions, drove back to the Vineyard for a few of her clothes. That evening I put on a dark suit and tie and went to pick her up in a taxi. Lilly was dressed and waiting with her hair set and combed out, sitting in a collapsible wheelchair just inside the hospital entrance. She had on some things I'd given her the last Christmas, a silk blouse, a pleated cashmere skirt and sweater and a string of old cloisonné beads I'd given her the Christmas before. Robin pushed her out to the taxi and I put her in the backseat with me, the wheelchair in the trunk.

I took her to the best Italian restaurant in Boston. We ordered straight-up martinis and wine and pasta and she faked getting most of it down and I pretended not to know she was faking, but her eyes glittered a little and the glitter was real. The head chef came out of the kitchen at her request, a handsome large woman named Molly O'Neill, and Lilly asked her how a mick got to be chef in a wop joint, and Molly liked her right away. The second time we went she ordered something special and Molly cooked it for her and seemed to understand without words why she couldn't eat more than a bite or two. The third time the waiter didn't give us a menu at all: Molly appeared as soon as she saw Lillian's wheelchair and sat next to her in the booth discussing different possible dishes.

It seemed to me that those discussions, the putting together of complex dinner menus Lillian couldn't hope to swallow or digest, did her more good than the healthy hospital food that was good for her, because the discussions fed something that was starving and the food did not. Lilly wasn't hungry. But that didn't matter because she was frightened, and that did.

I went on taking her out whenever she had enough strength and we tried other restaurants, but none that she liked as much, and one evening Molly asked us to her apartment and cooked a couple of Lillian's favorite dishes there. It was on the way back to the hospital from Molly's that we began to talk about doing a cookbook, because any kind of book meant writing and any kind of writing meant life. If you take only a little of the hopelessness out of sickness and death it's at least better than doing nothing and Lilly began to think about the cookbook whenever she could. We knew by then that we would never do anything about opening a restaurant—that was all junk talk—but this was not and we would do something about this.

The next day we asked Molly if she'd test the recipes for us and she agreed, and after that Lilly tried dictating food ideas into a tape recorder at night when she couldn't sleep. To make the book interesting we decided to precede each recipe with a memory: the day one of us had first eaten the dish or an incident connected with making it or some short remembrance of another time, another country, in which the dish appeared. The book would be divided into two, her half and mine, and we wouldn't show each other what we were writing until we each had a complete first draft. Once a week Robin would collect Lillian's tapes and send them to Rita to type up and when we were finished we would have a maverick book, a sort of cookbook/memoir, and we would swap and compare and help each other polish what we'd written.

Lilly brightened considerably at the idea and began to list the recipes she wanted so she could show me the list when I came to take her out. She got enough done to convince us both that the book would become a reality, but after the digital subtraction test, the overture to all the surgical procedures, her daily life changed. She had to batten her hatches then for what we both knew was coming, though nobody knew then how bad it would be. If we had known, or if I had, I would have stopped it, I think, because nobody has to go through that unless they want to, and nobody who knew the price and the smallness of the reward would want to.

One afternoon two of the specialists came to tell Lillian that they were in a dilemma. They couldn't do the first endarterectomy until her pacemaker was taken out and replaced, but they couldn't replace it, under a general anesthetic, until they were sure she was getting enough oxygen to the brain, and they couldn't be sure she was getting enough oxygen to the brain until they did the endarterectomy. "*You* talk to them," Lilly said when I went over that day, "I can't get it straight—you can't do *that* till you do *this*—but you can't do *this* before you do *that*. What in the hell does it mean?"

The nurse who was on duty said she thought it meant they wanted Lillian to have the pacemaker removed under a local anesthetic rather than a general.

"Forget it," Lilly said. "I'm not going to. If I die, I die, I will anyway. But I don't see why I have to die in pain and terror."

"Tell them," the nurse said.

She did but the argument went on. Lilly held ground and after a week they agreed to give her a general anesthetic rather than a local. The first procedure involved putting a temporary pacemaker in her leg while they removed the old pacemaker from the right side of her chest and implanted a new one in the left side. It was to take several hours and at the last minute they decided it was too dangerous without sufficient flow of oxygen to the brain: they would have to do the left endarterectomy first. Lillian hadn't made a decision about that, so things came to a standstill again and they went ahead with the semisurgical procedures.

The first of those was the digital subtraction test. It took a long time and I walked with her as far as they let me and then went back and sat in her room. I should have made some decision for her then but I didn't—when you're too anxious it's hard to think. First you must deal with your fear and then with your anger and after that with the unsettling experience of seeing someone you love wheeled around like a piece of meat, at the careless mercy of people you wouldn't sit down with, as if your heart and brain and gut had been trundled out with the garbage or left to wait in the hall. By the time it's over you're too shaky to think and by the time you think, it's too late.

After that test came the angiogram. It took Lillian a couple of weeks to recover and when they were ready for the endarterectomy she still hadn't made up her mind. She asked me to speak to the doctors and I did, but I wasn't in a legal position to make a decision for her and it occurred to me then that legalities were running all our lives: hers, mine and the specialists'. It was for legal reasons that they kept telling her more than she wanted to know because they were fearful of losing their insurance in case anything went wrong. If Mother Nature doesn't get us, the night nurse said, Father Time will—but it's the insurance companies that run our lives and tell us when to die.

So the doctors were no use to her in making decisions, because their hands were tied, they had to consider their insurance. But in the end, I think, I was the one who failed Lilly most, because I didn't need insurance. I should have had the nerve to follow my instinct, to brush them all aside, put Lillian in the car, buy a couple of cases of red wine and take her back to the Vineyard: I wanted to tell her to forget all of it and come home. That we would cook some of the meals she liked in the house and drink the wine and have as good a time as we could, and when it was over it was over. The hell with this, I wanted to say, the hell with specialists, screw these rules you never subscribed to, you've lived your own way, die your own way, I wanted to say, but I never said it. I was afraid of the things they told her might happen, much too afraid of watching her suffer and die. So if I wound up angry at the doctors I suppose the truth is that I knew they were doing their best and at the same time knew that I was not. I suppose I was angry at myself.

The day the final decision had to be made she asked what I would do if it were my life, and I said if it were my life I would do nothing. "That's good enough," she said. But at six o'clock that evening three of the specialists came in and went through a litany of the pain from strokes and other things that might befall her if she didn't go through with the surgery. They managed to make it sound like a test of courage and when they were done Lillian stood up and turned her back on all of us. She stood like that without moving for a long time, and I remembered the day out by Cape Poge lighthouse when I had loved looking at her back, the day I buried the dead twisted swan. The silence lasted several minutes.

"Okay," she said finally. "Okay."

It was the last time I was to hear Lillian's true voice. She said it from someplace quiet and deep and I'm glad she did because I can still hear it.

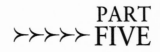

PART
FIVE

1,000% for You

➤➤➤➤➤ I

THE SURGERY DIDN'T kill her but it changed her into someone I didn't know or recognize. Her voice was not the same after that and neither was anything else about her: it was like listening to a different woman after that.

The night before the surgery I sat up with her till 3 A.M. when I knew she was asleep, and then went to the hotel to rest and change so I could come back in time to break the hospital rules and sit with her till they wheeled her out. She woke up a little after midnight and asked me to turn on the tape machine so we could talk about the cookbook. I knew what she meant, it was a way of extending things past surgery, and we argued a while about which recipes were whose and what anecdotes were worth telling. Her voice was already different, but only from fear, not the way it was to be after the operation, and we spoke of other things too.

LILLIAN: *Everybody finds out in the end about love, don't they— I guess nobody gets away with that.*
PETER: *Maybe not.*
LILLIAN: *Yes, but you see, I did. I thought, I've loved this man* * *from the time I met him till he died—as much the day I first slept with him as the day of his death . . . I thought I'd had a grand passion, in the real old-fashioned sense. And it makes you feel grand to think that. He told me I was beautiful, so I was beautiful . . . I knew I wasn't beautiful, but it didn't matter because he thought I was. It was responsible for the way I carried myself,*

* Hammett

*the way I walked. Only, now I'm not sure if I met him in the
Hollywood days whether I'd want to know him . . . I don't think
I would. Something about the impression of a young girl with
what he was, what he seemed, what he could accomplish . . . I
wouldn't be impressed now. The enormous frivolity, the showing
off, the throwing away of money as if there were no such thing
as tomorrow . . . but worst of all, the waste—the terrible waste
of talent . . . I wonder if I met him now whether I'd like him. I
wonder if any of the values I had were any good . . . I wonder
about the depth and truth of my values. . . .*

But fear can make you doubt anything and I kept that tape
only as a reminder of the dimensions of the shake-up she had
felt before surgery because I thought it might affect what she felt
after.

When they wheeled her down from the recovery room she
was already talking and that was when I knew she was going to
be different from now on. Lillian had always had a deep voice
and the rhythm of her speech was slow even when she was angry.
The new voice was high and jittery and fast, like the voice of
a nervous child, or the sound of fear itself, as if it had been
given speech inside her. She seemed to have no control over it
and I kept waiting for her to come back and take over but she
never did.

For a long time afterward she had a prolonged series of delusions caused by the surgery, waking nightmares that no drugs
seemed able to wipe out. When they wheeled her back she was
saying "Get off the window . . ." and "Get off me . . ." and
more often than anything "They're killing me" till I began to
think she was right. Then while they were shifting her from the
cart back to the hospital bed she spoke again. "Call the doctors
immediately . . . I don't have time for this, I ought to be working . . . tell them I'm having a meeting with my publisher. I'm
finishing a book . . ."

They gave her an antipsychotic drug called Haldol but it only
served to quiet her a little, it didn't affect the nightmares, and
it had an odd side effect that produced too much saliva in her
mouth so she couldn't speak without drooling. That went on for
a while till they increased the dose and then the drooling in-

creased so that by the time the cumulation of Haldol began to take effect she was choking.

The jumble of procedures and remedies in the next weeks were like watching someone trussed and tossed onto a roller coaster in full swing. To retain my sanity I kept a daily journal but there were days I forgot to write in it and other days when I didn't have the heart. A few people who cared about Lillian kept in touch and some of them came to Boston and waited outside her room. The ones who loved her enough didn't insist on seeing her when visits were forbidden by the doctors, but they sat in the hall on the off chance that she would need them. Hannah was often there and from time to time Rita, Molly, Mike and Annabel Nichols, the Herseys and Dick Poirier and for a long time Bill Doering, a Nobel-prize-winning chemist who lived in Boston. Most of them stayed a few hours, Hannah stayed overnight.

Seeing anyone Lillian didn't expect sent her into a frenzy of fear, so much so that the visits themselves were considered dangerous. But after a week I came upon a way of preparing her for visitors that seemed to work as long as the visitor was a very old friend. I would go in and say, "Hannah is here, but you can't scream at her—Hannah's got a heart condition." Then I led Hannah in by the hand as if I were her father and Lilly would calm down for a little while. Something about taking the focus off her own health and putting it on the other person's health had a sobering effect, though it didn't always last for long, sometimes no longer than a minute.

A few people who weren't able to come sent telegrams and letters and there was one enormous plant from Elizabeth Taylor that seemed to grow bigger every day. Lillian hadn't parted on the best of terms with Elizabeth but squabbles disappeared in the light of what was happening and she was pleased by the gift long before she was lucid enough to know where it came from. She liked showing it to the nurses and doctors as a sign of anonymous affection, as though the big awkward plant had grown there in the corner with her dreams.

The sequence of surgery-and-recovery was repeated in relentless slow progression as it might have been if there was to be no end, and for weeks the only change was in the list of names of people who phoned to ask about Lilly.

But there was one new person who came to see her regularly—a man who managed to get into her room more often than anyone else. His name was Mr. Fini and he did not exist except in Lillian's imagination, but after a while I began to think of Mr. Fini as more real and more of a threat than anything or anybody. By the third week after his appearance it was hard for me to remember that he was invisible to everyone but Lillian. I knew what he looked like, what he sounded like, and when all else failed I could smell him. By then he was so real I had to check back into my journal to figure what day it was that Mr. Fini had first decided to join us.

Thursday, 1:07 p.m.

Sonesta
She's in surgery.

Now I'm in room 1020—last week I was in 914. Last Thursday I flew back to L.A. (Lillian was said to be "out of danger," whatever that means) and Tuesday back here. The doctors decided to forgo the left endarterectomy for the moment and put the new pacemaker in. It's being done under a general because she's so afraid of pain, but she's been in surgery 2 hours now and they say at least an hour more.

This is the 4th surgical or semi-surgical procedure in the last 5 weeks—makes you wonder sometimes how much more she can tolerate. This morning before they took her down I made her laugh. She can't fake a laugh any more than she can stop a real one—that at least hasn't changed— it's useful now.

One day last week when Molly and Robin and I were in her room, she yelled at us and said the most insulting things she could think of to each of us. She was sorry as soon as she'd said them and that same night she woke up and told me about a dream she'd just had. In the dream Molly and Robin and I were out to get her—the 3 people she felt guilty about because of the way she'd behaved—we had a party in her room. First we tied her to the bed, nailed her arm to a board, wouldn't let her up, and then cut into her neck. She begged us to quit but we only got louder. She reached for the phone but instead found a "leather thing, shaped like a joint, smooth and round" (the tube in her arm?). The party got louder. She called the campus police. There was a "Mr. Fini" sitting outside her door all during the party. From time to time he slipped into her room, evil-looking and rotten-smelling, doing foul secret things, then he slipped out again and waited outside. The campus police came and stopped the party but nobody could get rid of Mr. Fini. She has no idea who Mr. Fini is—she says she never even heard his name before—she doesn't know him.

It's 1:26. Still no word. They took her down at 11:15.

Oct. 10

She's still shaky, still having hallucinations.

Sometimes it feels as if the only way I can pull her out is to enter into the nightmare with her. Mr. Fini, for instance—I'm getting so I can tell when he's in the room with us. Just a turn of L's head or the way she sniffs the air when he scuttles across the room. Last night I was watching her face when she didn't know I was there—she can't see anything in that light—and suddenly she stiffened and turned toward the door. I said:

"He's here, isn't he?"

"Who?" she said.

"Fini," I said. "I know he's here. He's in the corner by the window."

L's face went blank. "I don't know what you're talking about," she said after a moment, "Mr. Fini hasn't been here for days."

But she was lying. I could tell from her expression. She colludes with him a lot, I think, she's scared to tell the truth. Fini threatens her. Like that foul-smelling thing that winks at all of us in the dark—he gets her to lie for him.

She's much too thin now, 81 pounds and still losing weight. But the only thing she'll swallow without a fight is the malted milk I bring her from the hospital cafeteria every day, chocolate or strawberry. Otherwise she won't eat and the weight-loss seems to please her. I wish the doctors weren't playing into it so easily—they don't mean to but they're confirming the separation she's always made, the mind-body split. They're helping her hate her body.

Oct. 12

Anabelle, one of the best of her new nurses, just called from the hall and said, "The word is out." I asked what she meant. "Visitors," she said. "Strangers this morning, I kept them out of her room, but later on there was another man, and after that somebody named Alvin Sargent and his wife. He insisted on seeing her. I told him it would be bad for her, she's allowed no visitors—I showed them the sign on the door. But Mr. Sargent said he was awfully sorry, he was only in town for the day. She was white and shaky when they left. I try to keep people away," Anabelle said, "but the word is out, and I know the signs—Mr. Sargent won't be the last—I had a feeling he was carrying one of those miniature tape-recorders in his pocket." I said she was wrong, Sargent wouldn't do that, he's a decent man and fond of L, a little pushy, that's all, like most Hollywood people. "Just the same," she said, "I know what I know. But I'll do what I can."

Oct. 15

Anabelle called from the hall 20 minutes after I left to say L was down to 80.8 pounds—she's lost another two-tenths of a pound since yesterday. This morning L phoned me at 4 a.m. sounding like a bad actress imitating L—not her voice at all. She's been asking me to phone a real-estate agent and find a house in L.A., and she wanted to know if I found one. I said yes and she asked how much. I told her the asking price had been reduced from a million to 750,000, but the rental was 5,500 a month. L laughed. "That's Los Angeles for you—offer 3,000 and see what happens." I said I would. "It's very good news that you found a house," she said, "John Hersey will be happy to hear it—he's sitting right next to me, shall I tell him or would you like to speak to him yourself?" I said I'd speak to him. "Just a minute," she said. There was a pause, then Anabelle's voice again. "Miss Hellman made a mistake," she said, "Mr. Hersey hasn't been here for over a week. It's me she's looking at." I said goodbye and hung up.

Oct. 16

Anabelle says L's irrational at night and in the early mornings—lucid for a couple of hours in the afternoons. Sometimes at night she has to be "restrained"—i.e. tied to the bed. Then Lilly got on the phone with me. "Come immediately and bring Max Palevsky, I'm going to need money." I told her there was no problem about any money she needed. "Don't argue with me," she said, "there's something very ugly and strange going on here. Just come, and bring Max."

Anabelle says L has been talking about the hospital-people trying to kill her again—that she talked that way all night and most of the morning, trying to bribe the day nurse to make calls for help. The nightmare about being persecuted by everybody is easy to understand, what bothers me is that I think in a way she's right. What the doctors did for her seems to me very good for the doctors. But was it good for L? Why the endarterectomy; why the digital subtraction test; why the angiogram? Why anything but the pacemaker?

She thinks they're keeping her alive so they can torture her—I'm almost inclined to agree.

Oct. 17

Fini's back, I got a whiff of him in the hall and I knew from L's eyes. The new nurse says L is "lethargic at the moment—very weak, still having the audio-hallucinations from time to time." I asked her to explain and she said, "A little while ago Miss Hellman asked to go downstairs to the hairdresser. I told her she was too weak to go down, but the hairdresser could come up. 'No,' Miss Hellman said. 'I've got to use the phone down there—I want to call the U.S. Embassy and tell them I'm a prisoner in Mass General Hospital.' Then later she thought she was at Mr. Doering's house—and later she was lucid again and saying thank you to all of us for anything we did. She's like two different people—one violent, the other grateful."

Later on, I spoke to Dick P. He said Barbara Epstein called him—Dick wasn't in, but a friend of his answered the phone—and Barbara said, "You know, Lillian and I haven't got along lately." "I don't know anything about it," Dick's friend said. "Yes," Barbara said, "and I'm worried and concerned about her."

Before she went into the hospital L said, "Barbara Epstein and Lizzie Hardwick and Mary McCarthy and Martha Gelhorn and Dinny Johnson and on and on—it's like being hated by a ladies' club." I asked her once more to drop the lawsuit against McCarthy. "I probably will," L said, "I just want Mary to apologize, that's all—I don't think that's why the club-ladies hate me, they've always hated me."

I wonder if it's true. I think Barbara Epstein really likes her.

Oct. 20

LH this morning: "What a bitter world it's turned out to be . . . I can't see, I'm sick. And last week I died. I'm sure I died, I heard a doctor say, 'Well, she's gone'—and another doctor say, 'No, she's not, wait a minute.' "

Oct. 21

LH this morning: "Did you read about my death in the paper?"

I said I hadn't.

"I was dead," she said, "there's no doubt about it—I got a lot of telegrams."

I said nobody sends telegrams to dead people.

"Well, who did send them?" L said. "And if I'm not dead, why are you leaving?" I said I was only going to N.Y. for two days to discuss a magazine assignment and I promised her I'd come back afterwards and stay as long as she needed me, without ever leaving her again.

"I'm afraid it's too late for me now," L said. "What wouldn't I have given to hear those words 4 or 5 years ago."

Oct. 24—New York

Called the hospital last night—the nurse said she was hallucinating badly. She still sees people on the ceiling, people coming through the wall, people lying on top of her. But she wants the tape-recorder turned on and left next to her so she can dictate recipes. Nothing stops her working, not even delusions. I wonder if she remembers that Hammett died with an unfinished ms on his bed.

This morning she said to the nurse, "Did you see my obit in the *NY Times* the other day?"

The nurse said she hadn't.

"I know I'm dead, I'm not breathing," Lilly said. "Shut up and don't argue with me."

She still looks anorexic but there's something else in it too, something they're not seeing. Fini still sits outside her door, scuttling in and out of the room. The nurse said this morning that L refused a soft-boiled egg because it wasn't a 5-minute egg. But L doesn't eat 5-minute eggs—she eats 3-minute eggs, I remember the time in Vallarta when she sent the breakfast egg back to the kitchen until she drove the waiter crazy—it's not a thing she'd get confused about. I wonder if

Fini's telling her what to do. I have a hunch he is. She seems to be acting under orders.

It's as if she were putting up a desperate fight for life and saying screw it at the same time.

Spoke to Milton Wexler in LA, he has a friend in the Dept. of Psychiatry at Mass General named Steve Mattayse. Wexler thinks I should contact Mattayse. It sounds like a good idea, anybody Milton recommends is a blessing—I'll do it when I get back. Had the nurse tell her I was coming back tomorrow and L said, "Tell him to come today or not at all." As long as she's *that* kind of angry I can reach her.

Oct. 25—Boston

Got in tonight—L enraged at my absence—said she wasn't glad to see me, wouldn't say why she was angry, then started to cry. I asked her why she was crying. She said, "For my whole goddamn life."

She still has too much saliva in her mouth and when Dr. Yurchak came in she asked him about it. He said it was partly the medication, but also because her dentures don't fit since her weight loss . . . when Yurchak left she went on behaving with me like an infant punishing its mother for being away. I guess she really loves me.

Oct. 26 morning

I asked Anabelle to write down anything L said that seemed important—this morning she handed me this note:
"CONVERSATION 7 A.M. WITH MISS HELLMAN.
MISS HELLMAN—I want you with me always, Anabelle.
ANABELLE—I have cats, Miss Hellman.
MISS HELLMAN—Then fuck you."

Oct. 26 Boston, afternoon

L is still negotiating with death, I think—she admits she's been talking to Fini. I'm going to tell her that she's not in a position of strength yet. She's too good a negotiator to try bargaining from weakness, I'll tell her to get her stamina back, *then* take Fini on.

Oct. 27

Don't like her color. White, and that awful skull-look, the look people get toward the end, when you can begin to see the skull inside the face—the look of the dying. She's back on oxygen (the nurse says she complained of trouble breathing).

Later. Had breakfast with Steve Mattayse, Milton's friend. He's impressive. Said his father had the same psychotic symptoms after bypass surgery. Will try to get him past Dr. Yurchak to see L tomorrow. Mattayse would interest her, and he'll know how to talk to her.

Dr. Yurchak's treating her like a bad child. He doesn't understand that she's always behaved like a child. . . .

Oct. 28 morning

She' still in a private room on the intensive care floor. They're keeping her there so she can have oxygen in her room, but it's tricky because she keeps getting people to light her cigarettes. Over her head are two signs. One says "Oxygen Tank—No Smoking." The other says "Patient Care Reminder. Lillian Hellman. Legally blind. Wears soft lens R eye. L sided weakness. Thank you."

Oct. 30

She's done it again, Christ knows how she managed in an intensive care room, but the whole shelf under the window is a liquor bar—there's wine in the nurses' refrigerator and she's got two saltcellars under her mattress. She must be feeling better.

I told her about some of the things she said while she was delusional—then told her how I'd started to believe in Mr. Fini myself. She laughed, then said, "Lean over and let me kiss you." When I did she said, "I love you, will you take care of me?" I said, "I'm tired of that question—I *am* taking care of you." "Okay," she said, "just checking."

The nurse says Yurchak's sending a psychiatrist over. Way too late, but what the hell. Maybe I can even get them to come up with an internist. L was murder on Rita today— angry at her for announcing plans to return to N.Y. instead of staying here—"You're a dirty Catholic son of a bitch. You had a lousy marriage and your children are awful and I hate you." Rita just sat down and said, "Now, Miss Hellman, what can I do for you this morning?" L began dictating letters to her as usual.

A small sensitive-looking man came in just before lunch and said, "Hello, Mrs. Hellman, I'm the occupational therapist." "I'm a writer," L said, "butt out." He tried to pacify her and she got rid of him.

Donna (first morning nurse) told me that L slapped her and she quit. Then L apologized and they made up. The anger at nurses is getting way out of control.

Later

A psychiatrist just came, an obese man named [BLANK]. (If he can't cure his own obesity, what can he do for L?) Afterwards she quoted him as asking questions like "Why aren't you taking your medicine?—Why aren't you eating?—Why are you making so much trouble for the nurses?"

I called Yurchak later and said Lilly wants to see Steve Mattayse. (Wexler said to do it openly, that way.) Yurchak sounded angry. He said, "I was in to see her last night—she had her usual laundry-list of complaints—she won't do anything to help us get her strength back, she wastes all her energy on visitors, then sleeps through her physiotherapy. Then she accused *me* of . . ." He went on and on and I interrupted and said, "Dr. Yurchak, it doesn't matter what she accused you of, she's irrational and has been since the first surgery." "Well," he said, "I sent her a psychiatrist this morning and frankly I think her wanting to see this new man all of a sudden is kind of fishy." I told him she wanted to see the new man, Mattayse, because he'd been recommended as a person who might give her some comfort. "I'll talk to her about it," Yurchak said and hung up.

L's not mixed up at all now, she complains of *having had* delusions and bad dreams. Last night she said, "Peter, I dreamed you were on a binge."

"What kind," I said, "eating?"

"Screwing," she said, "I wouldn't like to tell you who—I wouldn't like to upset you."

I said I had a perfect right to know who I was screwing.

"Very small children," she said

"That's good," I said, "that can't wear me out."

L laughed. "Tell me something about your mother," she said suddenly. "I like laughing."

I wonder if Yurchak's going to be trouble.

Oct. 29

Mattayse went in to see her for half an hour and she looked like a different person afterwards: her color is back and she has sparkle. She wants Mattayse to come whenever he can. She said, "He's wonderful—I'd almost given up thinking doctors were human beings—God bless Milton Wexler."

There's a new sign on the door of her hospital room today, printed in heavy black letters: "LILLIAN HELLMAN. GENTLEMAN CALLERS ONLY."

                                                              Later

Two telegrams came for her today, both from L.A.

  1) *WHAT IS THIS, A JOKE? GET OUT OF THERE AND COME HERE.*

                                              PETER FALK

  2) *SINCE YOUR PHONE IS UNPLUGGED I THOUGHT I'D SEND YOU TODAY'S NEWS BY TELEGRAM. THE BAD NEWS IS THAT I HURT MY BACK AND PETER TELLS ME HE HAS AN OUTBREAK OF STRESS-RE-LATED FACIAL HERPES. THE GOOD NEWS IS THAT SUE MENGERS WANTS TO PLAY REGINA. LOVE,*

                                              ELAINE

                                              Oct. 29

Sally [the fourth day nurse] quit—L is being impossible.

Just spoke to Dr. Martin. He's a very decent man, better with her than Yurchak, I think. He says he wants to help her leave the hospital. All she needs is to be off the IV for 48 hours and feed herself—as soon as that happens they can discharge her. I'm taking him in to see her again tomorrow morning.

                                        Later, October 29

L's tape recorder must have been left on when I was in her room last Saturday. Along with L's new recipe ideas, Rita typed this into the transcript:

L: Let's not fight. We'll live together and be happy now.

P: You sound like a Hemingway character.

L: That's a terrible, terrible thing to say. I'm not a Hemingway character. I love you.

P: I love you too.

L: I love you more than you love me.

P: Hush up, Lilly.

L: Let's not fight. All you do is fight and call me a Hemingway character. Go screw yourself. I bet you screw every night in that hotel, don't you?

P: Sure.

L: Who?

P: Everybody.

L: One by one or gang bang?

P: I try to make it on a first-come-first-served basis.

L: Maybe we can make a little money on you.

P: We?

L: I'm entitled to some.

P: I'll give you ten percent.

L: What a kike you are. Hold my hand. I'm not going to die here, am I?

Nov. 1

She's not irrational any more, but she was angry when I walked in today—barking orders at everybody. I took it for a minute or two, then yelled, "Who the hell do you think you're talking to? Don't ever speak to me like that again." There was a silence. She said, "Then leave." "Right," I said, "goodbye." I started out. She called my name as I got to the door and apologized. Within a minute she was laughing. She's like a tiny baby now—crib-size. The hospital's her mother and I'm her father. What will happen when she has to leave?

Nov. 2

Yurchak called. He said she's to be officially discharged at 10 a.m. on Thursday—that's the day after tomorrow. It's not enough time to set her up with nurses in NY for the weekend—I'll have to ask them to keep her till Monday.

2 p.m.

Talked to Dr. Meltzer in NY—he said he'd try to help Rita set up nurses. Rita's flying to NY today. I'll go with L Monday in the ambulance.

Nov. 3

She's panicky about leaving the hospital. I fed her lunch

and she calmed down a little and I told her I'd be both her father and mother if she wanted.

"I want," she said.

When they wheeled Lillian out of her room and down the hall to the ambulance there was silence, but when the elevator doors closed behind her a cheer went up from the nurses' station. They were that happy to see her go. When the elevator started down we could still hear it, the voices diminishing in retrograde to a single sound that seemed to come from the depths of the machine, like a soft metallic sigh.

The ambulance ride from the hospital in Boston to the door of Lillian's New York apartment building made the ride across the Golden Gate Bridge seem like a frolic. The trip was to have taken six hours but it took over ten because of traffic and Lillian screamed till her voice gave out, made hoarse sounds till it came back and screamed again. The nurse gave her Valium but it might as well have been candy: the only thing that had a calming effect on Lilly was about midway when I blew my stack at her and said I was hungry. The driver pulled the ambulance off the freeway and stopped at a greasy-looking diner in some nameless back-water suburb. The place looked scruffy and uninhabited and Lilly quieted down and asked the driver to tell her immediately where we were. He said: "Bumfuckville, lady." Lilly said that was nice, she'd always wanted to go to Bumfuckville.

I ordered a cheeseburger for me, a chocolate malt for her, and we had lunch together in the ambulance. Lilly drank half the malt and said she thought I should know, before she died, that she had never approved of my eating cheeseburgers. I asked what was wrong with them and she said in her opinion cheeseburgers were against God and a man who eats cheeseburgers will do anything. I said in my opinion her primitive fear of cheeseburgers was an atavistic throwback to some early kosher rule about mixing meat with dairy products and Lilly said writers had disgusting minds. When I ordered another double cheeseburger for the road she chuckled but as soon as we were back on the freeway fear took over again and she went back to screaming.

About an hour out of New York we hit bumper-to-bumper traffic and she begged the driver to switch on the flashing red

light on top and turn on the siren. The rest of the trip wasn't
long but by the time we got to the apartment there was a headache of plague proportions on Riverside Drive.

I moved into a hotel and the nurse from Boston stayed on in
Lilly's New York apartment till things were organized. It took
about seventy-two hours to set up around-the-clock nurses and
Lilly slept a lot and decided that she was not going to be abandoned anymore. Early the second week she called me at my hotel
at four in the morning to ask my ring size. I said I didn't know
and when I went over that day she had Rita measure my finger.
I was too busy to pay much attention but two days later Lilly
showed me a pair of gold wedding bands she'd bought for the
price of one—she'd been calling jewelers around town looking
for bargains all week. The wedding rings were his and hers, and
when I said I wouldn't marry her she blew sky-high; then she
altered her tactics and tried reasoning with me and after that
some of her old charm. It went on for a week and when she
finally believed I meant no, she stopped speaking to me for two
days. The first day, out of revenge, she asked five men to marry
her: the doorman, a photographer she'd often used as an escort,
two delivery boys and Bill Doering. The only one she had any
real feeling for was Doering and when nobody took her seriously
she went on a hunger strike. But after another day she relented
and told Therese to cook up a mess of red beans and rice, my
favorite New Orleans food.

As soon as Lillian was all right I went back to Los Angeles,
back to work. Lilly was working on the memoir sections of the
cookbook and she called me every day to report her progress.
Sometimes she would call in the morning and say she'd dictated
a passage into the tape recorder the night before that was fine.
Then she would call back in the afternoon to say that she was
mistaken, she had pushed the wrong button, the machine had
recorded nothing. It was a painful and desperate and grinding
process but it was worth it because it meant that she was writing
again: if she could get through it she'd feel better and if she could
hold a book in her hands and know she had written it that way,
against those odds, she would feel triumphant.

Lilly's half of the cookbook took over a year to finish because she wasn't able to work continuously. After she finished,

the recipes had to be tested and then the book had to be edited; it would be months before it could be published. Now and then I flew to New York to see Lilly and she called once, excited as a child, and said she was planning a trip to Los Angeles. I didn't think she could make it and I was wrong: she made it twice. A little over a year and a half after the surgery at Massachusetts General Hospital, on the thirtieth of June, 1984, ten days after her birthday, in her own house on Martha's Vineyard, Lillian died.

The time between the surgery and her death passed in a galloping parade of small incident whose significance was apparently relative, since the parade did not appear small as it took place. The size of each event, viewed moment to moment, seemed monumental, as a tooth cavity feels to a probing tongue. The fabric of passing time was woven together by the constant problem of keeping nurses on the job. Lillian got rid of them the way a bird gets rid of an unwanted seed or a cat a bit of paper lying in its path: she flicked them away. She saw no reason to do otherwise and from her point of view she was right. If you wanted to make a story line of Lillian's whole life you would have to say that she broke the bonds around her as a child—that she became free, lived for years in the wild energy of freedom, was reduced to final confinement and rage as her body betrayed her—and sank into blindness, paralysis and death. It seems very simple viewed that way. But a year and a half before it was over it was not so simple.

When Rita called from New York to say that Lillian was headed for California to pass the winter and added that two nurses' registries in Los Angeles would no longer touch the case, things seemed impossible. Coast to coast, Lillian had tried female nurses, male nurses, practical nurses, illegal aliens and thugs and half-wits, but none of them could hold out for more than two weeks and most of them knuckled under after two or three days. During one long inglorious spew of rage and desperation she had skewered three in an afternoon: dismissively, without raising her voice, telling each of them off in precise and elegant terms that cut through to the core of whatever was vulnerable in that nurse's family, her training or her sex life.

Something had to be done but no one seemed to know what. Lilly had taken another furnished house in Beverly Hills for the winter, most of which she would be spending on her back in a rented hospital bed. She arrived in Los Angeles in mid-January, on schedule and safely thanks to Jonathan LaPook, who flew with her, kissed her and took the next plane back. From then on it was touch and go. The first nurse on the case lasted three days and left in such helpless anger that she drove into a tree on her way home. That was the day I figured some kind of boundaries had to be drawn, as boundaries are drawn for children, and if I didn't do it nobody would.

I went over to Lillian's that afternoon without knowing exactly what I was going to do. Lecturing her on the subject never had done any good, since her bedroom had become a battlefield and everyone who passed through it was destined to take sides: any criticism of Lillian's behavior only sounded to her like siding with the nurses and that disqualified both the criticism and the person who made it.

I parked in the circular drive and sat for a while looking at the house she had rented. It was a block-to-block tract home in the flats of Beverly Hills, the kind that was priced well over a million dollars, more than likely worth closer to three or four. Such houses appear very much as tract homes do in other places except that they are bigger here and have been redesigned on the outside to look Spanish or English, or otherwise quaint and expensive. Inside, the houses have been altered and added to much the way the Aztecs built their civilization over the conquered Mayan civilization, with such inexorable force by each new owner that the town itself has become a definition of what used to be called middle-class values, or lack of them depending how you look at it. In other parts of the world, if a couple shows you through their new home, they say: "This is the living room." In Beverly Hills they say: "This *was* the living room." Recently some people Lillian knew slightly, a middle-aged couple with a teen-aged daughter, had come home one night after a dinner party to find their house empty—two vast moving vans having backed up into the driveway and removed every valuable possession they owned. A month after the robbery it was discovered that their own teenaged daughter had tipped off the thieves, telling them the exact date and time of the couple's absence in return for ten percent of the swag—immediate cash the daughter needed to supply herself and her friends with coke and pot. It was the kind of incident that delighted Lillian, whose contempt for such people had formed so much of her life. That she should be trapped inside one of their houses now at the end of it seemed to mean that we can all be jailed by our nightmares if we live long enough, but in truth it probably said something else. Lilly had always been conflicted between her contempt for the rich and her desire to be one of them, and it was clear by now that she would never resolve the conflict.

I rang the bell and the nurse on duty answered and tried to smile. She had a pleasant face and the flat unfocused look of a person who expects the worst from life: she would last another three weeks, I thought. I had begun to evaluate nurses more by their staying power than for any other reason and I chatted with her a few moments and then went in to see Lilly, who was growling at Therese about something. I sat down and waited for her to explode and realized suddenly that the only thing I could do would be to start taking offense when she meant to give offense—to stop treating her like an infant. Since the surgery, I hadn't taken her remarks seriously, but ignoring them didn't help and her temper was no longer in her control.

She started almost right away. "I must tell you, Peter, that it pains me to find out you've been lying to me about everything," she said, "you're a terrible liar and . . ."

"Stop," I said.

There was a pause and Lillian said: "What's the matter?"

"What's the matter," I said, "is that I'm tired of the name calling, tired of putting up with your rage-attacks, I'm worn out. I don't care how nasty you are to nurses but don't talk to me that way or I'll walk out on you and stay out."

Lillian listened as carefully as she always did, then tested the waters gently once more. "If you mean what you're saying, you have no right to . . ."

I said: "I don't care what I have a right to or don't have a right to. Watch your mouth, it's about to get you into trouble."

There was another very long silence and Lillian turned her head away. "All right," she said, "let's talk about something else." She tried to speak without anger for five minutes or so and then couldn't sustain it. I knew it wasn't her fault and I no longer cared, I was too backed up with old anger at myself to give much of a damn, so when she called me a much worse name and got abusive all over gain, I stood up and said: "Good-bye, Lillian, I wish you well."

When I closed the door behind me I felt better. The nurse

came running out while I was starting the car and said Miss Hell-man needed to see me, that it was very urgent. I said to tell Miss Hellman I never got the message, that the car was gone when she came out to give it. The nurse looked stricken for a moment, then her eyes unclouded and she nodded.

It was ten days before Lillian was to go home to New York and I spent the time working and trying to ignore the communications that appeared to come in every orifice I knew in my house and one or two I didn't know. There were letters, telegrams, messages on the answering service, notes sent by messenger left under the front door and back door. By then I had worked myself up into a snit that had nothing to do with what was good for Lillian or wasn't: I couldn't have blown up at her that way if I'd been acting, so I had to mean it, and in meaning it I'd gone too far. When Therese called from a pay phone to say that Lillian was behaving herself with the nurses I felt justified. But the next letters Lilly sent made me feel worse.

April 5, 1983

DEAREST PETER:

I had, of course, a terrible day and terrible night, but that's for another day, if ever. I did call Hannah and I did call Poirier. Let me sum up what Poirier says, since it makes more sense than either one of us or Hannah . . . He said that he had heard me be abusive in Boston to nurses and to him, but he said to himself, who isn't abusive when they are dying, and as far as you are concerned, he said that we both had a habit of speaking in terms that were usually pleasant and funny. He also said that to all people there comes a time when these terms are not able to be stood any longer and could seem to the other person nasty instead of affectionate. As always, he made sense because I think that is exactly what has happened between us. In any case, if you want to hear what he has to say, you will call him yourself, but I am reporting it exactly.

This letter is being sent to you in a hurry and goes on Poirier's assumption, which is also mine, to make all apologies possible. If I ever really spoke disrespectfully or abusively, I did not know it, but that has nothing to do with apologizing for it.

I absolutely understand your feeling, because very often, Hammett used to hurt me in the same sense you believe that I did . . . for God's sake, believe me. I certainly never meant to be disrespectful and certainly not abusive, because you are a fine man and you know how much I love you—very, very much.

That much I will let nobody argue about—not even you—because if you have proved the love, so have I. Please do not let us part this way. Please do call me and let us meet once more and hold hands before I go away to be sick once more at the loss of you.

> More love than I can tell you,
> Lillian

The second letter that came was different. It was written by hand, not dictated, and it said: "I love you more than anyone ever. Please take me back. I will try to do better. *Please please* call me. L.H."

But it looked like this:

Something about a writer trying to explain feelings through blindness was more touching than anything else she could have said or done. I went out and got in my car and started it, then turned off the motor and came back in the house and sat down. Two days later another letter came.

DEAREST PETER:

As you know by this time, I have made perhaps 14 or 15 telephone calls and left 4 messages. I have also sent 2 letters by hand and I would do anything else I could. There now seems to be no chance that you will change your mind. The tough part of you is admirable. The over-tough part of you is what has hindered you. We are now, as we were that night in London, in the over-tough part of you. I am deeply sorry for that, because I would have made amends any way I could and will still, perhaps, someday try again. I have told you the truth. I love you now more than I have ever loved in my life before, and what I did, I did without knowing . . .

I think Dick Poirier summed it up better than anyone else, and I am going to quote it to you once more. He said, "Yes, you were abusive to nurses and I heard you one day be abusive to Hannah and one day you tried to be abusive to me and I stopped you. But even if you had been, I would have forgiven you, because who the hell faces death every minute of the night and day and cannot be allowed to be abusive?" . . .

I think I should be forgiven by you too, because I am not as yet well, and you know it. But I do not wish to urge you any more.

I think the loss of me will be as great for you as the loss of you will be for me. We were fine friends and very good to each other and will not find duplicates very easily. I tell myself that someday you will change your mind, but I do not believe it any longer, because Monday I am leaving and if there was a chance, you would not have been absent before I leave. You would have turned around and come back again if you wanted me, but there is no chance of that of course and so this

is to say goodbye to you. I send my love and my for-
giveness for what I think is your unforgiveness.

Lillian

The day before she was to leave I drove over and parked
once more in the circular driveway. Walking up to the house I
saw some people sitting with her and I circled around to the back
entrance. One of them must have seen me and said something to
Lillian because there was silence in the room when I walked in
and the other people stood up and left.

Lilly was sitting on the sofa staring without sight into the
sun through the window and I sat down next to her.

She didn't say anything and I could see that she was crying.
I kept still and she said: "I can't help what I am now, but I'll try
to help what I say. I'm glad you came back."

I don't remember much else except that she had a habit of
kissing my hands if she was grateful for something and she tried
to that day and I wouldn't let her.

She went back to New York the next day and for a long
time she was in control of herself with the nurses, enough at least
to keep them. She finished dictating her rewrite of the cookbook
and started another book right away, a book of stories about
children she had known; she got a sizable advance for that book
from her publisher and was happy about it. Then about a week
later she had an operator break through a phone call I was in the
middle of, saying it was an emergency.

"Forgive me for interrupting you," she said, "but I just found
out something terrible. If I die before I've finished my new book
I have to return the advance."

I laughed for a while and then told her if she were dead she
wouldn't care.

"That's the remark of a man who knows nothing about
money," Lillian said. "What can I do?"

"I'm not a lawyer," I said, "but it sounds to me as if you're
licked. Maybe you'd better not die."

"I'll call Ephraim," Lilly said, "and call you back."

Ephraim London was her lawyer, the one who was handling
the McCarthy lawsuit, and Lillian did call him, but he said more
or less the same thing I had, and he too broke out laughing.

So Lillian was condemned to life.

I went to Central America on an assignment and when I got back there were two more letters waiting for me.

630 Park Avenue
New York, N.Y. 10021
April 18, 1983

DEAREST PETER:

Perhaps I will try to do a piece of this letter every night. I am not sure. But I want so to be in some kind of communication with you that I guess I will try.

I thought tonight of calling your Mummie to say that if she heard you were injured [during your trip] would she call me. But faced with what might happen I backed out. That's because I suppose you would have to give her as the nearest living relative, whereas of course I didn't do that. I gave you as the nearest living person in Mass General. Naughty, naughty Peter, to give his Mummie. I am your nearest living relative.

It was a better day than usual because I went to Meltzer who said he was absolutely amazed at the improvement I had made. But of course he took all the credit for it, saying he predicted it and so on. He said I was in very good shape and he didn't even know why I need a physiotherapist anymore. If I don't, there would be quite a lot of money saved.

. . . I had a mild quarrel with Jack Klein, who refused to answer one more [money] question because he was too busy with income tax . . . But Rita and I did draw up a budget for Bob Towbin* and what I do spend every year is horrifying. The rate of inflation is so great that the one thing I remember about Pleasantville (and it is true that Pleasantville turned out a large amount of its own food, but we still had to buy coffee, sugar and such, and had more guests than I've ever had since and more servants) is that it cost $25.00 a week to feed everybody, whereas it now costs for the four of us an average of $125.00 a week, and more than that

---

* Lillian's investment counselor

of course if you count liquor. That would mean in twenty-five years . . . well, anyway.

I think perhaps I have solved the summer problem. I first hired what seemed to me a very nice colored man, and still seems to me a very nice colored man, but everybody here, including Therese, went on strike with too much publicity about AIDS among homosexuals. And Doering who came down to see me yesterday, and who said that chemists haven't the wildest idea where it comes from or how to cure it, and that a hospital in Denver closed down for two weeks after they had a death for fear of the nurses infecting other people, said he would never speak to me again if I hired the man. I then had to unhire him. But I think I have come up with a nice girl, except she talks too much . . . I can save some money because she is a practical nurse and she tells me she can work at night if she sleeps in my bedroom in the Vineyard and can get six hours sleep. I don't know if this is true or that it will work out, but I am going to take a chance. We may have to move some furniture into your room, but I will move it out before you come, if I know when you are coming. I think the only person who will ever know when you are going to do anything is Elaine May, but I am not sure, or maybe even Ray Stark. But then I guess he is small enough to listen to ground squirrels.

Richard Locke wrote me a silly note saying that he gave me his word that he did not recognize me in the *Vanity Fair* piece. And when Dick Poirier read it he threw it across the room. I wrote Locke a very nasty note saying that it was nice of him to apologize, but I didn't believe a word of what he said . . .

I had a wonderful dinner at La Tulipe with Ephraim London the night before last, who says that the McCarthy side is objecting to a jury trial which he, Ephraim, thinks is a good sign. He is a wonderful man . . . has never in all the years sent me a bill. As a matter of fact, a year or two ago I sent him a check and he never cashed it. When Klein asked him, it turned out that he had torn it up. So I sent him another check today that is not worth anything compared to what he has done. But I am hoping that he will at the end of the Mc-Carthy trial send me a proper bill. Nothing would give me greater pleasure than to pay Ephraim.

We had a pleasant conversation the other night. We held hands for a while and I told him I loved him and he said he loved me and then he said, "Lillian, if we had been the right age, I would have wanted you so much . . . But I guess neither of us could make it any longer." And I said I am not so sure because I always have wanted you. He said, "What a pair we would have made, and what a lovely affair it would have been." And that's exactly what I feel about him. Sorry, Peter. But you ain't here and I am not sure you are ever going to be. Well, well. None of that anymore. Or maybe some of that. Maybe, maybe, maybe because that's the part that has to be solved, in spite of your getting angry with me.

Hannah is coming back this weekend and that will make me feel better than I do now, although Meltzer's report made me feel cheerful. And so I will go to bed tonight and for once maybe I will sleep. I hope wherever you are you are safe. But of course I will not be sure until you come back. You are not to consider my health, and even if the slightest thing happens to your little finger, my health can now I think stand anything, and of course I will come immediately. To your little finger, I mean, because I certainly don't trust it to anyone else.

Goodnight darling, be well and stay well.
                                   Lillian

The second letter was dated a week later.

DEAR PETER:

This is Saturday night and I may have skipped a night because I don't think Friday night registered on the machine, or so the nurse tells me. I don't know why, because she turned it on. . . .

I have been depressed these last few days, maybe

because I think I am catching a cold, or maybe because in Mass General I went through every day with somebody saying please don't catch a cold, please come out of that chair, please put on another robe . . . As if catching a cold will kill me—and maybe it will—but I don't think so. I sleep too much. I cough too much . . . If I survived what I survived, then maybe I will survive a little old cold.

I just had a good dinner of roast chicken, baked potato and ripe pear. That's a fine dinner for me now, and I ate almost all of it. I am now almost ten pounds more than when I came out of Mass General.

I left Meltzer. I left him today because he sent me a bill for $150 for an office visit in which he did absolutely nothing except take my blood pressure. I think he is in love with some new lady. I decided he was getting too big for his pants, and I will go to a man he once recommended. I called the new man and said if this embarrassed him then of course I would not come. He said no, it would not embarrass him at all, so I will see him this week. La Pook thinks he is a very good doctor, and I think he is too. But I will talk it over with him anyway.

I will tell you, when you come back, my brilliant conclusion that there are men who should never fall in love, and Meltzer is one of them. Maybe it is true of all people, not just men.

Goodnight, darling, my mouth is too dry to go on. I will get Therese to bring me some chopped ice. The trouble is that I don't have anything to do with myself except to worry about troubles, and that's not my nature and never was, and I don't like all the drama and the possible drama ahead. Maybe I never liked drama at all. It's been a wicked time, but that's enough of that.

Goodnight, darling
Lillian

The day after I got back to Los Angeles from Central America, Warren Beatty took Lilly out to dinner. "I think I've come to interest Warren," she said afterward. "I don't know why—I can't imagine that a lot of women interest him, except sexually." I asked how many men had interested her, except sexually. "Not many," she said. "Most of us live by pretending to be more interested than we are."

She sometimes sounded like her old self, or the words did, but the music never did: the high jittery quality had been there since Mass General no matter what she said or how she said it, like the voice of a nervous girl—as if she knew she had a date somewhere, had known it for a while now, and was obstinately refusing to go.

In the winter she came back to Los Angeles for her second trip. Talli Wyler set up a small wing of her house—a suite of rooms with private access to the kitchen and the front door—and Lilly moved in for a couple of months. Talli's husband, William Wyler, now dead, had been a good friend to Lillian for a great many years and had directed two of the movies made from her plays; after his death, Talli kept up the friendship and took the trouble to help Lillian any way she could. Talli was a handsome and practical woman and she and I were distantly related: she was a Southerner, a cousin, another kind of survivor.

For the first week in Talli's house Lillian slept off her jet lag. Then she woke up and stared at the light from the window with a round-eyed gaze, as though she weren't quite sure what it was. I went over to Talli's as often as I could that month and read to her or had my meals there. Lillian was visibly weaker than she had been during her last visit. She was bone-thin and there was a smoldering feverish look now, as if her body were on fire inside, metabolizing itself quietly out of existence. But there was another look too—a look I thought I was the only one to notice until one afternoon when a messenger came to deliver a script and walked into her room by mistake. He was a man of twenty-five or so and when he came out of Lillian's room he passed me in the hall, nodded as he went by and said: "Some sexy lady you've got there."

I turned to watch him as he went on down the staircase to the front door. Then I asked if he was kidding.

"No, man," he said. "Kidding? Sexiest lady I've seen in a long time." He went out shaking his head and closed the door after him.

A seventy-nine-year-old woman dying on the installment plan would not normally strike a healthy twenty-five-year-old as sexy but I knew what he meant and he was right. It had been apparent for a while now, something to do with the burning out of bones, something that couldn't be defined in so many words, but it was unmistakably there.—Something to do with the burning.

The next day I went over to read to her and was having a cup of coffee between chapters when she said: "I want to ask you something. Close all the doors to my room, will you . . . tell me when it's done."

There were three doors and I shut them all.

"I want to know," Lillian said, "If we're ever going to bed together again."

"No, Lilly."

"Is that final?"

"Yes."

"All right," she said. "You can open the doors now."

I went back and opened them, waiting for the hurt feelings and the anger, but they never came. Lilly settled back and waited for me to go on with the next chapter. It took me a few seconds to realize that there was no trouble brewing and that she hadn't meant anything special by the question. She was just checking.

It was another week before it occurred to me that Lillian's age and condition had little or nothing to do with that particular subject. She had been a sexy woman all her life and the closer she came to death the more it showed in her face, possibly because everything showed more, but also because sex and death have the same urgency. The quality had probably showed when she was a child, I knew, and then I remembered that Lilly had once given me a photograph of herself taken in New Orleans at age four or five. Under it she wrote: "This only child sends a great deal of love to that only child from Audubon Park." For years I'd joked with her about the look in the child's eye and she had laughed and said I had a dirty mind. I wanted to tell her now that I certainly did and that under the circumstances I certainly was right.

A couple of days after that I walked into her room one afternoon with a box of chocolate truffles and found her lying in bed staring at the window with a look of silent calculation. "What is it?" I said.

Lilly turned her head slowly in my direction and then turned it back. "Thinking," she said.

I asked what about.

Lillian said very gently: "I just realized. There hasn't been a time in my life when I didn't have a romance going on in my head. I didn't know how to live without one."

I thought about that but I couldn't think of anything to say, except what I'd been going to say before: "I brought you some chocolates."

"Did you, darling," Lillian said. "That's nice."

We didn't talk any more and she rolled her head back in a slow way to face the light. When she touched the box of chocolates I thought there was a smile around her mouth but I wasn't sure, and I didn't like to ask.

A few days after that she asked me if I'd mind sketching out the rough draft of a story for her—one of the stories for the new book she planned, portraits of children. "I never will learn to dictate, not really. Maybe if you sketch it out on paper and then read it to me I can rewrite it my way."

I started to blush for her because I knew what it must have cost her to ask, and then decided I didn't know at all, and got mad at myself for my prudery. If a writer thinks that writing has stopped forever, then any way of getting it started again is a good way: I said again I'd do whatever I could to help, thinking she'd forget about it, but she didn't forget. That weekend I found a letter in my mailbox.

March 6, 1984

DEAR PETER:

This is a prelude to the story which I hope you will write for me as soon as you get through with all that television junk. This beginning can be amended in any way you like, but I thought it might give you an idea of what was in the back of my head.

My very warmest regards and respect to you and to your dear mother.

Lillian Hellman

I hadn't been writing television junk but I was finishing a short story and when I was done I read the five-page outline Lilly

had dictated and enclosed with her letter. It was about a child
she had once known as a girl in New Orleans, a religious little
girl who later became a nun called Sister Margaret. In her twenties, Lillian wrote, Sister Margaret lived and worked in a small
convent with some other nuns in El Salvador. The opening of the
story was told partly from memory, partly from the diary of a
little boy who was the son of a friend of Sister Margaret's, a child
who had suffered a crack-up and was confined to an institution.

The five pages were awkwardly dictated but wonderfully set
up, as only Lilly knew how to set up a story, and when I finished
it I wondered where she meant to go with it. Then I saw that
Sister Margaret was intended as one of the American nuns who
had recently been killed in El Salvador, and the little boy's crack-
up a result of his having been present during their rape-murder.

Halfway down the third page the little boy was introduced:
"The rest of Margaret's story is in the hands of a ten-year-
old boy. I know about the boy because he is the son of Carlton
Smith, who was with Peter Feibleman . . . when he went down
to San Salvador last year to do some work."

It was a good idea and a fine way to introduce the little
boy—but there had been no Carlton Smith with me in Salvador
or anywhere else. What was interesting about it was that Lillian
had come full swing. She had started, in her first book of memoirs, with fact—had come through her second book, which was
part fiction part fact, the book that contained "Julia"—had done
her last book, *Maybe,* about something that may or may not have
happened at all—and was now embarked on pure fiction—all in
the same form. She had completed the circle, with the reviewers
alternately praising and calling her a liar, and she didn't care
what they thought now any more than she'd cared in the beginning. She was too busy going her own way—determined, I guess,
to finish what she'd started—to find a form of fiction as fact that
worked for her no matter what anyone thought or didn't think.

I didn't rough out the story for her as she'd asked, largely
because imitating her prose would have sounded like imitation
no matter how well it was done, and also because I didn't trust
her judgment now in asking me to do it.

Instead of the story of Sister Margaret I brought her the
completed rough draft of the cookbook—not the recipes but the
memoir sections, her half and mine—and read it all to her out

loud. It took three days to read because she was too tired to
listen for long stretches but it was good to see her color come
back and I hadn't heard her laugh in a long time. It was an older
laugh now, more of a cackle than a gut chuckle, but it came from
the same place and she seemed happy from the beginning of the
book to the end.

When I finished she looked so relaxed it put us both off-
guard and she said without thinking: "Nobody can come between us now—no more anonymous calls—nothing."

I was at the door when she spoke and I stopped and turned
back. I didn't know what to say for a second, not because I didn't
know what she meant, but because I did. "There were no anonymous phone calls, were there?" I said. "You made them up."

The silence in the room appeared to grow like an invisible
sponge, sopping up every available thought. After a couple of
minutes Lillian said: "That remark pains me very deeply," but
she said it much too late and I was already laughing when I went
out of the room and down the stairs.

That same week she asked Billy Abrahams, who was editing
the cookbook/memoir, to fly down from San Francisco, and I
asked Elaine and Hannah and Talli to join us for dinner. With
Lillian's nurse that made seven and seven people made a dinner
party.

Nobody got very dressed up, but Elaine and I each put on a
clean pair of jeans and Hannah and Talli wore bright pretty dresses.
Billy wore a suit. Lilly had her hair done and was carried downstairs, but she walked from the bottom of the staircase into the
living room with her cane, the nurse following close behind. She
didn't like being helped so nobody got up to help her and Talli's
bartender made us all a drink. It had been announced the week
before that two unauthorized biographies of Lillian were being
written by people who had never met her and whose reputations
as biographers were not distinguished. Lillian brought the subject
up and suggested that a letter be sent to her close friends asking
them not to cooperate with the unauthorized books. Billy had
already consented to Lillian's request that he do her biography
himself. He settled down now to the kind of amiable gossip Billy
is good at and Lilly laughed and cheered up immediately; the
room seemed to buzz with goodwill and Hannah told a joke and
Lilly complained of the sauce during dinner and talked about the

horseradish she grew on the Vineyard, which was becoming more and more famous. She promised to send a jar of it to each person at the table and we chatted about the horseradish and Elaine, who smoked cigars in order not to smoke cigarettes, talked Lillian into doing the same. Lilly said she'd try, and Elaine gave her a cigar, and she held it like a rose for the rest of the evening.

I think that was the night Lilly knew for a fact that her friends were pulling for her more than she had suspected up to then. Things appeared to come together for her that night, odd bits and pieces coalesced, because after that a quietness settled in. She was often upset in the weeks to come but somewhere she knew that people were trying to help, and that pleased her more than anything and seemed to give her what had been missing since Boston: a certain twinkle.

In early spring she went back to New York and called to tell me that the trees in Central Park were budding. "Some of them are in flower," she said. "Wouldn't it be nice to hold your hand out once a year and produce a flower?" I said I was too old to be a tree and she said she hoped she wasn't. "I'm too old for a lot of things," she said, "but not for that—I'd make a nice tree."

She went on to say that Annabel had been coming to the apartment two or three times a week to read to her, as had Maureen Stapleton. "I have nice friends," Lilly said. "Don't I?"

Before she hung up I told her for the last time that I thought she ought to drop the McCarthy libel suit and added the worst thing I could think of. It was beginning to seem that she no longer stood for freedom of speech.

"I'll call you back," Lilly said.

In less than an hour she did. "I talked to Hannah and Dick," she said, "it's surprising, but they agree with you. Hannah feels very strongly about it—I've got a call in to Ephraim, I'll see what he says."

What Ephraim said was that he had already tried to settle out of court, offering to drop the demands for financial compensation in return for a written apology from Miss McCarthy, and the offer had been turned down twice. "If she won't apologize she must be waiting for something," Lilly said, "Ephraim says there's no doubt in his mind now that we'll win in court." I asked what Miss McCarthy could possibly be waiting for. "Me," Lilly said. "Ephraim just explained that a libel suit dies with the person who brings it. Maybe that's why the postponements—maybe they're waiting for me to die."

I said I doubted anybody was doing that and Lilly said she'd ask Hannah.

She spoke to Hannah a lot that spring. Hannah had always had a great quality of tenderness and comfort and by then she had accepted the role of Lillian's mother, which eased some of the envy over Hannah's three grown children. Lilly was often envious of women with children and being number one on Hannah's list of concerns now suited her well. They had sparred a lot over the years, as close friends do, but having a friend take over as a surrogate parent made Lilly feel safe, so it came as a sudden and quite brutal shock that spring when Hannah died. It happened without any warning at all and Lillian's voice, jittery as it was, took on a sadness that cut very deep. There was a brief note of triumph in it as well, the triumph of an elderly person who has survived another elderly person, but the triumph was short-lived and the sadness was not.

I went to see Lilly after it happened and spent the weekend in New York. When I walked into her apartment I was stopped in the hall by a new nurse who had been on the case for only a day or so and who wanted to warn me of the patient's condition. Miss Hellman, she explained, was half-paralyzed and almost totally blind: she couldn't eat, couldn't walk, couldn't find a comfortable spot in her bed, couldn't stand up. Miss Hellman, she said, was in terrible shape, and was probably dying.

I thanked the nurse for the information and went in and asked Lilly how she was feeling.

"Not good, Peter," she said.

I asked why not.

"This is the worst case of writer's block I ever had in my life," Lillian said. "*The* worst case."

She asked about the galleys of the cookbook and I said I'd be bringing them to the Vineyard soon—that I would try to get them for her birthday, on the twentieth of June. "I hope so," Lilly said, "maybe that will break the block."

Later that day Maureen came and read *Antony and Cleopatra* to her and after a while I shut my eyes and tried to listen blind, the way Lilly listened. It turned out to be a good way because Maureen can make you see with her voice. After a while you could see ships on the Nile and temples and tombs and Roman soldiers. When I opened my eyes she was still reading, but she wasn't looking at the page; she seemed to know the play by heart, as she knew much of Keats and Shelley and Donne when she read from them the next day. Listening to Maureen is not the worst thing that can happen to a person and I was in a better mood when I went back to Los Angeles.

Lillian went to the Vineyard at the beginning of the summer and waited for me there. The galleys were held up an extra few days at the publisher's, too late to bring them for her birthday, and I called to tell her so.

"You *can't* be late," Lilly said.

I told her it was only a matter of days.

"You don't understand," she said, "I want to work, I want to work, I want to work . . ."

I called the publisher and asked if they could step up the schedule a little, and they agreed to cut a day from it so that I could pick up the galleys in time to catch an earlier flight. It wasn't much of a difference, but a day was a day, and I called to tell Lilly but her line was busy.

There was a brand-new nurse on the job, a nice-sounding German woman who spoke with an accent. "They told me this was a difficult case," she said when I spoke to her very late that same night, after Rita had called to give me the news, "but I have had some experience with angry patients—so I didn't expect that Miss Hellman would be much trouble, and she wasn't. No trouble at all. When I came in, she told me to put my uniform on and give her a massage. It was her neck she wanted me to work on—only the back of her neck, of course, because she'd had surgery on the side of her neck. You know about the surgery on her neck?"

I said I knew about her neck.

"So," the nurse said, "I was working on her neck and I knew she was enjoying it—you can always tell—she took one of my hands and held it . . . so affectionate, you know—and then she began to squeeze my hand very hard—very, very hard—and she said: 'I think you and I are going to get along just fine.' Then she died."

I asked if Lillian had said anything else before she died.

"No," the nurse said, "nothing else. They sent an ambulance and tried to revive her in the hospital, but it was no use—it was all finished, you see. Miss Hellman had nothing else to say."

Lagniappe

>>>>> I

THE THING YOU NOTICE most about an osprey is not its wingspan
or its grace or even the way it plummets when it sees a fish—you
notice those things, but they aren't the main thing. The main
thing about an osprey is its eyesight. Not that the bird does it
well, but that it does it at all. How can it spot a fish from that
height? Why does it go way the hell up there to look? What kind
of vision is that?

I watch it every morning from my room and in the afternoon
from the deck outside. Sometimes we sit there for hours, Sadie
and I, and we watch other things too. There are two small rabbits that hop up from the beach grass in the afternoon and get
under the fence into the vegetable garden. The first week they
came the rabbits ate methodically, quietly, eyeballing Sadie and
munching their way down the two rows of kale and back along
the snow peas before they started on the arugula. In the beginning I chased them out of the garden and put up a chicken-wire
fence but they were very small rabbits then, only a couple of
weeks old, and they found a way to get under it. After the chicken
wire I tried putting down a long unbroken line of baby powder
all around the perimeter of the vegetable garden at the suggestion
of a neighbor who told me that rabbits won't cross baby powder
because it makes them sneeze. It took me several hours to do
because I put down two wide parallel rows of baby powder on
the theory that two rows are better than one, and I was happy
with the look of it when I finished. But that night it rained and
the next morning the rabbits were back in the vegetable garden.
After that I tried mothballs and several other things that other

337

people had told me about, but none of them worked for one reason or another. These rabbits could circumvent anything. In the end the only move I could make was to kill them, but I didn't have the heart by then and now Sadie puts up with them the way you put up with a tiresome relative or an impossible in-law. They aren't exactly pets, but it's clear that they're here to stay—the rabbits are part of the landscape.

Lillian would have scolded me, I know—she would have gone after the rabbits with whatever weapon was handy and skinned and cooked them for dinner. A kale-fattened rabbit, she would say, is a fine thing to eat, but Lillian isn't here and the rabbits are.

In summer there are twice as many sailboats in front of the house as there used to be when I first came to the Vineyard. Powerboats too, from big yachts to dinghies with outboard motors. The boats are especially thick on weekends and in August the beach often has two or three strangers sitting in bathing suits or walking up and down looking for shells. I could chase the strangers off, as some of my neighbors do, but it doesn't seem worth it—the bathers are like the rabbits—they're part of the landscape and I'm as used to them as I am to anything else. The fat ferryboats still come and go, they sit lower in the water these days because there are more people on them. Otherwise it's much the same as it was when Lillian died.

When Lillian died I forgot about her immediately. I was as relieved as she herself had been when Hammett died, as if an intolerable pressure had been lifted—I felt a thousand pounds lighter and I didn't think about her for quite a long time. It was only after I made the house mine and settled in that I began to wonder where she was, and when I did I was very angry at her. I wanted to feel nostalgic and soupy but I couldn't, I was too upset at her leaving me and I stayed angry for months. By then the attacks on her had doubled in the press—the attacks she had predicted—not only on her work but on her life. It began as a ground swell of simple debunking and pretty soon it was a hot blaze, much like book burning, with a couple of members of the ladies' club stoking the fires. It didn't stop my anger at Lillian but I found it annoying and I began to look for things to distract me.

For a while the legal machinery of death was a distraction—

Lillian's will was a mess. Rather than spend money at a big law firm to add a codicil every time she thought of one, she had gone to a less expensive lawyer toward the end of her life when she was scared of going broke. The less expensive lawyer rewrote the will for her and he did his best, but his best was not wonderful, and after she died the will had to be taken over and submitted to the surrogate court by a more expensive law firm for interpretation.

Lillian's will was something of a surprise. She had often spoken of setting up a foundation in her name for young writers and with her fears about money it was assumed that she would leave everything to the foundation in her name and perhaps a token gift to each of her friends. Instead she set up two foundations, but she left me the Vineyard house and half her royalties for life and some cash and several other things. She made me a fiduciary of her literary property, which included the literary property of Dashiell Hammett, and she made me her principal heir. It was enough to live on modestly for the rest of my life, and it was accompanied by a note saying she hoped that it would mean I could spend my time writing what she thought I was best at, which was novels. I sold the Los Angeles house in a matter of weeks and walked out before it was sold. Leaving Los Angeles made me sad and it was all right to feel nostalgic and soupy about that because the feeling didn't run very deep. I like Los Angeles the way I like brothels—I have a taste, I think, for corruption.

I moved to the Vineyard and whatever the internal anchor is that people drop once or twice in their lives, I seem to have dropped it here in the sand. That came as a surprise too because the Vineyard was the last place I thought I'd want to live when Lillian died. Too many memories and too cold in the winter, I thought—too dark is what I mainly thought—too everything in the winter. No place for a Southerner, not this Southerner anyway—not me, I thought. But I was wrong.

Another of the things I was wrong about was how I'd feel about Lillian when everything was over. After the dust had settled I was still angry at her but by that time the anger was different. Her will had made life comfortable for me and I thought about that for a while. Having money is a nice feeling, I was born into a family that had money, and I grew up having it but that was a long time ago. I had forgotten how nice having money is and I thought about it a lot after the will was settled: for two or three months I thought about money more than I thought about Lillian. That's how shallow I am.

I thought about missing her and at the same time feeling rich and then it dawned on me that I've never had a clean thought in my life that didn't have another thought like that one beside it. I've never understood the dualism of thought and maybe the reason I haven't understood it is because of what it says about me— maybe I'm not the little soldier I thought I was, I decided. It's true that I was loyal to Lillian but I wonder whether I would have been so loyal if she hadn't been going to leave me money: maybe it wasn't such a surprise. Maybe I knew all along. Maybe I've never faced what I am, and if I never have, maybe it's too late.

Laceration like that feeds on itself and I would probably have gone on with it indefinitely if two things hadn't happened to stop me. The first was my mother's suicide, final and successful. That shook me up for several reasons. My mother had never asked me for help in my whole life, but when she asked me to help her with her death the request was instantly familiar, as though I had always known she would do just that. But the final separation was even deeper for me than I would have imagined.

The other thing that stopped me from feeling sorry for myself was the ballooning attack on Lillian, which had by then reached the proportions of an international conflagration. You couldn't pick up a newspaper or magazine in America or even England without somebody firing a potshot at her and except for a few of her close friends, everybody and their uncle had jumped on the bandwagon, from Norman Podhoretz in New York to a dedicated hireling from Boston U. The texture of the assault was not new, it was still the work of the ladies' club, but the ladies had gone about their mission with true verve: the attack was in full bloom, though its original purpose was finished because the libel suit had died with Lillian. But certain knowledgeable people had been made angry and they went on with it all the same. There is no rage like the rage of the self-righteous, and Lillian herself had once observed that the drying up of gonads in the most delicate of literary ladies has a tendency to make them irritable not only during the drying process but long after the fact.

In a comparable way, a group of literary gentlemen took to picking at Hemingway's remains when he died on the grounds that his work had been the result of a false machismo. These gentlemen felt that they had more balls than Hemingway any day of the week. All his bragging and self-inflation had been used against him then, much the way Lillian's bragging and self-inflation were being used against her now, but nobody bothered to look at his writing just as writing. It was a transitory problem because of course in the end Hemingway's work is here to stay. His first book, *In Our Time,* is a wonderful book and some of the short stories are wonderful short stories and if the rest is flawed it's still among the best work of his time, and that's enough to keep a writer alive. Lillian's first play, *The Children's Hour,* is a wonderful play, and some of the memoir pieces are fine memoir pieces, and if the rest is flawed it's still more interesting than most, and that is enough to keep her alive. So when all the fuss is over, I thought, she'll still be around—but what about me? I'm past fifty now and by the time Lilly finally comes into her own and people start praising her again I won't be here to enjoy it.

That did it. At least it got my mind off myself and made me think of writing about her. The notion of saying something in print sounded like a good idea, though I had avoided it till then: it went on sounding like a good idea for about ten days and then it sounded like the worst idea I'd ever had. The pitfalls were endless; the truth is I was too close to Lillian and I am not a good journalist. In order to see her with objectivity I would have to rise hundreds of feet straight up above her and look down. But how could I spot anything from that height, why would I go way up there to look and what kind of vision is that?

I dropped the idea and if it hadn't been for a magazine I picked up three months later in a dentist's office, I doubt I'd have thought of it again. The magazine had yet another bulletin from the club, a piece assaulting Lillian on the usual grounds, but in such extreme detail that it was hard to read, as certain pieces sometimes are in *The New Yorker.* After about ten minutes of examination you wanted to say yes, that may be true—or no, it may not be true—but either way it only matters to another hippopotamus. Or in the jargon of a more pedestrian world, who gives a damn? It missed the point of Lillian.

Under that magazine in the dentist's waiting room was another magazine describing her funeral and the friends who came back to her house afterward, and that was more sick-making because its intent was apparently to make fun of other people's grief and drop a few names along the way.

When I sat down in the dentist's chair I took to thinking about Lillian's funeral—I had avoided remembering it since it took place—and about the things people had said over her grave. There had been several speakers present: I broke the silence and John Hersey closed it and Bill Styron and Jules Feiffer and Bob Brustein and Pat Neal and Annabel Nichols spoke between. The best of the speakers, I thought, was John, who moved back and forth, lean and lithe and spry, as if he meant to light up the earth next to her grave. But everybody else who spoke that day had something forceful to say about her too.*

Rose Styron gave a small lunch before the funeral which held it up twenty minutes and afterward people came back to Lillian's house and waited for Lilly to come out of the bathroom or walk up from the beach and say it was all a mistake. We waited for her to tell us that it was somebody else we had buried—that it was another of her practical jokes—that she wasn't dead after all—but she never came back, and soon everybody went home.

When I thought about that, I began to think about Lilly in other ways, and then I knew that I wanted to write about her whether I knew how or not. It seemed that everybody in the world had written about her lately except me and all of them had been out to get her. Every Southern lady has a right to believe that one Southern gentleman will stand up for her if she's assaulted and Lillian was being assaulted, and I am a Southern gentleman. So I had better get myself into gear and find the right way to do it, I thought, and as soon as I thought that, I knew what the way would be, because the only thing I was equipped to do was a kind of portrait. I couldn't pretend to be objective, not after forty-three years of a friendship, but maybe I could do it another way. Maybe I could tell a kind of love story about an older woman and a younger man, tell the story as what I am, a novelist, and hope for the best.

The morning I started work I was sitting with Sadie out on

* The speeches made at Lillian's graveside are given in the appendix beginning on page 351.

the deck. The osprey was off somewhere and I was watching the leaves of Lillian's horseradish plants, which had come up thicker and greener than ever. The horseradish was growing in a sandy place that was heavy with underbrush and purple wildflowers, about a fifth of the way between the vegetable garden and the sea, not far from the house. I was thinking about the configuration the plants grew in, when Lillian's caretaker, Melvin Pachico, came down to do some work and I asked him what kind of fertilizer he used on the horseradish plants, and he said he didn't use anything because they didn't need anything, they just grew.

"They're famous plants," I said, "people from all over the world used to write letters asking Miss Hellman for some horseradish."

"So I'm told," Melvin said.

"One thing I just noticed," I said, "the plants are growing in a perfect circle."

"They better be," Melvin said, "she planted them around the cesspool."

He went away and I stood there for maybe a minute and then I sat down by myself and laughed for twenty minutes and when I went upstairs to work on the portrait I was still laughing.

But when I sat down at my desk it didn't seem funny anymore, because nothing did. Nothing seemed worth telling about Lillian because all I really wanted to say was that something large has left us. But the largeness wasn't made up of large things. I kept remembering that speech from *Autumn Garden,* the one Lillian struggled with so long that Hammett told her to go out of the room and come back in an hour, and when she came back he had written it. The characters are middle-aged men: Griggs is talking to Crossman.

GRIGGS

So at any given moment you're only the sum of your life up to then. There are no big moments you can reach unless you've a pile of smaller moments to stand on. That big hour of decision, the turning point in your life, the someday you've counted on when you'd suddenly wipe out your past mistakes, do the work you'd never done, think the way you'd never thought, have what you'd never had—it just doesn't come suddenly. You've trained yourself for it while you

waited—or you've frittered yourself away. I've frittered myself away, Crossman.

The main thing I wanted to say about Lillian was that she
didn't fritter herself away. She used herself all the time, the best
way she could, and she was successful some of the time and not
successful some of the time, but she always managed to get on
with her life. It takes a certain kind of largeness to fall down with
a sizable thud, the kind that knocks the wind out of you, and get
up and get on with it. It takes a kind of largeness just to get out
of your own way.

But you can't say that, show that, in those terms—you have
to skip over the large stuff and give the smallest event the most
attention, since the microcosm is the macrocosm in most of us.
People who talk generalities are seldom successful at conveying
what they mean, but if you take a little piece of anybody's life
and look at it close enough you can see the whole life in it, the
way a trained eye can see an organism in a single cell, evolution
in a lifespan, a cosmos in a drop of water. In a charcoal sketch
you can see the meaning of a human being—unless of course the
hand drawing the sketch is not good enough—then all you have
is something that belongs in a waxworks museum. So the hand
had better be at least as inventive as it is true.

Before it's said by others let me say it for myself: some of
this book is invention. Whether it rained hard on a certain day,
how much time passed between this and that, which month
someone gave a party. That kind of memory is seldom for me as
specific as I've made it—the sense of a presence not always com-
municable in a canvas made up of snippets and patches, flashes
of remembered time without any connections. You can't convey
such a thing to another person. Instead, you want to extract from
the roots of a friendship those essences that give a scent, a quality; a necessary perfume. You look behind you. And then with
the straggly and dingy leftover threads you try to make something more than a fabric, you try for something of life, the only
kind of life after death I happen to trust, the life that remains in
the heart of the living.

But at first I didn't know how to do that for Lillian because
I didn't know how to do it period; so I started with a pile of
loose memories about this or that splinter of time, hearing her

voice. Because after the high jittery hospital-voice was silenced I could hear the other one, the true voice, without having to turn on a machine or listen to a tape.

"How old are you?"

"I'm only ten."

"I don't know what you mean by 'only'—ten isn't so young."

And I could hear my own voice later because I could hear the two of us, lewd and bawdy and loud, laughing in bed.

LILLIAN: *Shut up, Peter, wait till I die and write about it.*

PETER: *I don't want to write about it.*

LILLIAN: *Why not?*

PETER: *Because I don't want to sound like Alice B. Toklas is why not.*

LILLIAN: *Can't you write about me without sounding like Alice B. Toklas?*

PETER: *I doubt it.*

After that, I could hear the question she asked most, the question Lilly asked every time there was trouble between us, as soon as we got past the trouble.

LILLIAN: *Well, we got through it, that's the main thing—we came out fine in the end, didn't we?*

PAUSE.

LILLIAN: *Didn't we, Peter?*

PAUSE.

LILLIAN: *We came out fine in the end didn't we . . . ?*

But I never answered that question except to say I didn't know whether we had come out fine in the end, because it wasn't the end. Because, as affectionate kids of my generation used to say, it would only be the end when one of us was dead.

A few odd things surfaced while I was working. There was a letter from Lillian I hadn't read carefully when I first got it—a taped remark she'd made to me—a sentence she had written on the back of a photograph—an evening that Barbara Hersey remembered.

The night before she died, Barbara said, Lillian came to their house for dinner. The other person they'd invited was Gil Harri-

son, ex-publisher of *The New Republic,* whom Lilly had known
before; Harrison brought her a bag of candy as a present and
toward the end of the meal Barbara came out of the kitchen to
find the two of them sitting alone at the table. Lillian was leaning
close to Harrison and saying in a low voice: "You and I must see
each other alone sometime."

When they drove her home that night Lilly gave the bag of
candy to the night nurse and told her to put it in a very careful
place, and less than twenty-four hours later she was dead.

After Barbara, Elaine May called to say she'd found a letter
from Lillian that had been accidentally pushed, unopened, into
the back of a desk drawer. The evening after our dinner in Los
Angeles, Elaine had sent Lilly a box of cigars as an encouragement to stop the cigarettes, but after sending them she herself had
left town. The letter said: "I don't know whether I can accept
cigars from a woman I can't get on the phone."

There were others who called for other reasons. One of the
unauthorized biographers, a man named William Wright, called
several times, but Lillian had asked us not to talk to him so I had
no choice. When his book came out I had a look at it, and was
sorry that we hadn't been able to help because I think he meant
to do a good job, and because the only people who did speak to
him were people who hated Lillian. The acknowledgments in the
front of the book were like a list of her enemies. But even if she
hadn't asked her friends for silence, they would probably have
given it, since friends always tend to be silent about each other,
just as enemies tend to talk. The result, even with the best of
intentions, was a biography riddled with inaccuracy, larded with
untruth; and saddest of all, when the biography was published it
was not reviewed, Lillian was. For weeks it was as if her life had
been offered up for criticism, not a book written about her. It
made me wonder about the other people who would one day try
to write about Lilly and what those people would be like. A certain kind of biographer is not well equipped to discuss her motives since it's hard for a man to get inside a woman who's dead
unless he wants to be inside one who's alive: Lillian's sexuality
was at the root of her being, and apart from that, as a very simple-minded rule, men who hate women shouldn't write about them.

There were still others who called, the friends who needed
to say one last thing about her—say it to themselves as much as

to me. Mike Nichols: "I guess she was the best." Maureen Stapleton: "The funniest." Leonard Bernstein: "She was wonderful
and she knew it." John Marquand, Jr.: "She was awful and she
was worth it." *

One day while I was working, a gravestone that had been
ordered for Lilly by John Hersey arrived on one of the ferryboats.
It came by truck and the three of us drove out to the cemetery in
Chilmark and put it on Lilly's grave. She had wanted to be buried in the Chilmark cemetery because she liked it better than the
Vineyard Haven cemetery but when she died it didn't look possible. Chilmark is for the rich, you have to own three acres of
prime up-island land to get into that one, and Lilly owned only
a couple of acres in Vineyard Haven. Then it turned out that
Jerome Wiesner, president of MIT and one of the people who
had loved Lilly, owned an extra gravesite in Chilmark and by
some fluke he was able to give it to her. A few days after she
died, Lilly got in on a pass.

John and Barbara and I stood in the cemetery while the stone
was placed on her grave, a small piece of blue-gray slate with
LILLIAN HELLMAN, 1905–1984 written on it and a long writer's
quill etched beneath. I had thought it would be a sad day but it
wasn't, it was more like a family day. The sun made shadows
through the leaves on the slate and when I went back alone the
next week, the grave had a dappled look, a hush of trees over it,
and I was able for the first time since her death to stop thinking
that Lillian's oldest enemy, her body, had finally won the fight,
and that Mr. Fini had her. About a month after that, the earth
around the gravestone began to fill up with rows of colored peb-
bles and seashells people had brought up from the beach and left
there for her, like small natural presents.

One of the times I went back to visit her grave, I went on
driving. I drove all around the island by myself as though I had
somewhere to go, and then out onto the long strip of beach that
connects the island to Chappaquiddick. There's a riptide off a
point called Wasque there, where two currents meet, the best place
on the island for surf casting. I drove past some people with poles
on the beach and out beyond them past a bird sanctuary and a

---

* Marquand credits the origin of this remark to Donald Ogden Stewart
upon the death of his wife, Ella Winter, previously married to Lincoln Steffens.

pond, all the way to the beach at the Cape Poge lighthouse. I stopped there and got out of my Jeep to have a beer.

The water from Cape Poge ripples out forever to the horizon and the light is high and wavy like the sea. It's the kind of light that makes you wonder things—where does light go, or does it travel out forever? Can the image of a person always exist as pure light, always traveling out, and if you exist like that, how old are you—the age you choose, or the age your lover chooses?

The sky that day had the sort of mazy look that made me wonder what the final point of Lillian was—or if there was a final point. It's true that all good writers from time to time think they're full of pure nonsense and all good writers from time to time are right. How you get around such obstacles defines you, and Lillian got around them by dramatizing her life—but does that define her or is it just another loose floating fact?

After a while I opened another beer and tried to think about answering some of the people who had said bad things about Lillian but after a while I knew I couldn't answer them in kind or even get in the ring with them because I would only be hopelessly angry and tongue-tied, and because the only thing I have a right to say is something about Lillian herself, an affirmation, not a denial. It didn't take long to think that, and I didn't have anything else to think that afternoon, but just then I found myself wondering about the dead bird I had buried here in the sand and all at once I knew what it meant. It was one of those thoughts you struggle with for years, and just when you give up, the answer comes sailing in on a peripheral wave as if you had always known it. If I could tell about the day we went to the lighthouse—about the sun that day and Lillian's face when she disappeared in the light—about the strength in her back and the burying of the swan—then maybe it would be all right: if I could tell about what had been broken in her and what hadn't, if I could talk about the outraged heart of childhood. If I could make my own peace with that day.

Toward evening I got back into the Jeep and drove across the sand to a gas station on the main island. I put the pressure back in the tires and drove to the house and sat on the deck outside. I don't know what time it was when I went to sleep but when I woke up I was happy, and it was dawn.

The point of this book for me is not so much to prove anything as to be able to recognize one other living face—the task that scares me most, the one I'm not good at—to feel the presence of someone in the world as that person meant to be felt, and to remember. To say without sentimentality I have been witness to this separate person, this passage on the planet, to say she was here, and this is what she was like, take her or leave her.

The final point of Lillian, I guess, is that she was larger than her own life—big enough to make mistakes and know it, and live to accept it, larger than her critics—a great boom of a woman— loud enough in time to drown her attackers as well. She was, is, a lasting voice, and when all the storms in all the tiny teacups are done, it will still be heard. She has a final place. She is a writer.

LILLIAN: *We came out fine in the end, that's the main thing.*

PAUSE.

LILLIAN: *We did come out fine, didn't we, honey?*

Yes.

Graveside Eulogies

ON JULY 3, 1984, eight impromptu speeches were given at Lillian's graveside in Chilmark Cemetery on Martha's Vineyard. The first speech was my own, omitted here because it is a repetition of scenes and events already described in the text.

The other eulogies are as follows, reprinted by courtesy of *The Vineyard Gazette*.

JULES FEIFFER

On National Public Radio last Saturday night they played pieces of an old interview with Lillian, and as I listened to it I came up short, thinking, "Oh, my God, that voice." It had been a while since I heard Lil's voice in full-throated rasp. She had been too weak for the last year to hold up her rasp with her usual resonance. But that and her presence, even her thin, wasted presence, was still enough to dominate at dinner parties. I have often found myself marveling in dazzlement, envy and awe at Lillian's ability to hold the attention of a room with a story which when examined later had all the importance of a marketing trip to Cronig's.

She could take a marketing trip to Cronig's and string it out into three well-made acts, quietly dramatic, surprisingly suspenseful. Whom did she run into that she wanted to avoid? What slight would occur, what mishap at the check-out counter, the crisis of the meat counter, the incident of the vegetables, the adventure of the shopping cart, and all of this told in a growling, cigarette-gutted, booze-burnished croak, interrupted only by her own editorial asides. Isn't that extraordinary? Have you ever heard of such a thing? Have I gone mad? Maybe it's me: I'm sure it's me.

How the hell does she do it, I must have asked myself thousands of times over the years as I sat at the table, smiling, nodding, and smoldering with envy. And in what were alleged to be the more critical aspects of life—war and peace, the arms race, civil liberties, the rise and fall of the American Left—Lillian's voice was no less conversational, never polemical, never righteous except for an occasional, "forgive me," pronounced softly, but which meant that the person speaking didn't know what he was talking about.

When the talk was politics, Lil became more reflective, more quiet and more amused. She was drawn by irresistible instinct into public affairs: it didn't seem to be within her grasp not to take a position. I don't believe it was ever a matter of choice with her to play it safe or not play it safe, to defy the Un-American Activities Committee or to cave in. Others saw her as courageous at these times in her life. I don't think she ever saw it that way. She honestly knew of no other way to behave.

What made her angry, and continually angry, were the sorts of things that other people, including fellow radicals, learned over time to accept. Not to like, never that, but to get over, to let pass, to live to fight another day. Lillian couldn't learn to get over things. She was very bad at letting things pass. Her toughness was a matter of pride, principle, ego and a hard-nosed vision of the way things ought to be, and she didn't mind a fight. She complained about trouble, but as all of us who loved her know, a sizable side of her thrived on it.

And the influence she brought to bear on these troubled times was extraordinary. This is not a country that listens gladly to literary types. We listen to lawyers, we listen to lobbyists and journalists and other officially signified experts. But Lillian found a way of making herself heard. When she and I met in the early sixties, I was startled that someone that old could speak with such familiarity and fluency on issues that concerned my generation. Ten years later, I was startled that she could speak with equal familiarity and fluency with student revolutionaries who by and large had stopped speaking to me because of the generation gap.

In fact, she was cross-generational, and could effortlessly engage the old, the young, the middle-aged, the left, the middle, the right and just about anyone except on occasion, the women friends of the men she admired.

Over the last ten or twelve years of her life she was most concerned with the government's assault on civil liberties, and rather than write outraged articles on it, she got on the phone and brought together a group of lawyers and professors and writers and statesmen and a millionaire or two and formed the Committee for Public Justice. She chaired the meetings, helped raise the funds, helped get others to raise more funds, thrashed out agendas, and set up across the country a series of well-covered public meetings which described in detail the calculated erosion by the FBI, the CIA and the Justice Department on the First Amendment and our other constitutional rights. No other writer I know would begin to know how to do this, and she went about this work in a manner no radically different from the way she organized her menus for dinner parties.

Much has been written about her enemies. She picked them with care, and God knows they deserved her, but people who don't know her don't know about her friends. They were everywhere, had every kind of job, and every kind of politics, and found her in one way or another to be quite important in their lives. There is much to miss. I will miss the talks, the arguments, the extreme loyalty when it was called upon, and as much as anything else, the girlishness, the brattishness and incredible sense of fun.

WILLIAM STYRON

I'm Bill Styron, an old friend of Lillian's, like many of us here. She once told me that this would be the day that I yearn for more than anything in my life, speaking words over her remains; and she cackled in glee. "Ha, ha," she said, and I cackled back. She said, "If you don't say utterly admiring and beautiful things about me, I'm going to cut you out of my will." I said there was no possible way that I could refrain from saying a few critical things, and she said, "Well, you're cut out already."

That was the way things went with us. I think we had more fights per man and woman contact than probably anyone alive. We were fighting all the time, and we loved each other a great deal for sure, because the vibrations were there. But our fights were never really, oddly enough, over abstract things like politics or philosophy or social dilemmas; they were always over such things such as whether a Smithfield ham should be served hot or cold, or whether I had put too much salt in the black-eyed peas.

And I suddenly realized that this anger that spilled out from the lady, and it was almost a reservoir of anger, was really not directed at me or her other friends or even the black-eyed peas, but was directed at all the hateful things that she saw as menaces to the world. When she hated me and the ham, she was hating a pig like Roy Cohn, and I think this is what motivated her; and when one understood that the measure of her anger was really not personal but cosmic, then one was able to deal with her.

I was privileged, I think the word is, to take Lillian out, to be the last person to take her out to dinner; and I did so a few days ago here in Chilmark at La Grange, and it was quite an ordeal. We sat down, I had to get her into a chair, just the two of us, and we sat and she groped for the various things she had to grope for because as you know she was blind and quite radi-cally crippled; and we had conversation. We carved up a few mutually detested writers and one or two mediocre politicians and an elderly deceased novelist whom she specifically detested, and we got into this sort of thing; and we then started talking about her age.

I didn't tell her the snoop from *The New York Times* had called me up asking if I knew her age, and I said the only bio-graphical data I had at hand was that she was probably seventy-nine; and she was saying to me, which is wonderful, she said, "I don't know whether the twentieth of June was my seventy-fourth or my seventy-third." And I measured this, because she had been doing this all of her life, not as a vanity—though that was fine too, what's wrong with a little vanity—but as a kind of demon-stration of the way that she was hanging on to life.

I suddenly realized as I was sitting there that she was pain-fully uncomfortable. She said she was cursed by God with having from birth a skinny ass; so I had to go and put things under her constantly, which was fine. She said this bolstered her skepticism of the existence of God. And I told her something that she had always responded to, that it was made up with an ample and seductive bosom, and she smiled at that; and I suddenly realized that she, however, through all of this, she was gasping for breath and she was suffering. And it hit me that this woman was physically in agony, and there was something enormously wrenching about being seated alone with this almost fragment of a human being, suffering so much, gasping for breath; and yet, I had a glimpse of her almost as if she was a young girl again, in New Orleans with a beau and having a wonderful time.

And as these memories came flooding back, I remember that gorgeous cackle of laughter which always erupted at moments when we were together with other people or alone and it was usually a cackle of laughter which followed some beautiful harpooning of a fraud or a ninth-rater; and it was filled with a hatred, but it was usually hatred and anger which finally evolved into what I think she, like all of us, was searching for, some sort of transcendental idea which is love. And so, as we went out, I simply was in awe of this woman. I had no final reflection except that perhaps she was in the end a lover, a mother, a sister and a friend and in a strange way a lover of us all. Thank you.

PATRICIA NEAL

I will always love my Lillian Hellman. She has been and always will be a very important person to me; a friend whose fibers were woven into every aspect of my life. At my tender age of twenty, she was responsible for my Broadway debut in *Another Part of the Forest;* and a few years later, having come back from Hollywood, I appeared in her play *The Children's Hour.* At her New York home in 1952 I met Roald Dahl, who was to be my husband for thirty years.

Just last month, she got all dressed up to come to a fabulous party I gave for my youngest daughter, Lucy. Lillian wore a magnificent Russian amethyst necklace. She looked divine. She wanted to know all about my Lucy's future plans; she was very eager to help the next generation.

Just last week we discussed having a belated birthday celebration for my dear Lillian. However, at the airport in Boston, I learned of her death from a total stranger. How sad it is that she is gone. I will remember her with deep love for ever and ever. *Shalom.*

ANNABEL DAVIS-GOFF NICHOLS

Thirteen years ago, Mike brought me up to the Vineyard to meet Lillian. She was an important person in his life; and I was determined to make a good impression. The first evening I politely contradicted her on a literary reference; and on the way home I threw up on the plane.

Much to my surprise, we spent a lot of time the following years under each other's roofs. We had good times talking about food, planning meals, cooking and eating them. We had good times in boats. We had good times on beaches. There was a lot of talking, a lot of laughing and there was even one evening when in the face of male apathy, we got dressed very smartly and went to the local casino. During these years, she only gave me one piece of literary advice. She begged me to buy my infant daughter at least one garment which had nothing written on it.

Then she became ill and practically everything changed; everything, that is, except for the courage and the humor. I remember before a painful and very frightening operation, her calling me and displacing her anxiety into a half-hour discussion about what she should do with four pounds of sausages and half a pound of brie which she couldn't incorporate into the menu.

During the last year and a half, when Lillian could not do very much anymore—Peter already described the way her life had become and how painful every moment was, I could say every waking moment but they were all waking moments—she couldn't even sleep toward the end. And when we spent time together, I would read to her and we started to read Parkman's history; with excursions into unsolved mysteries in the newspapers about which we would develop perfectly acceptable theories as to what really happened. And she would also have me read the odd piece of work that I was doing, and then she would always apologize very sincerely if she dropped off before I got to the end; and this summer we went overtime to finish Norman Mailer's new novel, and she wanted to see how it came out before she came up to the Vineyard.

And after we read, she would talk to me about books, about the writers who had written them, about writers and writing in general. And each time I would learn something, sometimes an idea and sometimes just how to pronounce a word correctly.

She was to me a great teacher and a good loyal friend; someone to whom I had a chance to say good-bye, but who will always be with me, and someone without whom I still have four volumes of Parkman to get through.

ROBERT BRUSTEIN

Lillian wrote eight original plays and four adaptations—twelve in all, before abandoning the stage in the early sixties. Not all were of equal quality; at least three, I believe, will live as long as there is an American theater: *Toys in the Attic, The Autumn Garden* and of course, her classic, *Little Foxes.*

Skillfully constructed and imprinted with strong scenes, crisp dialogue and powerful characters, Lillian's theater was created largely under the influence of Henrik Ibsen, being an unvarnished tribute to contemporary social realism. Like Ibsen, she believed that drama had a function beyond mere entertainment, that it could be a vehicle for social commentary, psychological insight and, above all, rigorous examination of the rotting understructure of a corrupted society. Later in her playwriting career, Lillian made a conscientious and successful effort to loosen up her style by employing the more indirect, apparently plotless techniques of Chekhov, but she never wavered in her conviction that theater could be a force for change in an unethical, unjust, essentially venal world.

Lillian's major subject was money, how it is made, how it changes lives and what people do to acquire it. Money, in fact, is usually the hidden extra character of her plays, often the most important one. It can function symbolically but it also has a tangible, concrete, specific nature—in *Toys in the Attic,* money is stroked as if it were a domestic animal.

Lillian sometimes seemed to divide the world according to how people's loyalties were affected by money. As a result, critics accused her of writing melodramas rather than tragedies—to which she replied that tragedy, invented in a time when destiny was thought to be fixed, allowed no possibility for change. Still, like all good melodramas, her plays do seem to be a confrontation between good and evil, reflecting her own passionate friendships and fierce enmities.

This capacity for friendship was probably the force that

originally drew her to the stage, the most collective of all the arts, just as her disappointment with people eventually repelled her from it. Still, the wonderful memoirs she wrote in self-enforced isolation splendidly displayed her theatrical gifts, which explains why they are so easily adapted to stage and film. And it may be that her life, with its strong loyalties, combative courage and abiding hatred of injustice, will eventually be considered her greatest theater.

[Jonathan] Swift has sailed into his rest;

(wrote W. B. Yeats about one of Lillian's literary antecedents)

> *Savage indignation there*
> *Cannot lacerate his breast.*
> *Imitate him if you dare,*
> *World-besotted traveller; he*
> *Served human liberty.*

It is a fitting epitaph for Lillian Hellman and her theater.

JEROME WIESNER

The friendship of Lillian was for me an ever-expanding delight, with many dimensions and variations. I think she regarded me as her link to the world of science and technology, which she didn't understand and deeply mistrusted. Though we shared many interests I would like to remember her special caring for students and her excitement in helping them to learn and grow, and to recall too the enormous enthusiasms and love with which they responded.

Lillian taught for a time at MIT. At first she did this with some misgivings, asking what she could teach young scientists whose language she didn't even understand. I remember how startled she was to learn that they had never heard of Joe McCarthy. In the end they won her over by their quickness of mind and eagerness to learn. Incidentally, they learned all about McCarthy and many other kinds of evil by the time she was through. They also learned to admire a tough taskmaster.

Her public lectures were among the best attended the school had ever seen—the campus response to her was extraordinary for its warmth and admiration. In the years since then I have watched young people around the world light up at the mention of her name—for them she is one of the heroes and heroines of our time.

As I have thought about this respect, admiration and awe of her I have realized that sensitive young people recognized that her gift to them was not only her masterpieces but her caring, her courage and her example of how to behave in a crisis.

For young people growing up in a world in which so much of what is said or done by public figures is suspect, Lillian Hellman's writing and behavior provides inspiration and hope.

JOHN HERSEY

I'd like to say a few words about Lillian's anger. Most of us were startled by it from time to time.

Anger was her essence. It was at the center of that passionate temperament. It informed her art: the little foxes snapped at each other, we could see their back hairs bristle, we could smell their foxiness—they were real and alive because of the current of anger that ran through them, as it did through so many of Lillian's characters.

What I want to say is that this voltage of Lillian's was immensely important and valuable to our time. It electrified a mood of protest. The protest was that of every great writer: "Life ought to be better than this!"

This peppery quality took so many dazzling forms in her. You could hear it on the edge of that raucous laugh of hers. It decorated her mischief. I think it even lived in her taste buds—how she loved horseradish, mustard, Portuguese sausage! What a hot woman!

Her inmost fire, though, was not sensual. It was in the mind. It was a rage of the mind against all kinds of injustice—against human injustice and against the unfairness of death. In everything she wrote, and in her daily life, she fought against slander, greed, hypocrisy, cruelty and everything shabby and second-rate and dangerous in those in power. She was very, very angry at death—and not just at the end. Death became her enemy years ago, when Hammett died, and this enemy made her even more vibrant and alive.

What could calm this anger? Only the sea, and money, and love. Anyone who gave her the slightest flicker of love got in return a radiance of laughter and fun that was unbelievably enjoyable; this was the bright other face of the anger.

Dear Lillian, you are a finished woman, now. I mean "finished" in its better sense. You shone with a high finish of integrity, decency, uprightness. You have given us this anger to remember and to use in a bad world. We thank you, we honor you, and we all say good-bye to you now with a love that should calm that anger of yours forever.

Included in the eulogies reprinted in *The Vineyard Gazette* was the following:
[Mr. Koontz, a Vineyard charter fishing captain, did not speak at Miss Hellman's funeral. But for many years he was both friend and fishing companion to the late playwright, who loved the sea and the sport of fishing. His special appreciation of Lillian Hellman follows.]

JACK KOONTZ

Lillian Hellman was many things, and one of them was a fisherman. Some people love to fish or like to fish. Lillian placed no such verb between herself and fishing. She just fished. And she fished whenever she got the chance. If there is a patch of water where she is now, she is likely trying to coax a fish from it.

Lillian and I fished together for the first time six years ago. She and author John Hersey and I went out to Noman's Land and caught a box of bluefish. We had a good time. Lillian did not have a boat then. In the past she usually had a boat, she told me, and she wanted to own one again. I was not completely pleased with my boat at the time, so Lillian and I made a deal. Since fishing was difficult and even dangerous for her alone, and since she still wanted to fish, she would get a new boat and we would fish together. We fished every Saturday and the remaining days I used the boat for charter.

Lillian and I had many fine days on the waters around Martha's Vineyard over the past six years. Like any two fishermen, we had our ups and downs, but most of the time we got along pretty well, especially out on the water. She loved the water. Even when she was particularly ill and almost always uncomfortable, she relaxed when she went fishing. She never gave up on fishing. I suppose she was the sort of person who never gave up on anything she liked and cared about.

The first few years we fished together, Lillian was still strong enough to conquer a bluefish, or even several bluefish at once, when we used heavy umbrella rigs to try and fill the fish box. She would fight the crank on the reel as the fish struggled on the end of the line, and then state she was getting just too old and too weak to do this sort of thing. When she got the fish into the boat, she made it clear whose turn it was to catch the next fish, because after that it was her turn again.

The past two years, after her eyesight was nearly gone and walking without help became impossible, she decided to give the bluefish a break and, instead, to take on scup and flounder. I think she always liked bottom fishing better anyway, and she preferred to eat flounder. We would drift along the edge of Dogfish Bar, picking up a fluke every ten or fifteen minutes, and the inevitable speedboat would pass a little too close. I made sure she was sitting secure in the seat so she wouldn't be knocked down by the wake and I warned her when it was about to rock our boat. She always did the same thing. She sat until the boat began to churn in the wake, then she got angry, grabbed the rail, stood up and gave the guy the finger, hollering out that he had the whole ocean, so why did he have to bother us. Then we'd go back to fishing.

Last summer was tough for Lillian. She couldn't handle the rod by herself, her left side wasn't working so well then, and I held the rod steady for her while she cranked the scup or flounder to the surface. Then I'd hold the fish in front of her, so she could feel its size and shape. She usually caught the biggest fish. I don't know why, but she did. Perhaps it was because she had to work so hard to do it.

Not many people would have kept fishing as long as Lillian did. We were supposed to go fishing last Saturday, the day she died. She called me on Friday to check on the boat. She was anxious to get out on the water again.

Being on the ocean was good for Lillian these past few years and that she could still fish was important to her. She was angry about her failing health. When she fished she wasn't so angry.

She was a courageous woman. And she was a very good fisherman. I shall miss her.